THE ULTIMATE TRUTH

VENKATESH ADE

For

My parents, who always support me

Elon Musk, whose work inspires me

Dan Brown, whose novels inspired me to write novels

Contents

Prologue   *ix*

  1. Chapter 1   1

  2. Chapter 2   15

  3. Chapter 3   20

  4. Chapter 4   24

  5. Chapter 5   31

  6. Chapter 6   38

  7. Chapter 7   46

  8. Chapter 8   47

  9. Chapter 9   55

10. Chapter 10   66

11. Chapter 11   74

12. Chapter 12   78

13. Chapter 13   83

14. Chapter 14   86

15. Chapter 15   91

16. Chapter 16   97

17. Chapter 17   101

18. Chapter 18   104

19. Chapter 19   113

20. Chapter 20   119

21. Chapter 21   122

22. Chapter 22   127

23. Chapter 23   134

Contents

24. Chapter 24 — 137

25. Chapter 25 — 142

26. Chapter 26 — 145

27. Chapter 27 — 149

28. Chapter 28 — 155

29. Chapter 29 — 158

30. Chapter 30 — 166

31. Chapter 31 — 169

32. Chapter 32 — 178

33. Chapter 33 — 189

34. Chapter 34 — 192

35. Chapter 35 — 198

36. Chapter 36 — 202

37. Chapter 37 — 211

38. Chapter 38 — 214

39. Chapter 39 — 216

40. Chapter 40 — 219

41. Chapter 41 — 228

42. Chapter 42 — 235

43. Chapter 43 — 240

44. Chapter 44 — 248

45. Chapter 45 — 254

46. Chapter 46 — 262

47. Chapter 47 — 268

Contents

48. Chapter 48 — 276

49. Chapter 49 — 284

50. Chapter 50 — 288

51. Chapter 51 — 301

52. Chapter 52 — 308

53. Chapter 53 — 321

54. Chapter 54 — 325

55. Chapter 55 — 329

56. Chapter 56 — 334

57. Chapter 57 — 338

58. Chapter 58 — 340

59. Chapter 59 — 346

60. Chapter 60 — 353

61. Chapter 61 — 358

62. Chapter 62 — 363

63. Chapter 63 — 373

64. Chapter 64 — 377

65. Chapter 65 — 385

66. Chapter 66 — 400

67. Chapter 67 — 403

68. Chapter 68 — 410

Epilogue — 417

Prologue

At about 11PM, Joseph arrived at the bungalow of his master. This had made him a bit angry as it had ruined his nice plan. That night, he had planned to go for a horror movie with his girlfriend. But his master's urgent call had spoiled everything.

Walking closer and closer towards the bungalow, he said to himself, "Why has Sir called me at this time? Now, my girlfriend will surely break off with me."

Suddenly, he felt a bit nice after realising something.

If she leaves me for such a small thing, let her leave because this is not true love at all.

After walking a few steps, he reached his master's lavish and technologically advanced bungalow. Even at that time, the bungalow attracted his attention due to its elegant, simple, and futuristic aesthetics and features.

As he entered the gate, 2 fierce-looking robots scanned his face and allowed him inside, quickly recognising that he was the loyal assistant of the owner's house.

As he walked inside the region of his master, he scanned all the different types of advanced robots which were spread across the beautiful garden. There were robots which were assigned different tasks like grass-cutting, sweeping, watering the plants and cleaning etc.

Joseph's master was one of the greatest lovers and admirers of AI and robots in the world. His love for robots had created headlines all around the world, along with sparking controversy.

This is because he decided to start a company that would focus on cyborg engineering, thus greatly impacting the future of humanity. However, most researchers, including the government, opposed his plan, considering it to be very dangerous and harmful to the world.

As Joseph was walking towards the main door of the bungalow, he was feeling very unusual. He didn't know why, but his heart was telling him that something strange had happened.

With courage, he opened the metal door of the bungalow, wondering why his master had kept it open.

As he peeped inside, he could see nothing except complete darkness and silence. There was pin-drop silence as if none was inside.

Building some confidence, he said in a low voice, "M...May I come in, Sir? Where are you?"

His voice echoed into the darkness of the hall. But there was no response. He kept gazing with full focus and concentration.

Suddenly, he saw a flash of light before his eyes and was stunned after looking at the scene before him. The light was dim.

As he focused more, he saw a dark figure sitting before him on a big chair, on whose head a golden disc was undergoing circular motion. It was very bright and beautiful.

Joseph was very scared and confused. He was unable to process what was happening.

Suddenly, a voice announced from inside, "Don't get scared my dear Joseph! Come inside. The dark silhouette which you are able to see in front of you is none other than me."

Joseph took a sigh of relief. The voice confirmed that the dark figure was his master. But he was very surprised to find him in such an appearance.

Now, with more courage, he walked inside. The stamping of his feet was clearly audible in the silent hall.

Silently, he motioned near the big sofa and sat there. Just in front of him was the dark silhouette of his master, on whose head the golden disc was rotating in the air. After all, he was brilliant at such inventions.

Pulling in a deep breath, Joseph asked in astonishment, "What is this, Sir? Why have you suddenly called me here? And why are you not showing me your face?"

The master got up and started walking in periodic motion from left to right like a bob of a suspended pendulum.

He smiled and replied, "Joseph, now not only me, but you also have to hide your face. Not just from me, but from the whole world."

Joseph was puzzled. The incidents were really taking a toll on his brain.

"What?! I didn't understand."

There was a short silence. After a while, the master spoke in a serious tone, "My dear, today I have called you here to share with you a secret."

Joseph felt that he would now get a heart attack.

"Secret?! What secret, Sir?"

The master stopped in his tracks. Joseph was eager to hear the secret.

He coughed and said, "Joseph, the secret which I am going to share with you today has such a potential that it will change the whole world completely. Everyone currently alive on this Earth will get goosebumps if they just hear the topic of this secret."

Joseph's excitement accelerated after hearing that.

Leaning forward, he asked, "This secret has the potential to change the whole world?"

The master's voice turned dead serious.

"Not only does this secret have the capability of changing the whole world, but it will alter the entire course of humanity if revealed."

Joseph requested him to tell him what the secret was. And so, the master told him everything.

After knowing about the secret, Joseph's eyes widened. He felt adrenaline rushing through his whole body and his heartbeat increasing suddenly. His body was filled with sweat.

"Master! Please tell me what we have to do now. It all seems like a sci-fi movie."

The master motioned away from Joseph. A cool, gushing wind blew inside from the window, making the environment a bit cooler.

Looking outside the window, the master said, "Dear! We have to go on a very important mission as early as possible. Otherwise, the whole of humanity will face such a challenge which it had never faced till now."

Joseph understood the importance of their mission.

"The safety of humankind now lies in our hands. We have to act very quickly before the time slips away. And don't fear to eliminate all the thorns from our path."

He walked back near Joseph and leaned towards him, his eyes focusing on his eyes sharply.

"Now our goal is only one. To find the truth of the mystery and bury it. Or, more simply, destroy it."

Bhagavad Gita:

"Man is made by his belief. As he believes, so he is."-
Bhagavad Gita

Bible:

"For I know the plans I have for you, plans to prosper
you and not to harm you, plans to give you hope and a
future."- Jeremiah 29:11

Quran:

"And I did not create the jinn and mankind except to
worship Me."- Quran 51:56

Talmud:

"The day is short, the task is great, the labourers are
lazy, the wage is abundant, and the Master is urgent."-
Talmud

Science (Albert Einstein):

"The meaning of life is to give life meaning."- Albert
Einstein

The Universe is the answer. But what are the questions to ask? If we expand the scope and scale of consciousness, then we can understand what questions to ask -Elon Musk

Elon Musk, the greatest innovator of the 21st century and one of the most powerful men of the world

CHAPTER ONE

Mr. Liam Davis came running outside his office as if he was running a marathon race. He had come outside to observe the work which was going on. As he glanced upwards, which was his favourite activity, he could see the night sky stretching elegantly, containing the twinkling stars and the Moon.

Without wasting any time, he walked towards the launchpad, where several scientists, engineers, and technicians were working with sharp laser focus. As he was moving, one engineer came near him and said with a burst of enthusiasm, "Don't worry at all, Sir. Everything is perfectly fine. We all are constantly checking each and everything. There won't be any problem during the launch."

"Excellent! Work and check all the systems and everything. Don't miss a single detail, as the spaceship has to launch perfectly. Because tomorrow, humanity is going to take a giant leap in the progress of science."

Saying so, the engineer rushed to the launchpad to continue his work.

Mr. Liam Davis was a 50-year-old man who held the prestigious roles of the founder, chairman and CEO at the Newton Space Research Agency, commonly known as the NSRA.

As one of the prominent leaders in space research and technology, he likely possessed a deep passion for space exploration without having much experience in the industry. However, his extensive knowledge and leadership skills played a pivotal role in shaping the company's vision and success. In addition to being an important leader in the space industry, he was a gifted author who shook the world with his novels and also sparked controversies due to his views and opinions on the modern world and humanity's future. Many believed that he was too old due to his views. But he didn't care one iota about that.

The NSRA was located in California, USA. Its main goal was to advance space exploration technology and do everything possible related to the Universe.

With the brilliance and creativity of many scientists and engineers, the agency has made space travel cheaper, faster and innovative.

Mr. Davis, the king of the agency, was regarded as one of the greatest business leaders and innovators of the time. A tall, thin man with a small brown moustache, he was totally dedicated towards his work.

On that cold night, thousands of smart people were working with full determination to make an old dream come true. They had spent more than 10 years on that thrilling mission. And on the following day, humankind was going to enter a new era if the mission would succeed.

At about 6 AM in the following morning, almost the whole world was awake to witness the event. All across the globe, people were bustling with anticipation.

In the olden days, people used to gather around the launch area to watch the beautiful launches of spaceships and rockets, or they used to watch the events through their televisions at home. But within a short time, technology had advanced so much that now it was not necessary for people to gather around the launch area or even to sit in front of their televisions to witness the launches.

Because people were able to see the events and experience them even if they were sitting inside their houses, not just see, but experience as if they were physically present there.

This was possible due to another great tech entrepreneur of the world, Mr. Davis's best friend, Sir James Brown.

James Brown, a confident and dashing young man, had dropped out of college at the age of 23 and started his own company named **Virtual Eye.** Nobody had ever imagined or expected, but his company had revolutionised the way humanity accessed, used and interacted with AI, technology and everything.

Virtual Eye produced and manufactured various products like chairs, tables, beds, televisions, etc., blending them seamlessly with advanced technology. The company was also ahead in AI, robotics and virtual reality technology. They produced special goggles through which we could visit any place on Earth just by sitting wherever we were.

His vision and genius had brought a global technological revolution, which resulted in him becoming one of the greatest innovators and businessmen of the twenty-first century and also the second richest person of the world with an astonishing net worth of $230 billion!

In addition to this, Brown was a great philanthropist who donated billions of dollars in various areas like education, healthcare, technology, etc. He was a very kind and gentle person who was loved by everyone. He was regarded as the People's Entrepreneur.

Virtual Eye had contributed very much to the mission.

On that beautiful and historical morning, he was standing there, observing the spaceship which was going to launch and change the world forever. Many top executives of his company surrounded him.

Suddenly, Mr. Davis arrived near him, and they hugged each other. After all, they were best friends. There were a lot of similarities between them, like vision, mindset, and personality. However, the only thing that differentiated them from each other was their views on the modern world. Brown was a very optimistic person who was regarded as the people's entrepreneur. On the other hand, Mr. Davis was often seen as an ancient type of person due to his conservative views.

All the scientists and engineers gathered there at that time. Many teams of journalists had arrived there to report and broadcast the great moment. They were waiting for the 12 astronauts who were going to change the world in the upcoming time.

At about six- smart people came walking out of the NSRA and proceeded towards the launchpad.

The whole population was baffled and astonished after looking at the spacecraft. The technological spaceship had captured the hearts and minds of everyone due to its beauty and technology.

The spaceship was a work of art in itself, with finely detailed images of Sir Isaac Newton and Albert Einstein intricately carved into its polished titanium hull. Their images were rendered in a way that paid homage to their contributions to the laws of physics and the Universe. The surface was adorned with sleek, silver and golden accents, which contrasted beautifully with the images, emphasising the blend of historic and modern elements.

Virtual Eye, famous for its cutting-edge virtual reality technology, contributed to the spaceship's interior design and technology, ensuring that the astronauts had an immersive and visually stimulating environment during their journey. NSRA played a crucial role in developing advanced scientific instrumentation on board, enhancing the ship's capabilities for research and data collection during the mission.

SpaceX's signature raptor engines powered the wonderful spaceship. The aerospace technology giant had also contributed to the exterior design, the propulsion system and other advanced technology which made it very cheap and as swift as possible.

Inside the spaceship, astronauts had access to spacious living quarters designed to provide comfort and accommodate the crew for the duration of their journey. It was equipped with a hydroponic garden for fresh food production, waste recycling systems and a gym.

Cutting-edge navigation and communications systems, jointly developed by the 3 companies, allowed for real-time communication with Earth and accurate course corrections.

But the best thing was that it was fully autonomous and did not need any human intervention. There was a very smart and small robot, Z11, who was provided as the main assistant to the astronauts on their journey. If the astronauts ordered him, the robot would be able to switch the spaceship's mode to manual, and then it would return back to Earth amidst its journey in space. It was a giant leap in space technology!

As the 12 explorers walked near the launchpad, everyone was feeling very proud.

They had worn a very special spacesuit with a wide screen attached to the front. There were goggles around their necks, which would provide them protection from any harmful radiation or gases as they were going to work in such a place of which humanity had just dreamt.

As they arrived there, the journalists rushed towards them like cheetahs with their microphones and cameras.

The astronaut who was going to speak was the leader of the mission. Her name was Ms Lana Wilson, an attractive and beautiful girl.

Lana Wilson was a blend of beauty and allure. With lustrous, chestnut-brown hair, her eyes showcased her elegance and character. She was very fit, slim, and had a slender figure, which attracted several people towards her as if she were a magnet.

Lana was a born genius who had graduated with a master's degree in aerospace engineering at the mere age of 16 and then went on to become the Chief Technology Officer of Virtual Eye and an astronaut of NSRA. She was a very courageous and risk-taking girl whose problem-solving skills and critical thinking had brought her a great reputation. A handsome reporter approached her and began peppering her with questions, "Hello, Ms Lana! We all are really very happy to see you and your team ready for this amazing mission."

She nodded happily.

"Well, I would like to ask you your views and feelings about this mission."

Lana cleared her throat and replied with enthusiasm, "I am feeling very proud to be a part of this breathtaking mission which is going to be a giant achievement, not just for a country or a continent, but for the whole world. If we succeed, then the dreams and aspirations of many great people will be completed, and we will be able to explore and understand our Universe better."

"So, do you think that we would come across a lot of mysteries on the red planet?"

Lana and her team suddenly became emotional after hearing about the red planet. This is because the great mission of that day, for which the whole world had been waiting for 10 years, was held to take the astronauts to the red planet Mars. For a decade, thousands of scientists, engineers, researchers and executives were working super hard to make that dream come true.

The aim of the mission, envisioned by the tech wizard Elon Musk, was to create a huge research laboratory on Mars for doing research and discoveries on the planet. The laboratory was named the Universal Research Laboratory.

But before humans proceeded, robots were sent to the red planet in order to build the laboratory using their skills, as commanded by humans. It was an astonishing thing that before humans, robots had set foot on Mars!

It was a very important mission as humanity was going to set foot on a new planet for the first time to do scientific work. And a few years later, humankind would colonise the red giant.

The interview ended shortly as time was running up. The astronauts went near Mr Davis to take his blessings and later on towards Brown.

Mr. Davis kept his hand on Lana's shoulder and said, "My blessings are always with you! I am sure that our hard work will pay off. Sir Isaac Newton and many other scientists must be very happy today if our achievement from heaven really exists. Go on!"

Mr. Davis was Lana's father figure. He always treated her like his daughter. But 2 years back rumours had spread that they both were having an affair. But Lana cleared everything angrily, claiming that they were like father and daughter.

Brown's eyes were filled with tears as the astronauts touched his feet. And after that, they became ready for the mission.

But before the launch, a tall and thick charming man came walking out of the NSRA building. His eyes were looking very tired as if he had not slept for many months! But his walking style displayed his value and charisma.

Many reporters rushed towards him as if he was God himself. He was wearing a black t-shirt on which it was written in nice letters - **Occupy Mars.** Looking at this, there was no doubt that he was Elon Musk, the real Iron Man of the world, who, with his groundbreaking companies like SpaceX, Tesla, Neuralink, Boring, XAI, and PayPal, had changed the face of technology and business. Surprisingly, he acquired Twitter, thus entering the social media playground.

A female reporter leaned towards the billionaire tech entrepreneur's face and asked with excitement, "Mr. Musk! Colonising Mars had been your childhood dream. And today is the moment when humans are taking the first step towards that goal. How do you feel?"

Becoming joyful along with a tinge of stress, he replied, "Well, I am really on the seventh cloud today!

Because the first step toward my ultimate goal is in the process. If this mission goes well and brings success, then there is no doubt to say that mankind would colonise the red planet in a few years, thus becoming a multiplanetary species."

As time ran up, Musk stood beside Brown and Davis to witness the launch.

And when the crew members took his blessings, his eyes watered, showcasing his emotions. It was going to be a historical moment for mankind.

All across the globe, people were sweating profusely with tension and curiosity. Religious people were joining their hands, praying to their respective Gods, and spiritual people were meditating with full focus. Everybody was getting uncomfortable with every passing moment.

All were able to experience the joy of launch, thanks to the high-tech goggles of Virtual Eye.

At sharp six-fifty am, the spaceship took off from the ground and accelerated with a high velocity towards space. Everyone's eyes were on it. They were staring with full concentration on the computer screens without blinking their eyes.

Musk, Brown and Davis were staring at the spaceship unblinkingly. It seemed as if they had forgotten about the reality.

To everybody's joy, the mission was successful, and the spaceship escaped the Earth's atmosphere and headed into the mysterious cosmos! It was a giant accomplishment.

There was a grand celebration all across the world. The scientists, engineers and executives of the mission were dancing and singing with joy. Brown went and hugged Mr. Davis tightly. Tears started flowing from their eyes.

Elon Musk was not at all able to believe what had happened just then. He was bursting with excitement and exclaimed, "My ultimate goal is going to be accomplished now! Life will now become multiplanetary. Hurrah! "And then he burst into tears.

All the reporters were irritating Musk by throwing questions at him continuously. The news channel was continuously reporting about the achievement.

Mr. Davis and Brown motioned inside the agency, in Davis' cabin. On the other hand, Musk proceeded to the Tesla factory in order to solve some major issues related to his next project. His plan was to finish the work and have a peaceful and nice sleep.

The NSRA's eleven-storey structure was a marvel of modern architecture, blending functionality and futuristic aesthetics. The agency's exterior boasted sleek, silver metallic panels with large, reflective windows that

gave the building a high-tech and polished appearance. A colossal, abstract sculpture of Isaac Newton's iconic apple tree stood as a symbol at the entrance, signifying the agency's dedication to scientific exploration.

On either side of the building were huge sleeping quarters were the workers took rest or slept during overtime.

The first 3 levels of the building were dedicated to a huge house research and development labs, which were equipped with state-of-the-art equipment for designing propulsion systems, navigation technology, and materials. Engineers and scientists worked tirelessly to innovate and improve space travel.

The next 3 floors were dedicated to the construction of rockets and spaceships. Massive assembly lines, 3D printers, and robotics were constantly at work, producing the next generation of spacecraft. The floors we're bustling with engineers and technicians in clean suits, meticulously assembling and quality-checking each component.

The eighth level was the nerve centre of the agency. Mission control specialists monitored and managed space missions in real-time. On the ninth level, astronauts and crew members prepared for their missions, practising in high-fidelity simulators.

The tenth floor was the source and centre of knowledge and research. It was a quiet place containing huge libraries where scientists and all the other workers could delve into the depths of ancient and modern space history and theories.

The top floor hosted the agency's leadership, with spacious, modern offices overlooking the entire facility. The 3 tech leaders had their own separate office on this floor, where they worked insanely.

Mr Davis and Sir Brown were all alone in Davis's office, which was

situated on the top floor. They both were having tasty snacks and cold drinks with a bit of wine. There was a broad smile on their faces. It was the happiest moment of their lives at that time.

"I am now sure that we will get a grand success! The spaceship has been launched perfectly. Now, just a few months and humans will colonise Mars!" exclaimed Brown.

Finishing a glass of orange juice, Mr. Davis replied, "Yeah! And technology has advanced so much that space travel has become cheap and fast."

Brown ate a slice of cheese pizza and said, "We must be thankful towards the intelligent robots because of whom we are able to do this. Without their help, our mission would have been difficult."

Brown looked outside the window of the office towards the peaceful blue sky and said with depth, "May scientists find great and wonderful mysteries on the red planet."

And suddenly, Brown recalled something. He had to ask one question to Mr. Davis which had puzzled him for many days.

He stared at Davis and asked in confusion, "Bro, where did you go 10 days ago without informing anybody? It was like you suddenly disappeared."

But he observed that Mr. Davis was immersed in his own world, and his eyes were looking dead serious.

Brown leaned towards him and asked, "What are you thinking Liam?"

Mr. Davis looked straight into his eyes and replied in a sad tone, "James, I am feeling extremely sad after recollecting the saddest incident we ever had 2 months back. Our spacecraft and astronauts...."and he started weeping.

Suddenly, Brown's whole body started shaking as he recollected that disastrous and heart-wrenching incident.

Two months ago, NSRA had sent a crew of 5 astronauts on a very highly designed and technologically advanced spacecraft named XYZ-001. The mission was to land on the surface of the Moon to do some research. But unfortunately, before landing on the lunar surface, the spacecraft's direction and velocity changed due to something and the connection broke. None knew what happened to the crew members, even the spacecraft was nowhere to be found. Researchers claimed that it exploded, but the real reason was not known.

It was such a horrifying incident that none ever dared to talk about that. It was one of the saddest events in the history of space exploration.

Looking at the condition of Mr. Davis, Brown went near him. He kept his hand on his shoulder, smiled and encouraged him confidently.

"My dear Liam! Life is really very short and limited. Most of our life is spent sleeping, eating and settling. We always have stress and pressure hovering over our heads. There are various opportunities across our paths, and we try to take advantage of them to fulfil our passions and desires. And we end up putting our blood, sweat, and tears into the work we do. But unfortunately, we sometimes fail to accomplish our dreams. But the main thing is that we should not at all get discouraged as the Universe gives us more chances."

Mr Davis' eyes widened after hearing those beautiful words.

"We should stop getting disappointed by thinking about the past but should start learning from it and avoid repeating the mistakes. Then only we can hope for a better future."

Brown's smile broadened, and he said, "Liam, always remember. Life is very short. Don't keep crying for your mistakes. Instead, be restless and keep working for your passion and desires."

Mr. Davis hugged his dear friend tightly. Tears of love were flowing down from his eyes. With a lot of emotions he said, "You are really my best friend James! I wish our friendship will remain till eternity. We will always work hard till our last breath to make this world a better place."

Brown also started weeping. After all, those were tears of friendship.

But sometimes, the exact opposite happens. After all its life, anything can happen.

CHAPTER TWO

Faraway from Earth, the beautiful white spaceship was accelerating rapidly, thanks to the development in aerospace technology. With each and every passing moment, Earth was receding rapidly.

The inner walls of the spaceship had long, and thin screens attached to them. It was a total blend of beauty and technology. All that interior design was done by Virtual Eye. Brown had worked tirelessly for the project as he wanted to design the spaceship very elegantly. He had vast knowledge and a unique taste in design.

There was also a huge digital library inside which contained thousands of books on various topics like cosmology, engineering, physics, philosophy etc.

Digital means that the library didn't contain any physical books. It contained thin, transparent tablets on which the crew members could read any book of their choice and absorb the information. Each tablet was developed for a specific topic.

Lana, who was seated on the last seat, got up and proceeded towards the library. The other 11 crew members were sitting comfortably on the high-tech seats. The seats contained various buttons by pressing which one could go in his own virtual world. If one set up the theme of Antarctica, he would experience himself there.

As she moved towards the library, an invisible force made her keep staring at the astronauts. And suddenly, she became emotional.

Just as she was lost in her own thoughts, she suddenly felt a metallic thing touching her shoulder. To observe what it was, she turned backwards.

"What happened, Ms Wilson? What are you thinking so deeply?" a mechanical voice asked her.

In front of her eyes stood a small robot with a boyish face which was about the size of a 6-year-old kid. It was very cute with a human-like behaviour and face. It had small metallic legs and hands which looked like shiny metals. Its voice was a mixture of machine and human.

The robot was named Z11, and it was created to guide the scientists and provide them with all the information which they needed by Virtual Eye. He was very smart and intelligent and had vast knowledge of rocket science, history, philosophy etc. It was a multi-purpose robot, designed for helping humans in all ways possible. And really, he cared about humans a lot.

Lana returned from her thoughts and replied, "Nothing, Z11! I was just thinking about the rapid advancement in technology."

Z11 stared at her and said, "Yes, Ms. Wilson! Why not? If we will have such great tech entrepreneurs like Brown and Mr. Davis and Elon Musk, why will our world not move ahead in terms of technology?"

Lana nodded in agreement as the small robot talked more about Brown and Davis. It seemed as if it was the father of both of them who knew so much about both of them.

She was impressed by his knowledge. Leaning towards his face, she said, "Wow! You really have a lot of knowledge about both of them." "Yes! Thank you! I know very much about them. I even know that Mr. Davis worships Sir Isaac Newton very much, and Sir Brown loves Albert Einstein."

Lana thought, "Hmm. He is exactly right. They both love and respect the 2 great geniuses of world history. They worship them like God."

Suddenly, Z11 bent his head towards her face and whispered, "Are you aware that Sir Brown has lots of information about Albert Einstein?"

Lana was astonished to hear that. She was startled after hearing his words. But anyhow, she was interested in listening.

"What do you mean by that he has lots of information about Einstein? It is obvious because he is a very great fan of his."

The robot lowered his voice and replied, "No, Ms Wilson! You are not able to understand. By lots of information, I mean that Sir Brown...."

"Lana, ma'am! Come here quickly!"

The whole deep conversation between both of them was disturbed by the voice of Dr Zangger, the head of the planetary department of NSRA. He was calling Lana as if it was very urgent.

Lana glanced at him from a distance and asked with irritation, "What happened? Why are you shouting and calling me?"

Dr. Zangger replied with excitement, "Actually, there is an important voice message from Mr. Davis for all of us."

Hearing that the founder and CEO of NSRA had sent an important message, she rushed towards him, forgetting everything about her conversation with Z11.

While moving, she ordered the robot, "Please bring the tablet of cosmology for me and keep it on my seat."

As she reached Zangger, all the other 10 crew members surrounded them to hear the voice message.

Dr. Zangger, sitting on the chair tapped on his smartphone and eventually a thin blue projection ejected from a huge screen before them on the wall and started floating in the air before them. And soon after that, Mr. Davis' voice echoed throughout the room of the spaceship.

"We all are feeling very proud here on Earth that for the first time, human beings are being sent to another planet, thanks to the thousands of creative geniuses who worked hard for that. So, on the idea of James, we both are going to give a powerful and inspiring speech to the whole world at about 8 PM. Nobody knows why he suddenly called for that event, but whatever it is, we all would enjoy it a lot. I want all of you to witness the event live. Thank you."

A wave of thrill and excitement hit the bodies of the crew members.

"Wow! Such a great event where 2 of the most popular and loved innovators of our time, and after all our leaders are going to throw a powerful speech. It is really a great thing!" an astrobiologist Dane exclaimed.

Lana was sure that the speech was going to be very philosophical, emotional, along with a lot of drama. After all, great leaders need to be dramatic in order to change the world.

As she was thinking, Z11 came and handed her the tablet of cosmology.

"Happy reading, enjoy it." And he went back to where he was.

Lana silently sat on her seat and started the tablet. It had a beautiful design, was very thin and interactive. As she opened it, she thought of reading some great book. And she chose none other than the greatest cosmologist the world has ever had, Sir Stephen Hawking. She decided to read a book which was written by him.

As she searched for a book which would interest her, the elegant and simple features of the tablet attracted her attention, and she was impressed by that. Planets and stars danced as she scrolled.

In her mind, she kept admiring the creativity and vision of Brown, under whom she worked.

After handing her the tablet, Z11 motioned towards a window and started observing the receding space. He was designed and developed with such advancement and technology that sometimes it was difficult to distinguish whether it was a robot or a human. Because his conversations were like human beings.

Suddenly, as he looked out of the window, he said to himself, "The things that I was told will remain a secret. Because the time is approaching."

CHAPTER THREE

At about 5PM, a nice and sexy Tesla Model Y was parked outside a nice but small bungalow which was located at a very peaceful and lonely place, the crowd and noise of Los Angeles being 5 kilometres away. It was a very well-built house, with a touch of advanced technology.

The driver of the car came outside and motioned towards the metal gate of the bungalow. A thin, square-shaped screen was attached to the wall beside the gate. Below it was the name of the owner of the house. It was written in blue, and it seemed as if it was text on a mobile phone. The blue letters read:

Dr. Jacob Anderson

The blue screen suddenly came to life. The driver gazed into it as if a thriller movie was going to start.

On the screen came the face of a young handsome man who was in his thirties. He smiled happily and asked, "Is my car properly cleaned and ready?"

"Yes, Sir! It is looking very shiny now. There is not a single problem."

Saying so, the driver bid farewell to the man on the screen and left as he was in a hurry. And soon after that, the screen went black.

Anderson got up from his chair and turned off the ultra-thin computer before him. He motioned towards his huge cupboard, which contained his special and unique suits and tuxedos. He was very enthralled at that moment.

Dr Jacob Anderson was a celebrity figure in his time. He was a tall, charming and handsome man with a nice black moustache, who was 32 years old. He was famous worldwide for his expertise in various subjects like archaeology, astronomy, physics, artificial intelligence, biotechnology, philosophy and religion.

Out of all, the subject which interested him the most was artificial intelligence. He always warned people about the dangers of technology. Most of his time was spent gazing at the stars and wondering about the limitless mysteries of the Universe and of the past and doing research on them.

He had a degree in astrophysics from the prestigious California Institute of Technology, and he sometimes worked as an intelligence researcher at SpaceX and as a scientist at Caltech. The leader of the company, Elon Musk, had requested him to take the role of the chief product officer or something like that due to his extraordinary leadership and management skills. However, he always refused that offer as he was interested in being a simple researcher. He was an explorer and researcher who travelled around the world in search of various mysteries. His most special thing was that he was a multi-talented guy.

Once the great entrepreneur Bill Gates had invited him to his house as the billionaire wanted to learn about AI in depth. And Anderson was popular worldwide for his ability to teach and explain things as simply as possible.

On his desk at Caltech, there was a quote by Albert Einstein hanging,

'If you can't explain it simply, you don't understand it well enough.'

As he opened his cupboard by pressing a button, a bunch of shiny suits and tuxedos hung in front of his eyes. He was very confused as he was not able to understand what to wear. There were a lot of options.

After wondering for a while, he finally came to a conclusion. After all, time was running up.

Even though he was very careful about money and finances, he spent heavily on suits and tuxedos. And he decided to wear a black tuxedo for the upcoming event. He decided to wear that because he looked very attractive in black clothes, which attracted girls and young ladies towards him.

At about 7 PM, he dressed well and made his body smell nice by spraying a strong and fragrant perfume. Without wasting any time, he walked outside his house and left for the thrilling event in his Tesla Model Y.

Joseph's heart was throbbing at a large rate. His body was sweating profusely and also shaking. His once excited and happy face had suddenly turned pale yellow and tasteless.

Silently, he came out of his master's house and waited. There was a cool environment, and the sky was looking dark and greyish. He glanced at the sky and said with his heart, "Hey God! Please help me and my master today! Take care that our plan will be executed properly. Otherwise, we would get into big trouble."

Just as he finished praying, he saw his dear master approaching. The master was dressed in the clothes of a waiter, with a black mask which covered his face. He was a thin and tall gentleman with dark black hair and penetrating eyes. At that moment, he was looking like a great person.

He hurried towards Joseph. Looking at his assistant's sad and scared face, he said in a deep voice, "I know that the thing which we are going to do now is very risky. But we have to take risks if we want to make it work. There is no other option. Be calm; the lord is with us."

Joseph felt a bit relaxed, but still not enough to give him relief. With every passing moment, his tension was accelerating at a very high rate. But he couldn't do anything because the situation was such that even if he wanted to, he was not able to step back from his mission.

Anxiously, Joseph moved inside the car of his master to drive it. The master checked the time on his smartphone. It read 7PM.

After getting inside the car, he said, "We still have enough time. I think we will definitely succeed. Because God will also be with us because he also wants to stop a huge apocalypse from happening."

Joseph drove the car in the direction of their destination.

Looking out the window, the master said emotionally, "Sorry, lord! But I have to do this."

CHAPTER FOUR

The environment at the NSRA was filled with happiness and contentment. All the people who worked there were on the seventh cloud at that moment.

"If everything goes well, we will create a history for mankind. Our world will be completely changed after that," exclaimed Jonathan, a senior planetary scientist and engineer of the agency. He was among the top executives and famously known for his work on the strategy of building the Universal research lab on Mars.

A young man of 40 years, Jonathan Brooks was one of Mr. Davis's most loved employees. He was tall and handsome and possessed a charming aura.

All the other scientists were gathered around him. There was a true smile of satisfaction on their faces. They had strained for about a decade to complete the whole mission.

A middle-aged female engineer erupted with joy, "And there is no need to worry as the head of the mission is Ms. Lana Wilson."

Everybody nodded in agreement, admiring Lana's exceptional talent.

Taking a sip of hot coffee, Jonathan said with excitement, "Now I am just eager to hear the speech of Mr. Davis and Brown Sir. The top senior executives of our agency have to reach the auditorium to watch the event. I am sure that the speech will be a solid mixture of emotions, science and philosophy."

As the top executives of NSRA were getting ready to leave for the auditorium, a tall, strong and thin old physicist was also very excited about the upcoming event.

Dr. Andrew Johnson was one of the most respected astronomical engineers and physicists of the agency. He was a genius who was expert at solving the most critical and difficult problems. Even at the age of sixty- 3, he radiated restless energy and enthusiasm. He was extremely dedicated towards his work.

That evening, he was all alone, sitting in his department of astronomical observation on the eighth floor. The walls were dotted with complex but beautiful diagrams of various planets, stars and celestial bodies. The whole room was filled with computers, screens and other important objects. The room was designed so beautifully that it seemed as if one was standing in space itself. To experience that, all you had to do was to press a small white button near the door and the room would turn itself into space!

Dr. Johnson had activated that feature at that time. He was willing to experience the beauty of the cosmos in solitude. He was so immersed in its beauty that he forgot that he had to go to the event.

Suddenly, a voice yelled behind him, "Sir! Get ready quickly. We are getting late."

Moving out of his own world of thoughts, he turned back and saw Jonathan standing near the door.

Without wasting time in unnecessary discussion, he simply replied, "I know. I'll be ready." Jonathan left.

Dr. Johnson decided to dress and get ready quickly as time was running up. But again, his mind and heart were diverted towards his favourite thing - Space.

He motioned towards the largest screen of the department and sat on a desk in front of it. It was the desk on which he had sat tirelessly for various hours, observing space and doing research work.

He said to himself, "Before leaving for the event, I want to look at the beautiful and elegant Universe." He was also a bit puzzled, wondering why he was suddenly getting attracted to space.

He quickly pressed a few buttons and the large screen flickered to life in front of him. He leaned forward, observing the amazing space with full focus and dedication. With each passing moment, he was zooming inside it more and more. He was also able to see the spacecraft which was heading towards the red planet.

But suddenly, a very strange thing happened. As Dr. Johnson concentrated more on the screen, his eyes looked stunned and utterly surprised. His face looked as if he had gone bankrupt! He was unable to process or digest what he was looking at in front of his screen. He typed a few keys and did some calculations, but what he saw left him speechless.

In a slow voice, he asked himself, "Are my eyes getting weaker day by day, or...."

Lana was reading a book on cosmology on the smart tablet. She was reading and absorbing all the information with great focus, avoiding all the distractions. Reading has been her hobby since childhood, and she devoured hundreds and thousands of books.

Zangger, who was seated on the seat beside her, interrupted and asked, "If you don't mind, can I ask you one question, ma'am?"

Lana looked at him and nodded in agreement. She was always ready to question people and answer their questions. Because she had learnt that questioning is very important.

Zangger leaned towards her and asked, "What would you prefer most? Reading traditional or digital books? Because digital ones ruin our eyes and brains. And it will be a great problem for the future of our civilisation."

Lana kept the tablet aside for a while. She found his question quite interesting.

After thinking for a while, she smiled and replied, "Yes! You are right. There is really something romantic about traditional books. An indescribable natural feeling of love and satisfaction comes when we read a book physically. It does not harm our eyes and brains, but digital books do."

She paused, seeing that he was willing to say something.

He began, "So this concludes that digital books should be banned and there should only be the promotion of traditional books in the world. Otherwise, our coming generation will have to face a lot of health issues."

Lana sensed that he was unable to understand the main point.

"Zangger! Our world is developing at a rapid pace. We are already surrounded by gadgets and technology. You are saying that digital books cause a lot of health problems. But simultaneously, they provide a lot of advantages.

They are easy to access and use, there is no fear of losing or spoiling them, they are cheap, etc. Due to digital books, usage of paper is reduced, and trees are saved."

"What do you exactly mean?"

Lana gave a happy smile and said, "The main point that I am trying to tell you is that change is inevitable. With the passing of time, technology will develop constantly, creating many advantages and disadvantages. But instead of trying to eliminate the problem entirely, we should find a solution to it. Instead of complaining and crying over the difficulties, we have to take action to reduce them. And Brown Sir informed me that Virtual Eye is going to start producing special goggles for the protection of digital readers."

Zangger was really inspired by his words. A wave of confidence hit his heart.

"You gave a very beautiful speech, ma'am! I think that instead of being an astronomer and astronaut, you should have become the President of the USA."

There was laughter followed by silence.

On the other hand, the robot Z11 was standing peacefully and observing the space outside. All the crew members were enjoying chit-chatting and reading etc.

Suddenly, the robot started gazing deep outside. He was a very high-tech, general-purpose robot.

Out of all his features, he was designed with extraordinary and sharp sightseeing features.

At that time, he was gazing outside using that special feature.

But as he observed outside, he suddenly saw something that confused him a bit. He was not able to see it clearly as the whole scene was happening very far away from the spaceship. Although extraordinary, his features were not that extraordinary.

Dr. Johnson's whole body was shaking with fear and stress. Sweat was coming down from his forehead as he observed the screen more and more carefully. His head was spinning with a whirlpool of confusion and astonishment.

Between that, Jonathan entered the room. He got a little bit annoyed after finding out that Dr. Johnson had not dressed up for the event.

He exclaimed with irritation, "Sir! It's already 7:10. We have to arrive at the auditorium immediately as we all are the senior executives. And you are still not dressed!"

There was no reply. Dr. Johnson was not listening to anything. He was just constantly staring at the huge screen in front of him.

Jonathan was puzzled. *What happened to Sir? What is he looking at?*

He walked towards him silently. When he went near, he could see the image of the beautiful Universe in front of him on the thin screen.

Slowly, he kept his hand on his shoulder and asked in a low voice, "What happened, Sir? Why are you looking so startled and shocked?"

Without uttering a word from his mouth, Dr. Johnson straightly pointed his index finger at the screen in front.

Jonathan was becoming confused. He zoomed in on the normal-looking space image and stared with full concentration.

As he zoomed in, what he saw was shocking and unbelievable. His body suddenly pumped with adrenaline.

He turned back towards Dr. Johnson and asked in a fearful voice, "Is it am...."

"Yes," replied Dr. Johnson, his whole face turning confused.

CHAPTER FIVE

The shiny Tesla Model Y parked itself in the area of the VIP parking outside the huge and elegant auditorium. Anderson stepped outside quickly and motioned towards the auditorium, full of excitement.

As he walked, he could see men and women gathering all around, dressed beautifully and nicely. All of them looked very happy and enthusiastic. All the ladies were looking so hot and pretty that it seemed as if the programme was arranged for beautiful female models.

The time was 7:20. *Still a lot of time,* he thought.

As he turned his gaze from the beautiful ladies to the great auditorium, he was very impressed by its design and structure. The auditorium was constructed on the orders of James Brown, who had a deep love for architecture. But it was not just an auditorium but a beautiful architectural marvel.

The auditorium's exterior was an imposing structure, with a grand entrance which immediately captured the attention of the passerby. Two larger than life-statues of Albert Einstein and Isaac Newton flanked the entrance, their outstretched hands appearing to welcome the visitors. Their iconic visages were frozen in a gesture of intellectual curiosity, symbolising the pursuit of knowledge.

Above the entrance, there was a captivating scene that drew the eye. A finely detailed model of Mars, glowing in warm hues, was suspended in mid-air, bathed in soft, ambient light. It served as a fascinating prelude to the scientific and intellectual discussions that were sure to unfold inside.

The auditorium itself boasted a stately facade with architectural elements that exuded a sense of history and prestige. Large glass doors provided a glimpse of the bustling activity within as people gathered in anticipation of the speech of Mr. Davis and Sir Brown. The combination of classical architecture, artistic statues, and the celestial model of Mars set the stage for an evening of enlightenment and inspiration within the auditorium's hallowed halls.

Anderson understood that the speech was going to be very interesting as it was going to be a nice mixture of philosophy, humour and emotions.

But like all others, he was not able to understand why Brown had suddenly called up for that event.

As he started moving inside, all the men and women, after spotting the celebrity, began greeting him and shook hands.

Just as he stepped inside the auditorium, he could see that it was a very big, long and simple hall in which more than a thousand people could easily fit without any problem. At the end of the long hall, there was a nice stage, behind which a large, thin screen was hanging.

People had already captured their seats. Because nobody was ready to take any chances of missing the event. Volcanoes of curiosity were exploding inside everybody, resulting in the lava of happiness. All of the people were chatting and gossiping within groups.

The people who were invited to the auditorium to witness the event were not any ordinary or random people. They all were wealthy and famous entrepreneurs, tech CEOs, scientists, and businessmen.

Anderson wanted to pass the time by talking with somebody. But realising that it would be irritating, he decided to take his seat. After all, being famous is also very irritating sometimes.

When he was deciding where to sit, a gentle and polite voice greeted him, "Welcome to the event, Sir! I am very happy to see you."

Anderson turned back. He saw that the voice was of a young and boyish-looking man with messy hair and a small black moustache. He was looking like a high-school football champion and wore a plain black coat.

Anderson was unable to recognise him. *Nowadays, short-term memory loss has become my big problem,* he thought with shame.

Seeing him confused, the young man came forward and said, "Don't worry, Sir. I am the director of this auditorium, Ethan Garcia."

Anderson felt that he could spend his time with the director, but it seemed boring.

Before he opened his mouth, the director asked, "Sir! Half an hour is left before the event starts. If you don't mind, can you come along with me to another hall where I can show you some great things related to science?"

Anderson's brain released dopamine. He had got the best opportunity to spend the remaining time. He became excited to look at and observe the things related to his favourite subject - science.

"Yes! Why not? I'll be very happy about that."

"Okay! Just wait for 2 minutes. I'll return back after going to the washroom."

Anderson nodded in agreement, and the director left hurriedly for the washroom.

As time was passing by, more and more famous personalities were gathering inside the auditorium. They all were drinking juices and eating ice-creams of various delicious flavours that were provided there. His mouth started watering as he loved cold drinks. He made up his mind to fetch a glass of cold drink, which would be nice company when he would look at what the director was going to show him.

When he was walking towards the place to get that, suddenly a tall waiter dashed him. He had covered his face with a mask and was in a great hurry.

"S...Sorry Sir!" the waiter apologised.

Anderson kept staring at him as if he was Donald Trump himself.

The waiter looked a bit puzzled and asked in a fearful voice, "Wh...What happened, Sir?"

Anderson came closer to him. Examining his body from top to bottom, he said, "I don't know why, but it seems that I have seen you many times. But I am not able to recollect who you are. Your presence makes me say that you are a famous personality."

The waiter laughed falsely and exclaimed, "No Sir, what are you saying?"

Sweat was coming from his forehead.

He continued, "I am a small waiter, and you are saying I am a famous

personality!" and he gave a fake laugh.

"What's your name?"

"Nexus."

Anderson was astonished to hear that name. He asked him, "It sounds

totally robotic! I think that you are very scientific."

"Yes! I love AI very much. Playing with robots is my hobby."

"Nice!"

Soon after that, Nexus ran in a hurry and deeper inside the auditorium. He

was running as if the world was going to end. Maybe none can tell that.

Anderson kept wondering about the strange waiter. *How can an ordinary waiter keep his name like a robot? Does he love AI and science so much? But if he loves it, then today, he would have been a great scientist instead of a simple waiter. Some mystery is definitely surrounding him.*

The crowd was increasing constantly. It was sure that all the thousand seats would be occupied.

Just as Anderson was wondering about the mysterious waiter, the director returned. He saw that Anderson was looking at the crowd and thinking something deeply.

"Don't worry, Sir!" his voice was filled with energy, "You don't have to worry about catching your seat. We have arranged special places for you in the first row, where you will enjoy the event along with the senior executives of NSRA, Virtual Eye and SpaceX."

Anderson felt proud about that.

Immediately after that, Director Garcia took him upstairs through a nice, secret elevator where he was going to show him something.

As they reached the desired floor, the elevator door opened. In front of their eyes, they could see a vast hall.

Anderson observed various types of photo frames that dotted the walls of the hall. The frames contained the images of the most influential and popular scientists, innovators and philosophers of all time. The frames were designed out of advanced technology.

"I have visited this auditorium several times, but I haven't seen this room before! It is so beautiful and elegant! But why did you all keep it a secret?" Anderson asked out of rage.

Garcia smiled and replied, "No, Sir! You are thinking wrong. In fact, this room's construction and design has been going on since last month only. We decided to keep it a secret from the public. Only Mr Davis, Sir Brown and Mr Musk know about this. And now you. Our plan is to show this special small room of science to the public after today's event."

Anderson swallowed his short-term anger and immersed himself inside the small, beautiful world of science where the history and progress of science intersected.

Outside the auditorium, some 2 hundred metres away, Joseph was feeling nervous while sitting inside the car. He was continuously thinking about his master's dangerous plan, and also praying to God for its success.

If everything goes well, then it is great. But if some mistake happens, everything will go wrong. Everything.

At that moment, Joseph and his master faced the most important and worst period of their lives. They were going to do such a thing, which was completely going to shatter the whole world.

CHAPTER SIX

In the dimly lit hall, Dr. Anderson and Director Garcia stood in hushed anticipation. Their eyes were dying to observe the things which were in front of them. A soft spotlight illuminated an extravagant exhibition showcasing the greatest achievements of science and historical moments.

As they approached the central exhibit, a lifelike recreation portrayed Elon Musk driving a sleek electric Model X with none other than Nikola Tesla seated beside him, conversing animatedly. The car seemed to glide effortlessly through space, a nod to Musk's SpaceX ventures.

On one side of the exhibit, equations of profound significance floated like ethereal and eternal thought bubbles above a charming and captivating portrayal of Albert Einstein. The great physicist appeared in deep contemplation, and the equations, such as $E=mc2$, seemed to emanate from his very being, symbolising his groundbreaking contributions to the world of physics.

The scene was a mesmerising fusion of past and future, a testament to the remarkable strides in science and ingenuity of humanity, leaving Anderson and Garcia in awe of the boundless possibilities that science and innovation could unlock.

It was really an impressive exhibition. As they moved and saw more things, Director Garcia told him something.

"See here, Sir!"

Amid the grand exhibition, the area surrounding the statues of Isaac Newton and Albert Einstein stood out as an extraordinary display of historical significance. Holograms, as if plucked from the annals of time, materialised in front of the statues.

To the left, Sir Isaac Newton appeared as a holographic figure, demonstrating his groundbreaking discoveries of the 17th century. His image showed him thinking deeply under an apple tree while equations and diagrams floated around him, symbolising his foundational work in classical physics and the laws of motion.

On the right, the holographic form of Albert Einstein emerged, casting a thoughtful gaze upon his theories of relativity and the curvature of spacetime. His presence challenged the Newtonian views of the world, as space and time seemed to warp and bend around him.

As the 2 brilliant scientists stood face-to-face in the holographic realm, a video featuring Mr Davis played on a screen strategically positioned between them. Mr. Davis posed a thought-provoking question to the audience, "Which of these brilliant minds deserves more respect?"

The question was a topic of debate as the visitors would ponder upon the transformative impact of both Newton and Einstein on the course of scientific history.

Anderson felt that the question was logical. He was constantly staring at the screen.

Director Garcia became excited to hear Anderson's views on that topic.

Anderson thought for some time, gave a smile and said with full confidence, "You know what Garcia!"

The director moved closer.

"There are several reasons and explanations which say that both of the great men should always receive the same respect."

Garcia was impressed after realising that Anderson was speaking from his heart and soul.

"You see, dear. Sir Isaac Newton did what needed to be done at the time when it needed to be done. He has got his name engraved in the books of history only because of his thinking and curiosity. He was just obsessed with truth and wanted to understand the nature of the Universe. His creativity and smartness paved the way towards the beginning of a great era of science and astronomy.

On the other hand, 300 years later, nature brought a great scientist, Albert Einstein, into existence to modify and correct Newton's theories. And so, he did that out of his genius and creativity. If Einstein had not taken birth, we would have considered some of Newton's wrong views on space, light, and time. Because of Einstein, we are able to understand the nature of motion, time, light and the Universe very well. After all, none is perfect."

A cool wind blew inside the hall, making a nice environment.

He concluded at last, "The main thing is that both of them have played equal roles in our world. It is the duty of a scientist to challenge the theories of the previous pioneers of that field to give a proper explanation of the cosmos. Therefore, my main point is that Newton and Einstein should be respected equally."

Director Garcia's eyes widened after hearing the answer. He was feeling like he was standing in front of the descendant of Socrates or another great philosopher.

A smile flickering on his face, he said, "Sir! Today, you have taught me a very new perspective on life and its problems. I have understood that each and every person in this world contributes something to humanity. We must respect everyone, as in the case of Einstein and Newton.

Anderson recalled a beautiful quote from Paulo Coelho's The Alchemist book,

"Everyone on Earth has a treasure that awaits him."

Now, they moved deeper inside the exhibition hall. Suddenly, Anderson saw an interesting thing and stopped to analyse it.

There was a small statue of the world-famous biologist of history, Charles Darwin, who, with his theory of evolution, directly challenged the religious beliefs about the story of the creation of life on Earth. The statue was laughing at a small 3D model of the Bible beside it. It was meant to show that science is superior to religion. On the other hand, a hologram materialised above the 3D model of the Bible with the text,

'Laugh as much as you want. But in the end, you will realise that nothing can be explained without God.'

"Oh! That same age-old conflict between science and religion!" hushed Director Garcia with an odd expression.

Anderson smiled softly and said, "The conflict between science and religion will never end until and unless both of them start cooperating instead of arguing."

Garcia sensed that Anderson was very serious about that topic.

Glancing at the models, Anderson continued, "Science and religion both play an important role in our world. Science gives our lives a thrill, a wonder for solving mysteries, and an adventurous spirit. And religion provides us with a moral compass and solace."

"Sorry for disturbing Sir, but science is not controversial. It is factual. People fight over whether Vishnu is the creator of the Universe or Allah is, but they never fight whether gravity is real or not. Because its effects are the same for everyone, whether you are a priest or a scientist. But religion is awful."

Anderson chuckled and replied, his voice calm, "Who says that science isn't controversial? The technology which we are creating today has the ability to rewrite our life! Genetic engineering, biotechnology, artificial intelligence, virtual reality and many more."

Director Garcia looked startled.

"What I mean to say is that science and religion are equally important. Life and the world are dual. Each and everything depend upon each other. Everyone exists for a purpose; nothing is random. Even the tiny electron shows a dual nature, so why not the entire world?"

Garcia was impressed.

"Even though science can find absolute truths, there are some deeper truths which cannot be grasped without religion and spirituality, or stated more simply, without God."

"Great!" Director Garcia admired Anderson's wit.

Anderson wanted to explore the hall more, but suddenly, Garcia's smartphone rang.

He answered the call.

"Sir! I have to immediately move downstairs. The event is going to start in 10 minutes. Let's move."

Soon after that, both of them hurried downstairs from the secret elevator.

All the crew members were sitting on their respective chairs to watch the upcoming event. They were bustling with anticipation and excitement.

Leaning towards the large screen in front of them, Lana thought that the night was going to be very thrilling and satisfying. Her eyes were dying to see the speech and ears were dying to hear it.

The time was 7:50 PM. The whole auditorium was filled with popular tech entrepreneurs, businessmen and scientists. The first and second rows were filled with the top executives of NSRA, Virtual Eye, and SpaceX. They were very well dressed.

As soon as possible, Anderson motioned and sat in that row along with them. Everybody welcomed him with smiles. He felt happy. The event was just 10 minutes away. Everyone's eyes were on the stage.

Amidst that, Anderson felt an urge to go to the toilet. Before leaving, he asked the president of the launch of NSRA, "By the way, where are Dr. Johnson and Jonathan?" How can such important people miss this speech? Where are they?!"

The executive replied in confusion, "Actually, they said very strangely that they have got some very important work, so they will watch the event from where they are. We are trying to ask what exactly has happened, but they are saying that nothing of tension has happened. Everything is fine."

Anderson was startled to hear that. *What important work do they have now after every important work is completed? What the hell are they doing?*

Without wasting much time over that, he quickly proceeded towards the toilet. Time was running up.

After 2 minutes, he returned back. But something very strange happened at that moment.

As he gazed out of the auditorium through the main door, he saw Nexus, the strange waiter wearing a black mask who had accidentally met Anderson some time ago.

Nexus was standing and looking at the auditorium. After scanning it, he turned back and disappeared into the darkness of night in a very strange manner.

Anderson felt his pulse tighten. He was getting more puzzled as he thought more and more about the mysterious waiter who had named himself like a robot. He felt like catching him, but the speech was on the edge of starting. So, he went back and sat in his seat.

The master walked in disappointment towards his car. With each footstep, his heartbeat was accelerating. Joseph came outside the car after seeing him coming.

He asked fearfully, "Sir! Is everything alright? Have you completed the task?"

The master nodded in agreement.

Joseph stood with silence there. He was unable to open his mouth to speak. It seemed as if his tongue and vocal cord were gone on a long vacation. And suddenly, tears started flowing from his eyes.

Seeing Joseph totally broken, the master went near him and tried to encourage him, and he pulled his black mask down.

Behind the mask was a handsome and genial face with a dark black French beard and moustache. His eyes were shining like diamonds.

He said in a very low, but inspiring voice, "Dear Joseph! Your becoming emotional is sure because we have literally done such a thing which we had never imagined in our lives. But the situation is compelling us to do what we are doing. Otherwise, humanity will face great danger. I will never be able to forgive myself if I fail this mission. So don't get sad as humankind's wellness is our ultimate aim."

Joseph felt inspired by his words. He realised that he had to do it in order to stop a major apocalypse.

Both of them entered the car. Joseph asked his master, "Should we head towards our next destination?"

The master again pulled his black mask down and replied, "Yes! Move the car where it is destined to go. There will not be much crowd at the airport at this time as everyone's eyes are on the event."

"I think that something very mysterious is going to happen within an hour on our planet!" shouted Dr. Johnson as he moved away from the screen towards Jonathan.

"Yes! According to the calculations of our supercomputer, the strange circular meteorite will be crashing on our planet sooner. And that, too, right behind our agency!"

The hearts of both of them were throbbing at a very fast rate. They were utterly shocked after finding that a circular meteorite, about the size of a bed, was going to hit the surface of the Earth, right behind the NSRA! It was going to be a very mysterious night.

Jonathan said, "It will be good if we still don't inform anyone about this. Let them enjoy the event nicely. After that, we will tell them."

Dr. Johnson took a chair and sat beside Jonathan. They both started watching the event live on Jonathan's smartphone. That was the best way to pass their time till the meteorite would land.

What was going to happen, nobody knew. But it was sure that the upcoming incidents would be exciting, stressful, and mysterious.

CHAPTER EIGHT

The auditorium was completely filled with famous people. There was not a single place even for standing. A few celebrities to name among them were Mr Walter Smith, the chairman of a famous electric and futuristic car company; Mrs Diana Martin, the CEO of the largest television manufacturing company; Mr Jack Solomon, the physics guru of Stanford University; and many other brilliant minds. All of the population present there were extremely interested in space technology and space itself.

At sharp 8 PM, the lights of the long hall were turned off. It was totally filled with darkness.

Soon after that, the lights on the stage came to life. Director Ethan Garcia came walking, with a broad smile on his face. He looked very confident and excited.

On the huge screen behind the stage, there was written:

"A Historical and Philosophical Speech by 2 great tech entrepreneurs of our era."

Garcia stood in front of a digital desk at a corner of the stage. He pulled a deep breath, gazed at the thousand people in front of him, and announced in a voice filled with a lot of energy, "Welcome, all my dear ladies and gentlemen! Tonight is going to be very exciting and inspiring. As we all know, humankind has done a great thing today after launching the spaceship, which is going to take humans to Mars, so Sir James Brown has organised the event to celebrate it. The main reason is still unknown as to why he has suddenly called up for this event."

Everyone wondered about that mystery, including Anderson.

Why has Sir Brown called up the whole world for this event? The spaceship has not yet landed on Mars, so why this speech? There is really something that he wants to tell the whole world. But what is it?

Garcia continued, "But what mankind has done today hasn't happened overnight. It was the blood, sweat and tears of thousands of scientists, engineers and executives who made this old dream come true. It took 10 years for the robots to build the Universal Research Laboratory on the red planet, on the commands and instructions of humans."

The air of the hall was filled with emotions.

"All of us at this moment are wondering why Sir Brown has suddenly organised this event. It has created a sense of mystery all around the globe. Yes, or no?"

"Yes!!!"shouted the audience in chorus.

Adjusting his necktie, Garcia said in a loud voice, "Okay! So, let's hear the answer to the mystery from the mouth of the person who has created it! I would like to welcome the 2 great tech leaders and best friends who are changing the face of technology in the twenty-first century. Please welcome our beloved celebrities, Mr. Liam Davis and Sir James Brown. Give them a huge round of applause."

The auditorium was hit with a wave of happiness and enthusiasm.

The audience hooted and shouted loudly the names of the 2 innovators as they came on the stage.

Mr. Davis had worn a full blue coat in which he was looking very charming. On the other hand, Brown had worn a dark black plain suit. His young age was making him look more attractive and handsome.

Both of them sat on 2 digital chairs, which were kept on the stage for them. They were feeling very proud at that moment.

The audience already knew that Musk was not going to attend the event as he was sleeping peacefully to regain the strength of his body which he had lost due to his long working hours for the Mars mission.

The hall became totally silent. There was pin-drop silence. Everyone's eyes were on them. People all around the world were watching the event live.

Sir Brown took the microphone and greeted everyone with a simple hello.

There was the same reply.

"My dear fellow business friends, genius scientists, researchers and all my people, we both are very enlightened and happy as you took the effort and interest to attend this event to hear our speech. We are very glad to see you all."

Mr. Davis took the microphone and said, "But before proceeding further, I have news for all of you that is very good for Brown."

All were eager to hear the news.

Mr Davis turned his gaze at Brown and announced loudly, "I would like to tell you that today, about 2 minutes ago, my dear buddy and business partner Brown became the richest person in the world, overtaking Elon Musk with a net worth of $245 billion!"

There was a huge round of applause. The sound of clapping was accelerating like a rocket.

Anderson thought *Brown Sir deserved that as he was a genius and a hard-working person.*

"I had never ever dreamt of becoming the richest person in the world," Brown said, "I had always just dreamt of becoming a big innovator in order to push the bounds of science and innovation with my companies. That's the reason why I entered into the business world after dropping out of Stanford."

There was laughter.

"Today, I am not happy because I have become the wealthiest man alive on Earth, but because I have contributed to the world through my groundbreaking innovations and technologies. My trillion-dollar company, Virtual Eye, has changed the technological landscape, contributing to the world to a large extent. And this is only possible due to futuristic vision and hard work."

He paused, giving Mr. Davis a chance to speak.

"Yeah! James is absolutely correct. We always think about how we can develop our civilisation so that humanity has a very bright future. As the chairman and CEOs of our respective companies, we always put our heart and soul into our companies' projects."

Mr. Davis took a small remote from the small square-shaped table kept between their chairs and gently pressed a button on it, pointing towards the huge thin screen behind them.

After he pressed it, to everyone's surprise, a clear and HD image of Neil Armstrong flickered on the screen.

The audience was unable to connect it.

Seeing the gossip which began among the audience, Sir Brown laughed and said, "My dear fellows! Don't get startled. This is just the beginning."

Anderson glanced at the screen with complete focus. He knew what was going to happen next.

Sir Brown turned a little serious and, while examining the image, said, "This man has captured the hearts of all the people around the world due to the extraordinary role he has played in the history of mankind, as we all know. Neil Armstrong was the first person to set foot on the Moon."

Everyone was staring at the American hero's image with pride.

Brown looked at the people and said, "20 July 1969 was the day when humankind took a giant leap when humans first stepped on the Moon, whom our ancestors prayed, and people still pray. It was an unbelievable achievement."

There was silence for a while.

Mr. Davis changed the slide, and the image of the evolution of humans was visible on the screen.

He continued, "Homo Sapiens evolved on this planet some 4 billion years ago, when a single cell started multiplying and multiplying until the first DNA was formed, thus creating life. However, it is still a mystery how we actually came into existence."

Anderson was immersed in the speech. Such topics always interested him.

"Our ancestors thought only about eating and sleeping. But as time progressed, so did the intelligence and brains of them. Eventually, civilisations developed and collapsed, religions developed, which inspired us and gave us a sense of purpose, and cultures emerged, which connected us together."

Mr. Davis spoke, "But everything was not great until science entered the field. The first human who set foot on the soil of Earth must have never thought that his descendants were going to fly above the skies, reaching other celestial bodies. But that happened. Because every possible thing first seems impossible. That's the rule of nature."

The screen now featured the beautiful images of various scientists and geniuses who completely changed the course of human history. Clear images of Newton, Galilieo, Copernicus, Einstein, Tesla, Edison, Darwin, Hawking, Ramanujan were visible.

Mr. Davis continued, "Our ancestors of the stone age period didn't ever imagine that the hands by which they were making simple stone tools and hunting animals, will one day make rockets and spaceships. They never thought that we would ever use a great device like a computer. If we travel back in the past and bring a stone age man in our own time, he will feel that he is standing in heaven by looking at our unimaginable world."

Brown began with a soft smile, "Newton and Einstein wrote and rewrote the laws of the Universe, Tesla and Edison lit up the world with their world-changing inventions by harnessing one of the greatest forces of nature - Electricity. These men are the ones because of whom we all are having a comfortable and leisure time."

Everyone became emotional.

"These guys dared to imagine the impossible, and eventually, they ended up changing the world. But why so?"

The question of Mr. Davis hung in the air.

"This is because they were just obsessed with the truth. Their curiosity and boundless love for wisdom and reality led them to cross all the human limitations and touch the skies just by using their brains."

The slide now featured a captivating image of Benjamin Franklin and his famous quote.

"Investment in knowledge pays the best interest," began Sir Brown loudly,

"This quote is worth reading again and again. Education is the solid base of our building, which is our life. The only way to serve the world happily and die peacefully is to gain as much wisdom as possible. The first step towards creating an exciting and bright future is to get a proper education. Each and every individual who is born on this Earth should be educated properly. Then only we can hope for a great future."

The audience was getting more and more inspired by the golden words of the 2 innovators.

Anderson felt very happy when they talked about the importance of education.

Lana and the other crew members were watching the show in amazement. Lana's eyes were totally focused on the 2 showmen. She was really enjoying it.

Standing at the back of everyone, Z11 was also watching the speech with full interest.

Suddenly, he looked at Sir Brown on the screen and said to himself in an emotionless voice, "Within a few minutes, everything is going to change."

CHAPTER NINE

"What will the future look like?" asked Mr. Davis to the audience. The question created complete silence in the hall. Everyone present there was constantly thinking and wondering about the answer.

Mr Davis looked confident. A smile lingered across his face.

"How the future will look depends upon how we shape it today," Mr. Davis spoke with full energy, "Our present actions will affect the future. It depends upon us how we act today for a better future. Technology is developing at a very great speed, and it is inevitable. Technology gives our life an adventurous journey and purpose."

Everyone agreed.

"But with great technology comes great responsibility. We have to ensure that the technology which we will develop doesn't harm us."

There was a short silence. Everyone's guess was correct. The speech was very philosophical.

Sir Brown scanned the hall and said loudly, "In the year 1969, Neil Armstrong set his step on the Moon, which is a satellite. But within a few months, mankind is going to step on Mars, which is not just a satellite but a planet! Our constant struggles of 10 years are going to pay us back soon."

Mr. Davis changed the slide, and the image of Mars was clearly visible in the background of the dark space.

"My dear ladies and gentlemen," Brown continued, "Open your eyes and souls! We are now not far away from becoming a multiplanetary species! Everything is going to change completely!"

Inspiring and energetic music started in the background, which energised the audience.

Mr. Davis continued the track, "Our ancestors would have never imagined that their descendants would one day extend their consciousness to other planets. Just within a year or 2, we would start doing agriculture on Mars and eventually start building human colonies! Humanity is now standing in front of a door, which, if opened, will take it into an entirely different world. That's really exciting."

People around the world who were watching the event realised that it was really a historic speech.

Sir Brown threw a jovial expression and exclaimed, "Just imagine, guys! Today, we played football matches between Argentina and Manchester United, cricket matches between India and Pakistan, etc. But now we are not far away from the day when we will play matches between Mars and Earth! And people will hurry like mad dogs and chimpanzees to buy the tickets as they do now!"

There was laughter, followed by silence.

"And with rapid progress, a day will come when we build a stadium that floats in space between the 2 planets, and people will watch the match by sitting in their own spaceships!"

Cutting his speech in between, Brown said, "And we will go for our summer vacations on the red planet or a distant galaxy from Earth just as we go from the US to London."

The audience was stunned. They were all lost in their own imaginary worlds where they are travelling in space in their own spaceship. It was awesome.

Suddenly, Mr. Davis asked everyone a question.

"Why is it so important for life to become multiplanetary? Why are people like Elon Musk so determined and dedicated to achieving that goal? Why?"

The question directly attacked the brains of the audience.

Before anyone could answer, Sir Brown smiled and said, "Today, Dr. Jacob Anderson is present among us. I would like to hear the answer to Liam's question from the mouth of the genius Dr. Anderson. Please welcome him on the stage!"

Anderson was suddenly struck by an arrow of surprise. He had not thought that he would be called on the stage. But after all, the best things always happen unexpectedly.

Without wasting time, he proceeded towards the stage with courage, accompanied by a bit of nervousness.

The whole hall echoed with thunderous clapping.

He went and stood before the digital desk where Director Garcia was standing, who then moved aside.

Anderson pulled a deep breath and said enthusiastically, "Thank you my seniors, for giving me this wonderful opportunity. I would really like to answer this question."

Clearing his throat, Anderson stared confidently into the audience's eyes and began, "Friedrich Nietzsche, the most influential and controversial philosopher of the twentieth century, has made a very famous statement which has a deep meaning hidden in it. He said, 'Anyone who has a way to live can bear any how.' I will not go deep into the statement."

Everyone's eyes were focused on him.

"People often forget or fail to find why they are doing what they are doing. There is a great difference between why and what. But the former one is really very difficult. In this case, we have found and can find many ways *how* to become a multiplanetary civilisation. But *why* are we dreaming of it? Why are we investing so much money, time, and energy into it? Why?"

Sir Brown and Mr Davis looked at each other. They thought that they had done absolutely right by giving Anderson a chance to speak.

"We all are now hoping to make the future exciting by making life multiplanetary. But by all, I mean a very few people. Even today, many people criticise the concept of this. They say that we should focus on improving the Earth before searching to settle on other planets."

Director Garcia realised that Anderson was correct.

"But I say to all those critics," he turned a bit angry, "That in order to make human consciousness survive forever, we have to extend that consciousness beyond Earth. Anytime an asteroid can hit the surface of our planet and wipe off life completely as it did 65 million years ago to the dinosaurs. Will the critics survive to criticise us then?"

There was a huge laughter. Anderson was a master at mixing seriousness with humour.

"Okay, so let's assume that we develop the technology to stop asteroids from hitting our planet. Even then, our own foolishness will kill us. This is because we can only be responsible for the end of our species as we have all nuclear weapons, deadliest strategies and desire for power and money. Even if we earthies end ourselves, our consciousness can survive on Mars and beyond that if we extend it beyond the red planet."

There was pin-drop silence.

"In an interview at Vivatech, Elon Musk said a golden line that we should always remember.

'The light of consciousness is like a tiny candle in a vast Darkness, and we should do everything we can to prevent that candle from going out.'

Our Universe is so large that we can't even imagine its size. And it is still expanding. We haven't found any evidence of life. It can also be like we are all alone in this world and have the greatest gift of consciousness. So, we need to save this consciousness at any cost. How would you feel when the Earth on which you were born, played happily, studied, wondered about the mysteries of the cosmos, loved someone, laughed and cried, became angry and then forgave, gets destroyed, or the life on it gets destroyed? Who will then appreciate the greatness of Newton, Socrates or Picasso? Our every struggle will be of no use if everything will end. We have to do something so that the human consciousness survives forever. Our future generation should immerse themselves totally in finding the secrets of life, the Universe and everything. And making life multiplanetary is essential for that."

Anderson adjusted his tuxedo and said in an emotional but energetic voice, "Which future do you think is bright and exciting? The one where you see roads and buildings after waking up, or the one where you see stars and planets after waking up?"

There was a huge round of applause, accompanied by praises and admiration for Anderson. His words had really created a huge impact on the hearts and souls of everyone.

"Thank you all for your love and support!" Saying so, he walked back to his seat. He was feeling proud of himself at that moment.

"Thank you so much, Dr. Anderson, for making a mystical and emotional

environment here," said Brown with a smile.

Mr. Davis breathed and said, "I'd like to take a moment to delve into the

intriguing story of Elon Musk's childhood, a story that played a pivotal role

in shaping his ambitions of making humans a multiplanetary species

through the creation of SpaceX."

Everybody became more enthralled and interested as Mr. Davis decided

to talk about the genius billionaire tech entrepreneur, who with his companies, brought a great technological revolution in the world from

space, automobiles and transport to the brain, payments and Artificial

Intelligence. But simultaneously, they were feeling very disappointed as he was not present to speak at the speech.

Anderson felt very proud to be alive in the time of such a creative and innovative person like Elon Musk. Such genius people give birth once in decades.

Mr. Davis was suddenly hit by confidence and excitement as he started

the story.

"As we all know, Elon Musk has been a voracious reader from a young

age. His insatiable and unending curiosity led him to explore a wide range

of topics, from science fiction to engineering and space exploration. Musk's

childhood fascination with books, especially those centred around space and science, ignited a spark within him."

Anderson seemed lost in the speech as Mr. Davis continued.

"One of his favourite books, *The Hitchhiker's Guide to The Galaxy* by Douglas Adams is a comedic science fiction series that captures the imagination and humour of intergalactic adventures. This book, along with other classics of the genre, sparked Musk's desire to venture beyond the confines of Earth."

Sir Brown became emotional as he was also a great fan of the book by Douglas Adams. He then remembered the day when he and Elon were discussing the meaning of life on a cold evening.

Mr. Davis increased his speed, "Elon Musk's reading obsession instilled in him a profound appreciation for the potential of space exploration. He saw the boundless possibilities that the cosmos offered and believed that humanity's future should extend far beyond our home planet. This passion and vision led him to establish SpaceX, a company dedicated to revolutionising space travel and ultimately making humans a multiplanetary species."

Everybody's heart suddenly turned sensitive as they heard the inspirational story. Director Garcia was hearing him without blinking his eyes.

"Today, as we witness the incredible progress of SpaceX, including our both companies and Elon Musk's unwavering dedication to his childhood dreams, we are reminded that sometimes, the books we read as children can become the blueprints for the extraordinary futures we create. Musk's journey from a bookworm to a visionary entrepreneur is an inspiration to us all as we work together to expand the horizons of human exploration and consciousness."

The silent auditorium suddenly erupted with the noise of thundering clapping from the audience. Some people's eyes started watering as they heard the powerful success story of Elon Musk.

Looking at Mr. Davis, Brown said, "Really! If we dream about something and work super hard for it, one or the other day, we finally get success. A few months later, when the astronauts step on Mars, Musk, Sir, will be beyond his imagination and belief. He will realise that his ultimate dream has been accomplished. A great, proud and historic moment!"

There was a huge round of applause again. Everybody was very happy.

That day, the audience felt proud to be human instead of just becoming proud of being an Indian, an American, a Russian, or a Brazilian.

Mr. Davis smiled and said with confidence, "Before giving success, God takes everyone's test. The one who passes it definitely achieves the dream he wants to achieve. The test includes just 3 simple lessons - faith, courage and perseverance."

The hall once again echoed with the sound of clapping.

But amidst all that, something strange happened. A handsome young man, who was the CMO of Virtual Eye, Robin, was seated just beside Anderson. He noticed that Anderson was suddenly sweating as if he was very worried about something.

Leaning towards him, he asked in confusion, "What happened, Sir? Why are you looking so worried and tense? Has something happened?"

Coming back to reality, Anderson gave a fake smile and fluttered, "No! N....Nothing. I am totally fine. I am just feeling a bit tired and uncomfortable due to the stomachache I have had since morning. Nothing else."

But Robin still felt that Anderson was hiding something from him. But what, he was unable to understand.

Anderson's body was sweating profusely. His heartbeat was also increasing. But why, he also didn't know.

I don't know why, but my inner voice is strongly telling me that something very bad is going to happen soon. But what bad can happen during such a happy and joyful time?

Anderson was not at all able to understand what was going to happen. He just decided to have some faith.

Lana and the crew members felt great when they saw Anderson's speech. Lana was also becoming very emotional.

Z11 came near her and asked in his mechanical voice, "Why are you becoming so emotional, ma'am?"

Smiling like a beautiful angel, she replied, "Dear Z! You will not understand as you are not a human being, but just a robot. Robots don't have feelings and emotions, but humans do have."

Nodding in agreement, he moved back and again stared at the screen.

But suddenly, Lana's curious brain again started exploding with questions which were very difficult for her.

Robots don't have consciousness, and they don't have emotions. They can just act how we programme them. I don't think that they will ever be able to think. But one question has always troubled me since childhood.

"What will happen if robots try to help us for our own benefit, but in a very different way that we may not like?"

"Just 15 minutes more, and the mysterious meteorite will land near our agency! Thanks to its size. Otherwise, something bad might have happened," exclaimed Dr. Johnson as he gazed at the computer screen.

Both of them were just thinking about what mystery the meteorite might bring along.

But at the same time, Sir Brown's mystery was just about to be solved.

• 65 •

The auditorium turned silent again as Sir Brown was willing to speak. He picked up a shiny glass from the table on which Einstein's picture was engraved. He decided to move further while drinking cold coffee. It was his favourite thing, and he always drank it during such important events. Before the start of the event, he had ordered Director Garcia to keep that glass ready so that he could drink it while telling the world his important thing. The glass was very special to him because it was gifted to him by Mr. Davis, his dear buddy.

Taking the cup in his hand, he got up from the chair and walked ahead on the stage. Director Garcia thought that he was going to say something important.

He smiled and said, "My dear friends, I would like to ask you one question. Please tell me who my favourite scientist is."

The hall echoed with the name of Albert Einstein. Everyone knew that Sir Brown worshipped Einstein as if he was his God.

"Yes! You all are absolutely correct. I have idolised Einstein since my childhood. He is a sort of God figure to me. I feel that I am the greatest fan and devotee of him who is alive on this Earth."

Suddenly, Mr Walter Smith, the chairman of one of the most popular electric car companies, stood up and asked in astonishment, "Sorry to disturb Sir Brown, but I want to know why you are suddenly talking about your hero, Einstein. It seems a bit puzzling."

Everyone found the question logical, including Mr. Davis.

Sir Brown threw a smile at the audience and replied, "Mr. Smith! The whole world got surprised today after getting to know that I suddenly organised this event. And conspiracy theories started spreading all around on the internet and social media that I am going to share some very important information with everyone through this event."

Walter Smith exclaimed with surprise, "Means are you really going to share something very important with the world today? That's why you organised this event?!!"

Sir Brown's expression showcased his excitement.

"Mr. Smith, always remember that things don't happen randomly. Each and everything in this world happen for some or the other reason. Same is with this event."

"Okay, but then why are you talking about Einstein instead of sharing the important information?"

Sir Brown put his hands in his pockets and replied loudly, "Mr. Smith! The main topic of this event is none other than Albert Einstein!"

The audience was shocked to hear that. They were unable to believe their ears.

What the hell is this going on? Brown Sir organised this event to share some information about Albert Einstein to the world? But what information? Thought Anderson.

Mr Davis asked, "What are you saying, James? It is not just a surprise for the whole world, but also for me! You planned this event to share some important things about Einstein? And you didn't tell me. But why?" And he gave an odd look.

"I have kept this information secret from everyone around the Universe. None knows about this except me."

Saying so, Sir Brown walked towards the huge screen, taking the remote from Mr. Davis. The eyes of all the people, especially scientists, were on Brown. They were eager to hear what he was going to say about the scientific genius - Albert Einstein.

Lana, Zangger and all the crew members were staring at the screen on the wall in front of them as if an alien was speaking with them.

"My dear friends! Don't put much stress on your brain. Just relax and enjoy what happens next. Now, I am going to tell you all such a thing about Albert Einstein about which none would have ever imagined! Just relax and enjoy. And remember that after the revelation, the entire future of humanity is going to change! Entire future."

His words sent an invisible force inside the souls of the population.

He smiled gently and said, "Einstein was considered a dumb and boring kid by his teachers and classmates. None expected that he would succeed in future."

Brown's gestures were impressive.

"But as we all know, the people who are thought to be foolish and different are the ones who end up changing the world like Einstein. His work on the special and general theory of relativity, photoelectric effect, cosmology, wormholes, time and many other complex physics topics changed the face of science forever. Even though he is not with us today, his name will be echoed through the corridors of time forever."

Brown changed the slide and a new image flickered on the screen. But that image shocked all the people who were watching the event.

Anderson was startled. *What is the name of God? What the hell is this!!!*

It was the image of a newspaper. The headline of it was **'Einstein Dies!'**

Anderson's pulse tightened as he focused on the image. He, including everybody, were left speechless after looking at the news of 18 April 1855 when Einstein took his last breath and left the world.

Mr. Davis observed that Brown was pressing his stomach slightly while drinking cold coffee. But he didn't pay much attention as his mind was focused on Einstein.

"18 April 1955 was the day when humanity lost a great science hero who helped to revolutionise the entire physics by rewriting the laws of the Universe. He is also regarded as the person of the 20th century," began Brown with sheer enthusiasm.

"Albert Einstein changed the entire course of science with his groundbreaking discoveries and theories. Such types of people take birth once in a hundred years. Today, we all know almost everything about his life and work. He is an inspiration for today's science geeks."

He finished the glass of cold coffee and kept it on the table.

"But everything is not known completely. There is always some mystery about each and every one of us if we examine them closely. After all, the Universe itself is filled with countless mysteries. The same is true with Einstein. Even though we know a lot about him, we all have forgotten one important thing about him, which remains an unsolved mystery to this day."

Gossip started taking place among people. At that moment, everyone was just thinking about what humankind has forgotten about the scientific hero.

Sir Brown was walking slowly from left to right and vice versa, with a broad smile on his face.

Finally, he decided to reveal the secret.

Taking a deep breath, he announced, "Guys! Be ready. Open your eyes, ears and hearts as I am going to tell you the secret which is going to alter the entire course of mankind."

Anderson and the audience were staring unblinkingly at Brown. Their hearts were beating as if they were performing an intense dance performance. Just after a few moments, they were going to hear a breathtaking secret about Albert Einstein.

Sir Brown stopped and said, "The secret is as follows:

When Einstein was admitted to a hospital in Princeton, New Jersey, USA, he died at about 1:15 AM in his sleep. But the nurse who was present there said that he spoke something in German before his death. But she was not able to understand as she didn't understand German.

To this day, Einstein's last words remain a mystery for everyone."

The revelation sent a wave of shock and thrill all across the world. None had ever imagined that Brown would tell some secret that will directly link with Einstein's death.

Within a fraction of a second after his announcement, there was a huge chaos and gossip all around. Almost each and every person was astonished to hear that.

Director Garcia became very impatient. He said to himself, "Oh God! A truth that has been lost for several years will now finally be revealed."

Mrs. Diana Martin, a beautiful and charming tech leader got up from her seat and asked Sir Brown, "Means if I am not wrong, do you know something that directly connects to the last words of Einstein?"

Brown smiled and replied, "Mrs. Martin! I don't know something which directly connects with the last words of Einstein. In fact, I know the exact last words of Albert Einstein."

There was complete silence in the hall. Everybody's face had become expressionless. On the other hand, Brown was looking happy and excited.

Now Brown was going to tell the world what Einstein's last words were.

He was moving slowly from left to right like a pendulum. But simultaneously, he was pressing his stomach very much.

After stopping at a place, he announced heartily, "So my dear beloved people! Now listen to what the great Albert Einstein said before leaving the world."

All the people stopped breathing, and their hearts were throbbing.

He continued, "Before his death, Albert Einstein said that...."

But alas! A very heart-wrenching thing happened before he completed his sentence.

To everyone's surprise, the smart and handsome innovator suddenly collapsed on the stage, pressing his stomach and shrieking in pain.

There was a huge chaos in the auditorium. All the senior executives of NSRA, Virtual Eye and SpaceX got up and rushed on the stage. Director Garcia and Anderson also ran.

While running, Anderson thought, *my doubt was correct. I was strongly feeling that something bad was going to happen. Hey God! Save Brown Sir!*

But it was too late.

There was a very loud noise behind the NSRA.

"The meteorite has landed! The meteorite has landed!" shouted Dr. Johnson with excitement. He was calling Jonathan, who was seated in one corner of the room and glancing at his smartphone.

Dr. Johnson was surprised to see that Jonathan was not responding even after hearing the loud noise of the meteorite. Becoming annoyed, he ran towards him and shouted in rage, "Hey! The meteorite has landed! What are you doing? And Brown Sir is announcing something about Einstein's last words, right?"

Without giving any reply, Jonathan kept staring at the tiny screen of the mobile phone. And suddenly, a drop of tear fell from his eye on the screen.

Seeing the drop of tears, Dr Johnson grabbed the phone from his hand and examined it. As he glanced at the screen, his eyes widened, and his mouth remained open.

He quickly fell to his knees with disappointment and shouted at the top of his voice, "Brown Sir!!!"And tears rolled down his cheeks including Jonathan's.

CHAPTER ELEVEN

There was a huge chaos at the auditorium. People were shouting and running away. Everyone across the globe was shocked to see the great technologist and billionaire struggling for life on the stage.

On the vast, smooth stage, in front of the 2 chairs, Sir Brown was lying down with his hands pressed on his stomach. He was shrieking in pain.

Mr. Davis knelt beside him, his face filled with sweat and eyes with water.

Director Garcia immediately called the ambulance, but Anderson told him that there was no use. James Brown was already dead.

Mr Davis covered his face with his hands and started weeping. The whole Earth trembled with shock that night. All over the globe, there was utter sadness and nothing. Everybody's beloved billionaire had left the world very tragically.

"No! James Sir! That's impossible!" shouted Lana at the top of her voice, throwing her mobile phone away with a large force. Her eyes turned red, and she started weeping after looking at the dead body of Brown on the screen.

Dr. Zangger and all the other crew members completely collapsed after that traumatising incident. They all totally forgot about the mission for sure.

Lana, still weeping, said, "But how can this be possible? How can a strong and healthy man like him die suddenly? Was it a heart attack or something else?"

Everyone, along with Z11, agreed with her.

Dr. Zangger said in a very disappointing voice, "Yes. He didn't have any type of health issues or disorders. So how come he died suddenly?"

"Murder!" replied Lana with a bit of annoyance.

"There is definitely someone behind this who has killed Brown Sir out of jealousy and enmity. And I vow to find and punish the criminal."

Surprisingly, Lana ordered Z11 to switch the spaceship to manual mode and return to Earth. The acoustics of the spaceship were unable to believe what she said. All the crew members thought as if they were watching a dream when she gave that order.

"What the hell are you saying, ma'am?!! Are you fine? We are on a mission which is extremely important for the whole of humankind. How can we return back?" exclaimed Zangger with astonishment.

Lana's face turned red with anger, and she replied in a loud voice, "I also know that Zangger! But this is not good. The person who worked tirelessly for 10 years for this mission will not be able to see it. And after all, Sir Brown was like a very close relative to me. After the death of my parents and family, he and Mr. Davis took care of me. I cannot let this injustice happen. I vow to find that criminal and punish him badly for taking the life of such a kind person."

Everyone was left speechless. They were feeling very emotional.

"Z11! Dare you to argue this time? Switch the mode to manual and move the spaceship towards Earth."

Seeing Lana's anger and sadness, the robot followed her commands without arguing.

There was a long silence inside the spaceship. Not a single crew member dared to speak against her after seeing her anger and annoyance. None had ever imagined that Sir Brown would die at the mere age of 35.

Lana wiped her tears. But even after wiping so much, there was no use because they were not going to stop.

All the crew members were unable to understand why Lana was so damn serious about finding that criminal by herself. Yes, it was true because she worked very closely with Brown. But still, they wondered how she could stop such an important mission in between. The main reason remained a mystery to them.

Lana gazed out of the spaceship window. With tears flowing down from her eyes, she said, "Don't worry, James! I will surely catch the evil soul who has killed you. You will get justice at any cost. It's my promise."

Far away, near the airport of Los Angeles, California, a car stopped. Joseph and his master came out of it, the master completely disguising himself, even changing his identity and name.

Suddenly, as they were walking towards the airport, Joseph shouted, "Sir! Breaking news! Brown Sir died just 2 minutes ago at the auditorium. The internet and social media are going crazy."

Hearing the devastating news, the master's eyes filled with tears of sadness, including that of Joseph's. Quickly, he took out his smartphone from his pocket and opened something.

"We did not have any option excluding this dear Joseph! I don't know why, but God has chosen us for this purpose. We have completed our first task sincerely and successfully. Now it's the time to proceed further."

Saying so, both of them hurried inside the airport. They had to catch a flight for their next mission.

But before that, one question kept troubling the master. *Who is the one who told me to do all this by texting me? And how come he knows about this secret along with Sir Brown?*

CHAPTER TWELVE

Anderson's eyes had become red. They showcased his sadness and emotions at that time. He had been very excited for the speech, but now conditions had changed everything.

Director Garcia immediately informed the police and asked everyone to leave the auditorium. All the cameras and everything was switched off. The executives of the 3 companies, including Davis, were forcibly removed. He was not at all ready to leave, but Anderson convinced him to leave. And with extreme disappointment, he left.

Now, only Garcia and Anderson were left, along with some security officers of the auditorium. The auditorium, which was filled with happiness and excitement a few moments ago, had suddenly become a silent area. There was total silence. Anderson and Garcia were not able to develop the courage to look at the lifeless body of Brown.

Director Garcia walked silently towards Anderson and asked in a low voice, "What is the reason for the death of Sir Brown according to you?"

Anderson thought for some time. It was difficult for him to think about the death of the person with whom he used to work closely.

After a few whiles, he replied, "I don't think that Brown Sir died due to some health issue or disorder. Almost the whole world knows how strong and fit he was. And recently, he didn't have any issues. All this leads to just one conclusion: Brown Sir is murdered by someone."

"Murder! Who? Why? Why would someone want to murder such a great personality?!"

"To silence the information of the secret which he had! Do you remember that before dying, Brown Sir was going to tell the world the last words of Albert Einstein? The killer doesn't want Brown Sir to share the secret, so he killed him."

Director Garcia was shocked to hear that. But he was puzzled.

"But what is so special about the last words of Albert Einstein that the killer directly took the life of Brown Sir? Do they share some very great information?"

Anderson became serious and replied, "Yes. I feel that they contain very valuable information. That's why Brown Sir organised this event. They really carry some information which is no less than a treasure."

Amidst their conversation, the area surrounding the auditorium was filled with the sound of sirens. By hearing that, Garcia and Anderson understood that the policemen and the Forensic team had arrived.

"I think the police and the Forensic team have arrived. Everything will be sorted out now," exclaimed Director Garcia.

Anderson nodded and looked at the entrance door.

From the huge entrance door of the auditorium, a tall, dashing and muscular police officer came walking. It seemed as if he was a WWE champion due to his rigid body and biceps. A smart, but nerd-looking scientist wearing a white coat, black jeans and spectacles was coming along with him towards the stage.

Two police officers were following them.

Within a minute, they hurried towards the stage and were unable to believe that they were looking at the dead body of Brown Sir.

The police officer and the scientist motioned towards the dead body.

"Hello, Director Garcia and Dr Jacob Anderson! I am the COP of this city, Mr. Abner Ardolf. I will be the chief investigation officer of this strange and sad case."

There was a short silence.

Pointing towards the nerd scientist, he said, "Meet him! He is the head and the chief scientist of the top Forensic Department of Los Angeles, Dr. Nathan Bell. He will be the main person who is going to undertake the responsibility and the task of doing research on the body of Brown Sir."

Adjusting his wire-rimmed and squared-shaped glasses, Dr. Bell walked towards Anderson and said confidently, "Don't worry! I will quickly find out the reason for Brown Sir's death. Then it will be easy for us to find the criminal."

Anderson nodded.

Soon after that, the 2 police officers picked up the lifeless body of Brown from the stage and put it into the ambulance to take it into the Forensic lab.

Far away from the auditorium where one of the most traumatising and devastating incidents in the world of business and technology had happened, in a small house, Mr. Liam Davis, the founder, chairman and CEO of NSRA, was lying on his bed as if he was ousted from his own company and gone bankrupt. But the thing which had happened was far worse than that. His dear friend and business partner, James Brown, had left him forever.

Staring out towards the full Moon outside the bedroom of his window, he said in a low voice to himself, "Nights are really very beautiful. Sometimes, they fill wonderful colours of happiness into one's life, and sometimes, they snatch away all the happiness from someone's life. Nobody has any idea of how their nights are going to be. But this time is really very great."

A cool and gushing wind blew inside the room.

"It is the time when a hard-working student sacrifices his sleep for his studies in order to achieve his goals. An entrepreneur puts his blood, sweat and tears into the work of his company all night. But God should never fill the dark bands of sadness into someone's night because it is the time when all the people, whether poor or rich, kind or cruel, hard-working or lazy, forget everything and try to have a few moments of silence and peace. But if they are not happy, they will not be able to sleep well. Their whole night will be worthless."

Continuing looking at the dark sky outside, he kept talking to himself.

"Once, a great and powerful king asked one of his wise ministers a question. He asked him who was the happiest person in the whole world. Whether it is a soldier, businessman, or a doctor. The minister smiled and replied, 'The only happiest person in the whole world is the one who sleeps peacefully at night. This is because a person who is sleeping peacefully is totally relaxed and happy. He is not at all sad.'

But today's incident will not let me sleep at all. My night has become worthless now."

Slowly, Mr. Davis grabbed a small photo frame which was kept on his table. It was the frame which showcased the images of him and his dear Brown.

He kept observing the frame for a long time. After some time, tears were flowing down from his eyes.

Gazing at the picture of Brown in the photo frame, Mr Davis said emotionally, "I remember a quote, my dear James. 'A strong friendship doesn't need daily conversation, doesn't always need togetherness, as long as the relationship lives in the heart, true friends never part.'

My dear James, even if you are not present with me physically, you will always remain with me emotionally, for our friendship is eternal. Friendship has no beginning and no end."

CHAPTER THIRTEEN

"I think that the person who has killed Brown Sir has some great reason to do this. He just wants to keep Albert Einstein's last words secret. That's why he did this. Otherwise, why would anyone do this?"

When Anderson put forth his opinion, all the other 3 became silent.

After a while, Dr. Bell said, "Hmm. If we consider your case Dr. Anderson, then we can conclude that the last words of Einstein contain some very valuable secret which has the potential of changing the whole world. And someone wants to keep that secret a secret, so he murdered Brown Sir."

"Exactly! You really understood my point," exclaimed Anderson.

COP Abner then blurted out, "A murder?! But I don't think that this is a murder. Or even if we consider that this is a murder, as there is a very high probability of it, I feel that the killer did this out of jealousy or some personal enmity with Brown Sir. Because what secret can the last words of Einstein contain?"

Anderson rejected COP Abner's opinion and said, "No Sir! My inner voice is telling me that the last words of Einstein carry such information that it has the potential to change the whole world. That's why he arranged this event to share that. And somebody who doesn't want to get the secret leaked out killed him."

He paused after that. Joining all the fingers of his hands, he started thinking about the matter deeply. COP Abner was not at all satisfied with his explanation and opinions.

After a while, Anderson cleared his throat and said, "Now all we have to do is to focus on 2 things: Finding the criminal and the last words of Einstein. Then only we can solve this entire case."

Saying so, he walked down from the stage. Before leaving, he turned back and said to COP Abner with a smile, "Sir! I know that you have great experience in cracking complex cases. I don't have any. So, you focus on finding the killer, and I will find Einstein's last words. Our views on this mission are very different. Let's work hard and solve the problem. Time will only tell who among both of us is correct. Time will only tell whether the criminal has personal enmity with Brown Sir or he wants to bury the mystery that Brown Sir knew. Now, I am proceeding towards my work. Please keep me updated about your findings. Bye-bye, everyone."

As Anderson walked out of the auditorium in a happy mood which was mixed with seriousness, the other 3 kept wondering over the challenge which he gave to COP Abner.

Dr. Bell was very astonished. *How can he take such a difficult challenge?*

He said, "Dr. Anderson has given you a challenge Sir! I am really excited to see who is going to win it."

"It is his habit!" blurted Director Garcia with an unusual enthusiasm. "It is in the blood of Anderson, Sir, to accept challenges! And remember that whenever he takes on any challenge, he definitely wins it. I am very confident about it."

He paused in between as he thought about something. "But this time, I am not sure whether he will win this challenge. This is because the case in front of us is very complex. Einstein, Brown Sir's death, etc."

As he finished, COP Abner walked a few steps ahead and said with a confident smile, "You know what! This challenge is not meant for winning or losing. I know Anderson very well. He is very smart and sharp-minded. I know that he is not at all interested in winning or losing. He is a very dedicated person who is now going to put his blood, sweat and tears into his research until he finds the last words of Einstein."

Adjusting his hat, he smiled and said, "I swore that I will not sleep peacefully till I solve this case and give justice to Brown Sir."

COP Abner walked towards the entrance door. But before leaving, he said with energy, "Speaking in Anderson's words, time will only tell everything."

CHAPTER FOURTEEN

As Anderson sat inside his Tesla Model Y, he started driving it without switching to autopilot mode. But as he started the car in a hurry, he heard someone calling him from behind. As he looked back from the window, he saw Director Garcia running towards him rapidly.

When he reached the car, he was breathing heavily and panting.

With a huge question mark on his face, he asked, "What happened, Garcia? Do you have something to tell me?"

Wiping the sweat from his forehead with his elbow, Garcia replied in a soft voice, "If you don't mind, Sir, can I accompany you to help you find the secret? Because I am very excited. If you give me the permission, then...."

"Permission granted!" replied Anderson with a broad smile. He requested Garcia to come and sit in his Tesla.

Garcia became very happy when he got the opportunity to work with Anderson.

He asked him, "But Sir, I have one doubt: why did you give me permission to help you so easily?"

Anderson smiled and replied, "Because I am fond of people who are really interested in science, philosophy and life's big questions. And since I met you, I have seen within you a desire, love and passion for science. That's why I granted you the permission."

Garcia was feeling very nice.

"One should work with a person who is not very intelligent in that area but is extremely interested. However, one should not at all work with a person who is an expert in that area but not at all interested. If you are interested, your intelligence will develop gradually."

Garcia felt himself seated beside a philosopher. He highly appreciated Anderson's thinking and personality.

Without wasting time, Anderson started the Tesla and sped it out of the auditorium.

"But where are we going, Sir? Now the time is 9 PM."

"We are heading towards Brown Sir's house, which is located near NSRA. There, we will investigate his rooms and eventually his whole house to see if we get any clue about Einstein's last words, which he was told before his death."

Turning the car towards the left, he exclaimed with confidence, "I swore that till I don't find Einstein's last words and the mystery behind them, I will not sleep peacefully."

Garcia thought with humour. I *feel that Dr. Anderson and COP Abner are twin brothers. Both are dedicated to their work and after all, they take on some difficult and challenging tasks.*

Anderson thought in his mind, *I strongly feel that the last words of Einstein hold such information, which, if revealed, would change the world completely. It might contain information which is very precious due to which Brown Sir kept it a secret, even from his dear friend Mr. Davis.*

Anderson was very determined to complete his mission. He accelerated the car towards Brown's house.

The top executives of NSRA, Virtual Eye and SpaceX were gathered at the large meeting hall of NSRA. Their faces were pale yellow as it was the worst day of their career.

The President of NSRA, Mr. Richard Braun, was not speaking to anybody.

He had not drunk a single drop of water since witnessing the death of the great genius. But after all, everyone was facing the same situation that night.

Upstairs, in the Department of Astronomical Observations, Dr. Johnson and Jonathan suddenly went mad. What miracle happened? But both of them behaved like small kids aged 7 or maybe less than that as they stared at the huge screen in front of them. Another great problem might have arrived, according to their faces.

"First of all, we have not informed anybody about the small bed-sized a meteorite that landed behind our agency a few hours ago. And now this another unexpected and unimaginable problem came hovering over our heads," exclaimed Jonathan with a sense of craziness.

Taking a deep breath, Dr. Johnson replied, "But now we have to inform everybody about both these things. So, let's go downwards!"

When the 2 brilliant engineers moved downstairs into the large meeting hall where everyone was seated in a completely dark mood, they immediately blurted out the whole situation to them.

As everyone heard them, they all were left speechless. Nobody was ready to believe what they were saying as it was a very unexpected thing.

Suddenly, a young, beautiful, and charming lady who was the CDO of

Virtual Eye got up from her seat and, wiping her tears, shouted, "What the hell are you both talking about? How can this be possible? Mrs. Lana and all the other crew members are returning back to Earth without informing anyone? This sounds really strange and crazy!"

All of the executives of NSRA Virtual Eye and SpaceX were dumbfounded after hearing that news. *What would Elon Musk feel when he came to know about it?* I wondered about all the SpaceX executives.

Mr. Bill Adams, the CPO of Virtual Eye, asked surprisingly, "Did you try to ask them why they are doing this?"

"We tried 5 times, Bill! But they are neither replying nor receiving our call. I think that they will return within an hour or a little bit more as the spacecraft is accelerating towards Earth as if it is light itself," replied Dr. Johnson.

Firstly, the death of Sir Brown had already jammed everyone's brain with darkness and emotional pain. In addition to that, Lana and the other crew members were returning back to Earth without informing anyone, thus leaving the Mars mission incomplete.

Bill said in a disappointing and confusing manner, "What is this all going on? A few hours back, we all were on the seventh cloud, and now we see what has happened. Tonight, 2 shocking things came back-to-back."

Dr. Johnson became very serious and replied to him in a deep voice, "Shock and surprise are not over yet, Bill!

There is a third thing which you all aren't aware of. When I tell you this after the crew members return, you all will not be able to sleep the whole night."

Everyone's mouth widened, and their neural network was disturbed.

And after a short silence, Dr. Johnson finally said, "Or maybe not for countless upcoming days."

CHAPTER FIFTEEN

Sir Brown's simple white bungalow, built with a strong admiration for Steve Jobs, was situated approximately 2 kilometres away from the NSRA in an isolated, serene location. The bungalow's architectural design was a testament to simplicity and elegance, much like Steve Jobs' philosophy.

The exterior of the bungalow was pristine and immaculate, painted in a brilliant shade of pure white. The walls were smooth and unadorned, creating a seamless and uncluttered appearance.

The front yard of the property featured a remarkable and eye-catching statue of Albert Einstein, a nod to the fusion of science and art celebrated by Steve Jobs and Brown's eternal love towards his hero. The statue portrayed Einstein holding the Universe in one hand, signifying his profound impact on the field of physics and cosmology. On the other hand, the cradles of a notebook emphasise the importance of creativity and innovation in scientific endeavours.

Below it, the words of his second wife (also his cousin), Elsa Einstein, were written in an elegant font and style, which she had said after

visiting a place where the Hubble telescope was located. She had flaunted her husband's intellect by saying, '**What you all do here by observing through the telescope, my husband does on the back of a notebook.**'

Surrounded by lush greenery, the bungalow exuded an aura of peaceful seclusion, making it a fitting tribute to Sir Brown's appreciation for both Steve Jobs and scientific greatness.

When Anderson and Director Garcia moved out of the Tesla Model Y, Garcia was surprised to see the simple design of Brown's house. He said to Anderson in a confusing voice, "I had never ever visited his house. But I had thought that it would be very great. But it is so simple."

With a smile, Anderson replied, "Because Brown Sir was a true follower and an admirer of Steve Jobs! And you very well know that Jobs believed that simplicity is the ultimate sophistication, like the greatest artist and multi-talented genius, Leonardo da Vinci. That's why he has designed his house so simple. By the way, beauty is not required in the house, but in the heart of the person who is living inside it."

After that, they proceeded towards the gate of the house, where they saw a guard who was completely lost in his mobile phone, seated on a smart chair designed by Virtual Eye.

Anderson began politely, "Dear friend! May I have your attention, please?"

Suddenly, the guard jerked backwards and got up after seeing him.

Hesitatingly, he replied, "Oh! Dr. Jacob Anderson.... Come...."His voice was breaking continuously, and his eyes had become red. Anderson quickly understood what had happened and calmed down the guard, who was feeling very bad after the death of his beloved master.

Hugging Anderson tightly, he screamed in pain, "Why does God always do this with such kind and innocent people? Brown Sir never ever treated me like a guard! But he always treated me as his dear friend. Yeah, sometimes he yelled at me due to my lack of attention and incomplete work, but it was for my good only. Sometimes, he used to drive people and his employees crazy during work time, as he had a passion for perfection, as Steve Jobs did.

But that was due to his goals and his vision of making humanity's future bright and prosperous. Why did God snatch away such a person?"

Anderson and Garcia again became emotional after meeting that guard.

Wiping the tears flowing from his eyes, Anderson motivated the guard and said confidently, "Don't worry, dear friend! COP Abner is working along with the Forensic department to know how Sir was killed. And eventually, we will find the killer. But for now, I, along with Garcia, am going to research Brown's whole house to find some trace of any information related to Einstein's last words. If you wish, you can help us."

"Sure!" replied the guard with a real feeling of motivation and determination.

And all 3 of them walked inside the house with the aim of finding the mystery of the genius scientist's last words.

The time was 9:30 PM. There was complete silence all around. Even the sound of the dog's bark was not coming as there was none around. The leaves of the trees were static, like huge rocks. The sky was totally clear, and there was no sign of bad weather or rain.

All the senior executives of both the companies, including that of SpaceX, were waiting for the spacecraft to return. Not a single person was feeling the urge to sleep. That night was definitely going to be remembered in the history of their companies. But one thing was that none had informed anybody in the world about that strange thing. Now a few moments more, and the mystery would come to an end.

At midnight, Dr. Johnson saw something heading towards the agency from the sky with great speed. But as the tiny object started coming closer and closer, Dr. Johnson looked joyous. And after 2 minutes, he shouted, "Guys! Holy shit! Holy shit! The spacecraft is coming! See here!"

As he shouted, everyone came running outside as if God himself had arrived on Earth to give some blessings to his subjects! Everyone's eyes were on the white spacecraft that was coming towards them. After a minute, it finally landed with accuracy in the middle of the agency.

As the door swung open without making any noise, Lana and the other crew members came outside with a disgusted and completely disappointed face.

Jonathan, Johnson and all the other top executives ran towards them to find the reason why they had come back, leaving the Mars mission incomplete.

Holding Lana by his strong hands, Dr. Johnson asked her in a loud and commanding voice, "What the hell are you all doing here? Are you going nuts? We all had spent 10 years on this mission. And you left it in the middle? Why? I want the answer."

All the other executives started asking her and the other crew members the same question back-to-back.

Zangger and all the other members were not able to open their mouths for uttering a single word. Now, only Lana was going to speak.

Staring into the eyes of Dr Johnson, she began after clearing her throat, "Sir! We all witnessed the event of Brown and Davis, Sir, through the spacecraft. And what we saw was traumatising. We never imagined that an event as beautiful as that would turn into mere darkness." Her eyes filled with tears, and her voice became low as she spoke. Her heart throbbed at a fast rate, and her forehead filled with sweat.

She continued, "So it was my decision to return back. This is because we couldn't enjoy the success of landing on the red planet in the middle of the death of our beloved Sir. And now I have taken the decision that until I don't find the criminal," her tone became louder due to anger. "I will not go to the red planet or any other mission." She said that she walked angrily inside the NSRA and straight inside her office.

Everybody thought that she had gone mad after looking at the death of Brown Sir. Zangger went behind her while the other crew members were given some food and water. Only Dr. Johnson was left near the spacecraft. He was staring at the sky with a heart full of pain and sadness. But suddenly, a metal-like thing touched him from behind. Surprisingly, as he looked back, he could see before him the small human-like robot, Z11. Johnson bent down near him and said in a low voice, "Hey! How are you, our little genius?"

Z11 replied in a more human-like voice than a mechanical one, "Actually, I don't have emotions, but still seeing all of you is human sadness; I think that I have to help you in some way."

"Thank you so much! When we need help, we will definitely inform you."

But before Dr. Johnson could say anything more, Z11 suddenly started behaving in a very strange way. He activated the flight mode inside it and, without informing Dr. Johnson, flew high up into the sky and came back in less than a minute, very precisely and accurately.

"Hey, what did you do that for?"

Z11 started speaking and shouting, "Oh no! A meteorite was detected at the back of the agency! A meteorite was detected at the back of the agency!"

Dr. Johnson held the boyish and naughty robot and said in a low voice, "Please don't shout! I have to inform everybody, and I will within a few minutes."

But the impatient Z11 kept irritating him by continuously insisting that he tell everybody. After all, it was a robot and was coded in such a way that it should inform humans as quickly as possible when it detected anything strange and foreign within a diameter of 5 kilometres around the space agency. So, after all, it was doing it as it was coded.

Finally, Dr. Johnson agreed due to the growing demand and decided to quickly inform everyone by calling a meeting in the huge meeting hall where all were sitting.

As he moved there, Z11 was walking behind him like a small boy with metallic legs, he thought in his mind. After *all, robots don't have emotions, and they only do things that are beneficial for humanity, for we have coded them like that.*

CHAPTER SIXTEEN

As the door swung open, the 3 men walked inside. The guard quickly pressed an icon on his mobile phone, and all the lights in the room turned on.

The living room was simpler compared to the outside structure of the house. The walls were white as milk, with not a single layer of dust or dirt. Completely clean. There were just 2 sofas, which were highly digital and looked as if they were floating up in the air. A huge theatre-like thin screen was attached to one of the walls, with statues of Nikola Tesla and Thomas Edison beside it; Tesla was holding a big electric rod in his hand, looking very smart and cool, and Edison was holding the electric bulb which he had invented and eventually changed the world.

As they walked further inside, Anderson thought, *it is incredibly crazy to see the 2 rivals of electricity together. By looking all around, it perfectly resembles the house of a true science and technology lover.*

After examining the living room, they finally reached a closed shiny metallic door. There was not a handle or anything else on it, except a small traditional blue button.

The guard pressed it. And to Anderson and Garcia's surprise, a thin blue screen floated in the air in front of them and a melodious female voice said, "Password Please!"

"The people who are crazy enough to think that they can change the world are the ones who do."

Within a fraction of a second, the door opened.

"The famous quote of Steve Jobs is the password!" shouted Anderson with excitement.

Brown Sir really thought and changed the world.

And they stepped inside the room.

Just after stepping inside, a wave of enthusiasm and confidence hit Anderson. Suddenly what happened, his whole stress got relieved, and he felt better.

Soon after that, he ordered Garcia and the guard to search each and every corner of the house, to see if they found anything, and he himself decided to investigate the study room.

Brown's study room was designed very elegantly, with virtual 3D images of the Solar System hanging all around and the beautiful Universe. It seemed as if Anderson was walking in the Universe. Such futuristic technology was Virtual Eye's technology.

He started investigating first into the study table where lay piles of white papers, with the complex design and sketches of the future products of Virtual Eye. Also, there was a digital library beside the table, where there were tablets related to various books from spirituality and philosophy to cosmology. James Brown was an avid reader like other great people.

Anderson began questioning himself.

None knew that Brown Sir was going to reveal the secret that he had only known on this planet. Even his dear friend Mr. Davis didn't know about it. This means the words have a valuable secret. But what are the words? And where are they, except in the mind and soul of Brown Sir? He must have written them somewhere. But where? Because he was not careless that, he would write it anywhere where anyone could get its access easily.

Thinking over where to search next, he investigated the study table. Garcia and the guard kept searching the whole house.

"What the hell are you speaking? Sorry to say but have you both gone nuts?" exclaimed Bill Adams, who was very angry towards Dr Johnson and Jonathan's behaviour.

All the other executives in the meeting hall, including the 11 crew members, were dumbfounded and shocked after hearing about the mysterious meteorite which had landed just behind the NSRA.

Lana was sitting on a chair, her face completely sad. She was not able to handle the traumatising incident of Brown's death. That's why the news of the meteorite didn't create any impact on her.

Unable to handle it, she walked back to her office. Nobody dared to stop her this time. They knew that she should be left on her own for some time.

Dr. Johnson and Jonathan decided to speak up. Coming towards Bill,

Jonathan began in a voice that was filled with sorrow, "Hey, dear all! You

know what? We both were compelled not to share this news with any of

you. This is because, firstly, Brown Sir left us all unexpectedly, and we all were totally disheartened and full of stress, tension, and pain."

He paused when Dr. Johnson proceeded further, "So we felt that if we

share this new problem of the strange meteorite with you, you all would get more stressed at that time. So, we decided to tell you after you return back and calm down. Unfortunately, before we could inform you, we saw the spacecraft returning, so we delayed it. But we really say sorry to all of you."

All the annoyed and disappointed executives started to calm down. They showed some mercy on both of them as they were compelled not to inform anyone due to that tough condition or situation. But after all, they now had to solve the mystery of the small meteorite which had unexpectedly landed a few hours back behind the NSRA. But in such a situation, they needed to urgently call an intelligent detective personality, who should also have knowledge of science, space and archaeology. And Dr. Johnson clearly knew who was to be called. Without wasting a single moment, he took out the smartphone from his pocket and dialled a phone number that was among the most important contacts section of his call log.

Speaking with the receiver for 2 minutes at a corner of the hall, he turned back towards everyone.

Dr. Johnson exclaimed with positivity, "Guys! The master of strategic thinking who is famous in the world as a polymath is coming soon to help us. None in Virtual Eye, NSRA and SpaceX has as much knowledge about meteorites as him, for sure."

Nobody understood who Dr. Johnson was referring to except Jonathan.

He smiled and said, "Guys, he is talking none other than about Dr. Jacob Anderson."

CHAPTER SEVENTEEN

Anderson's whole body started shaking as soon as the call ended. He could feel the same thing which he felt after looking at the lifeless body of Brown. Now, it was time for him to face a new mystery.

He quickly shouted, calling Director Garcia and the guard, and walked hurriedly into the living room, the stress gradually increasing.

As soon as both of them came running, Garcia became overjoyed and asked, "Did you find Einstein's last words?"

Anderson adjusted his collar and replied, "Leave that matter for a few moments and listen to what I am saying."

As both of them listened to him carefully, their bodies pumped adrenaline. Their ears went crazy after hearing about the meteorite.

"What the shit is all going on? A meteorite which landed just behind the NSRA? Lana and the crew members returned, leaving the important Mars mission incomplete," exclaimed Garcia, his mouth wide open.

The guard wiped the sweat from his forehead with a white napkin and said in astonishment, "What will the world think after knowing that they cancelled such an important mission? I think Ms. Lana couldn't see the death of Brown Sir, so she did it."

"Yeah! Now, I have been called immediately by the NSRA to do some research work on the meteorite. I am now leaving immediately. But you both keep searching for the genius' last words. Bye-bye."

Anderson walked out of the house in a hurry towards his Model Y. The NSRA was just 2 kilometres away from there. But before starting the car, he said to himself, *what is this all happening? First Brown Sir died mysteriously, leaving the crazy secret of Einstein's last words. And then, the Mars mission is cancelled by Ms Lana. A meteorite has landed behind the NSRA, which is hard to believe.*

He checked the time on his watch. It was 10 PM. The next few hours were going to be very stressful for him.

Faraway from there, at the airport of Los Angeles, California, a plane was ready to take off. There was not any crowd there and only a dozen of passengers was in the plane. None at that time was feeling happy to travel. The pilot of the aeroplane, Griffin, was also not in the mood of flying the plane after witnessing the devastating event. But whatever it was, he had to do his duty.

Joseph and his master were sitting on the last seat of the aircraft. Their faces were totally emotionless. Joseph wanted to drink water, but he was not in the mood to do so. What they had done was not excusable by the world.

Soon, the in-built audio of a female announced, "All the passengers, please be ready! The plane is going to take off within a minute. We will keep you informed about the news around the world. Have a nice and safe journey ahead!"

Just after a minute, the aeroplane took off from the airport. The place where it was going to take the passengers was one of the most famous, controversial and amazing places in the world.

As the plane lifted from the ground and started its journey, the master said to Joseph, "The Pyramids of Giza are one of the most mysterious wonders in the world."

CHAPTER EIGHTEEN

Anderson hurried towards the place where the meteorite had landed, just behind the NSRA. As he drove his car by the main buildings of the agency, he couldn't see a single person there. Everybody had gone to examine the meteorite.

Taking a left turn, he was now able to see several top executives of NSRA, Virtual Eye and SpaceX in front of his eyes. They all were discussing something very seriously, in front of something.

Z11 soon detected the car and started shouting in his irritating mechanical voice, "Tesla Model Y coming! Tesla Model Y coming!"

As he stopped screaming, everyone's eyes went towards the car that was coming nearer and nearer and finally stopped.

Dr. Jacob Anderson rushed towards them. Even in the middle of that stressful night, he showed sheer intensity and courage.

He stopped near Dr. Johnson and exclaimed with confusion, "What has happened? Consecutive 3 unimaginable things in one night. Brown Sir's death, cancelling of the Mars mission, and now this fucking meteorite!"

Dr. Johnson nodded in silence.

After a while, as the gossip and talks started increasing between the executives, Jonathan came towards Anderson and said, "Sir! Now, you are the one who will be the head of this mission of doing research on this strange meteorite. Landing it just behind our agency is really unbelievable."

Anderson's body was sweating profusely after seeing the intense sadness in Jonathan's eyes. He saw a ray of hope in his eyes for him. Clearing his throat, he replied with confidence, "Don't worry! I will take this responsibility. Even though I have sworn to find the last words of Einstein, I will work here also. We cannot say, but maybe this meteorite can help me in finding some clue about that mystery."

After a while, Anderson asked both of them, "Where is Ms. Lana? Is she alright?"

Jonathan's face became sad, and he replied, "She is sitting all alone inside her office. You know what, she is really very disappointed and broken."

"I think someone should go to inspire her. That would be helpful for her."

Soon after that, Dr. Johnson sent Z11 to entertain her. The robot did as commanded.

At about 11 PM, all the top executives of the 3 companies went back to their homes, completely startled and broken.

Only 3 people were left on the barren land at the back of NSRA. Jonathan, Dr. Johnson and Anderson.

"Let's examine the meteorite, Anderson, Sir," said Jonathan. And both of them soon followed him.

The sky was totally clear and dark. The Moon was shining brightly. Anderson had the habit of reading books peacefully, staying up late at night in such weather. He loved this type of weather very much. But that night ruined his habit and everything.

After walking hundred metres, they reached the place where the unexpected meteorite had landed, impacting its surrounding area, not much as it was just about the size of a bed.

But its impact was so severe that the surrounding area near it became totally dark and black.

When they observed, to their surprise, they found that the meteorite had stuck deeply into the ground! It was unbelievable!

When 3 of them peeped down into the pit, they were not at all able to see the meteorite. Jonathan pulled out his small torch from his pocket that was gifted to him by Brown Sir on his 40th birthday. It was one of the greatest inventions of the Virtual Eye.

The torch, unlike traditional ones, was very small in size, and it had such power that it could penetrate deep into darkness. There was a small button on its back, which, if pressed, produced a small, thin blue hologram in the air. We had to type the name of the thing we wanted to search for. After pressing okay, the torch produced a thin ray of light, which directly stopped near the searched object if it was there! The use of that torch was mostly done in research and investigation-related fields and studies.

The torch detected the meteorite, but it was not clearly visible as it was stuck deeply into the ground. They had only one option - Remove the meteorite from the ground.

Anderson gave an odd look and said in a very deep voice, "Guys! This is really a very great problem. The meteorite has stuck deeply under the ground. And it is very difficult to take it out as we do not have such fast technology. I think I have to return back to my investigation of Einstein's last words till this meteorite is removed from the pit. And after looking at the situation, it is clear that it will require a great deal of time."

But just as he stopped speaking, someone yelled from behind, "No! You are wrong, Dr. Anderson! The process will not require a great deal of time. It will be completed within a few minutes."

As the 3 men turned behind, they saw a tall, middle-aged man coming towards them who was in his fifties. He had worn a simple night dress. As he approached closer, everybody was surprised to see him. He was none other than Mr. Davis!

He was walking towards them with a broad smile on his face. It seemed as if he had a solution to their problem.

When he finally reached there, Dr Johnson started peppering him with questions.

"Why did you come here at this time, Sir? You should rest at home. Where is your car?"

Mr. Davis scratched his neck as a mosquito bit him and replied, "I came with my car only, but I have parked it at the entrance. Leave all that. The reason for my coming here is to give you the solution to this meteorite problem."

The 3 intellectuals were unable to believe that Mr. Davis had the solution to the problem.

Anderson motioned near him and asked, "Can you really pull out this meteorite from the pit? And how did you come to know about this meteorite?"

Without giving any reply, Mr. Davis pointed his index finger towards the sky. He then told them that Z11 informed him about the meteorite as the robot felt that it was important to inform him as he was the CEO of the company.

As they shifted their gaze to the sky, they saw a group of 5 strong robots flying towards them, holding a large cylindrical machine in their hands. It was like a sci-fi movie scene.

Anderson was suddenly immersed in his own world of thoughts.

Until now, AI and robots have mainly entered into a few sectors like big tech companies, industries and mainly rocket agencies. But sooner or later, they will enter into each and every field and also become the daily use of the common man. The first step is already over as robots have become capable of building research laboratories on Mars with human commands. Even though it is on Mars, it will be on Earth also one day.

Within a few seconds, the group of robots landed accurately, without causing any damage to the mysterious cylindrical machine which they had brought along with them.

After completing their task, they exclaimed in chorus, "Mission accomplished! Cylinder brought safely!"

On the commands of Mr. Davis, they again flew back, this time a bit faster as they didn't carry any load except that of their bodies.

The cylindrical machine was about the height of a medium-sized cupboard. A highly sharp and pointed metallic shape rose above it which gave it a scary look as if it was made to kill somebody. There were various buttons on its curved surface and also a thick blue screen where its total charge could be seen in percentage.

On the backside of the cylinder there was a door which was of the same colour as that of the cylinder, complete silver.

But before Mr. Davis could explain what it was, Jonathan screamed with excitement, "Oh! I understood. It is a drilling machine, and the sharp part which is rising above it is the main thing that will drill this whole fucking pit!" .

Stopping him from further spitting out his unwanted logic, Mr. Davis said, "No! Its functions are very unique. Let me explain it to you."

He moved towards the cylinder. All the 3 men's eyes were on him. They were very curious to know its functions.

After all, it is the universal fact that curiosity is the thing which drives mankind to achieve unimaginable feats.

Standing confidently beside the machine, Mr. Davis smiled shortly and began explaining the features of that unique machine.

"If you press this golden button, the backdoor will be opened, and a series of small machines will come out fantastically and start digging the ground with their ultimate mechanical and electrical power. Then the meteorite will be visible."

He pointed towards a shabby silver button and said, "After that, we have to press this silver button, and then a miracle will happen. Another robotic machine will come out, which has an extremely high tensile strength to hold the meteorite or any object weighing between 8000 - 70,000 kg. The whole process will just take 10 minutes due to the advanced technology used in creating this machine."

Everyone's mind was completely blown off. They were looking at such technology that none had ever imagined.

Moving closer towards the CEO of NSRA, Dr. Johnson asked with a puzzled expression, "But Sir, did you develop this technology secretly? But why? Why did you keep it a secret?"

Mr. Davis paused for a while. He was thinking something.

None dared to ask him any question while he was sunken into his own world of thoughts. They knew that if they disturbed him, he would get furious.

Mr. Davis replied in a low voice, "Actually I made this machine to give it as a birthday gift to James as he had a love and passion for archaeology. So, I didn't inform anyone, except the group of 5 robots which brought this cylinder here a few minutes ago. They built this under my guidance."

Without wasting any more time in the discussion, Jonathan requested Mr. Davis to start the work.

"Yes! Let's begin!" replied Mr. Davis.

He pressed the golden button and typed a few lines on the keypad that was built on the surface of the cylinder. A loud noise came, and 10 brick-sized machines came outside at full speed and started digging the pit under which the mysterious meteorite was hidden.

As the machines were drilling the pit, Anderson asked Davis in a low voice, "I want to ask you one question. If you don't mind, can I ask?"

He knew that Mr. Davis was not in the mood to speak much at that time, but his curious brain still couldn't stop him from asking questions.

"Yes! Ask."

"Sir, I wanted to know what the use of that black button is, which looks like the shabbiest of all. You didn't say anything about that."

Mr. Davis' forehead suddenly filled with sweat. He looked very uncomfortable.

Anderson was startled to see that. With some courage, he asked, "What happened, Sir? Why are you suddenly sweating so much?"

"Actually, I have started facing a problem these days: if I stay awake late into the night, I start sweating. I also don't know why, but doctors said that my body structure is like that."

Anderson gave an odd look. He was not satisfied with that answer.

"You know what! The function of the black button is very special. If you operate it, then the machine itself will move, use its upward sharp part, and start digging the ground, creating a passageway that can lead you under the ground to do what you want to do. Even from a large distance."

After a short silence, he continued, "But the most fascinating thing is that once you have done the whole work of digging, you can easily come back, and the machine will make the ground normal again."

Anderson was very amazed. He felt that it was really the invention of the year, but unfortunately, that of a robot. But whatever it is, its benefit is for humanity.

As they discussed it more, the whole noise stopped. They both were surprised to experience that. But as they looked, they saw that the meteorite was pulled out safely by the machines and they went all by themselves back into the cylindrical machine.

Seeing the bed-sized meteorite in front of them, all 4 of them were amazed. A sense of excitement and curiosity hit in their heart and soul.

Anderson thought, *Now the next hours are going to be truly amazing, mesmerising and mind-blowing.*

CHAPTER NINETEEN

The Forensic Department of Los Angeles is famous worldwide for its top scientists, researchers and biologists. Many genius minds of the world worked there. The department did not have any specific name but was very well-known for its groundbreaking research. It not only worked and explored dead human bodies but also ran a lot of scientific research on the whole human body and the bodies of other life forms. Dr. Nathan Bell, a thin and nerdy researcher, was the head of the department. He had earned a PhD in human anatomy from Johns Hopkins University, Baltimore, Maryland.

He was in charge of running a quick investigation into the dead body of Sir Brown.

That night, he was sitting in his office, which was separated from the rest of researchers and scientists.

He was sitting on his chair in front of his desk, thinking about something so deeply that he had forgotten to blink his eyes. His face was totally tasteless. Because at that time, like Anderson, he was also under a huge building of stress tumbling over his head. His responsibility was to find the exact reason behind Brown's death. The task was not as simple as he had thought.

Sitting cross-legged on the chair, he said to himself, "This is the most difficult case of my career. I am unable to understand anything. We ran a series of tests on his body but found nothing useful. He didn't have a cardiac arrest, a blood vessel burst or anything else. There is no poison in his body. There is also no trace of blood on his body. He was not shot. But then, how did he die?"

As he kept peppering himself with endless questions, his mind started

He was becoming more annoyed and irritated. Because if they didn't find any evidence or the reason why Brown died, they couldn't find the criminal, who then might create huge havoc, for none knew who he was and what was going on in his mind.

While thinking about that, he scrolled down the messages on his phone, which had been texted to him by COP Abner an hour ago. He had shown his problem and difficulties by saying that they couldn't find anyone who could be suspected of the crime. They also checked each and every CCTV footage of the auditorium but unfortunately found nothing helpful.

He became more upset by scrolling through those messages. But his impatience led him to think of messaging the COP once again. But as soon as he touched the keypad of his mobile phone, the door of his office opened. As he turned himself there, he could see his junior scientist Samuel before him, who was very younger than him, with a huge beard and ugly-looking moustache. He asked permission to come inside, and Bell granted him. He quickly kept his mobile phone in his pocket and stood up. Samuel came closer towards his desk and said, "Sir! You have to come quickly and as early as possible with me to the research room where we have kept Mr. Brown's body for doing research." Bell became silent as he spoke. He could sense that something amazing but bizarre had happened.

Samuel continued, now his voice turning impatient and breathless, "You won't believe what we have found while doing another complex research on his dead body. It is really unbelievable and mind-blowing! Please come quickly, Sir."

Bell's doubt was correct. *Something great happened during the research*, he thought again as he followed Samuel out of his office. With each approaching second, his heart pounded rapidly, and sweat filled his whole body.

Walking a few steps, they finally reached a large and elegant room.

In the dimly lit research room of the Forensic department, Dr. Nathan Bell and Samuel cautiously approached a cluttered desk where the lifeless body of Sir Brown lay beneath a white sheet. The room was filled with a tense atmosphere as 15 researchers, dressed in white lab coats, huddled around the examination table. Bright overhead lights cast a stark illumination, revealing an array of scientific equipment, microscopes, and

evidence bags strewn about. A prominent whiteboard on the wall displayed diagrams and notes related to the case. The air was heavy with the scent of chemicals, and the room was permeated with an aura of intense focus and determination as the experts worked diligently to uncover the secrets behind Sir Brown's untimely demise.

As they walked inside, they saw 15 scientists and researchers who were the most talented and intelligent and were chosen specially for that case, were surrounding in front of a long metallic desk on which there lay the body of Brown.

As he approached, Bell started getting more tense after looking at all the top researchers of the department standing there in utter disbelief and shock. They all looked very startled, and their faces were cowardly.

As soon as he reached there, one top scientist, who was in charge of the neuroscience research sector said to him in a very fearful voice, "Sir! Thank God you came here. We are really dumbfounded and don't know what to do."

All the others nodded in agreement.

Getting more stressed, Bell asked with a tight face, "What has happened? Please explain it to me."

The scientist replied, "You know what, Sir? As soon as you left here, we randomly started looking deeply into Brown Sir's body. But we didn't find anything interesting."

After a temporary pause, he began, "So, after so much frustration and irritation, we finally decided to take a great risk."

"W... What risk?" asked Bell immediately, his face turning yellow due to tension.

"You won't believe it, but we decided to use that tiny robot to explore the dead body."

As he said that, Bell's jaw dropped. He was left totally speechless after hearing what the neuroscience researcher said. Blood drained in his face.

"Means, if I am not wrong, you all used that tiny, crappy and shitty tiny

robot which we had invented 2 days before and decided to throw it at the end of the week to explore Brown Sir's dead body?"

The whole room became silent as he asked that question. All of them suddenly moved and stepped backwards as they saw his face turning red with anger, and he gets more annoyed.

Walking close towards the researcher, he erupted annoyingly, "What the

hell are you all doing here? Without my permission, you decided to use that shitty nanobot for the exploration of Brown Sir's body? Are you all going nuts? Have you all taken a high dose of Red Bull this evening or something else? You all are well aware of that crappy robot! It is completely useless. It has a high danger of damaging the dead body parts and blocking useful organs inside the body. Using that is like digging your own grave! If you have used that, I am sure that now we won't be able to find anything inside his dead body, because each and every organ would have been damaged till now! Its strange functions cause the whole dead body to go off the track!"

He became very angry towards them. That is because previously, they had used that tiny robot to find out how 3 dogs and 2 cats had died. Unfortunately, even after so many modifications, the robot always blocked the organs of the body and spread its strange radiation or something that made it impossible for any human being to touch that dead body! Anyone who touched it got a high voltage current, and the internal organisation of the dead body would go nuts. So, they decided to throw it, but unfortunately, the researchers used it without informing Bell.

As he kept forcing them to give him an answer, Samuel told the neuroscientist to be aside, and he decided to tell Bell the truth.

He began in a low voice, "Sir! What you are thinking is completely wrong.

We know that you don't love risks very much, but we have found such a thing with the help of that robot, which will truly amaze and simultaneously shock you."

Everybody supported him and convinced Bell to come near a desk that was situated a few footsteps away from Brown's dead body. Continuing arguing annoyingly, he decided to come.

As soon as they reached the desk, Samuel said, "Now see here, Sir, you will come to know everything."

As he pointed out, when Bell turned his eyes towards the digital board that was attached to the desk on the wall, his eyes felt numb. He was totally surprised to see it. He felt adrenaline rushing through his body, and his heart was pounding rapidly.

The neuroscientist, to whom he had scolded very much a few moments ago, came beside him and spoke sarcastically, "Dear Sir! Sometimes taking risks is also very important in order to achieve immediate results."

CHAPTER TWENTY

COP Abner looked anxious as he gazed at the photo of Brown's dead body on his phone. He felt as if the whole world had suddenly changed overnight. None had ever expected that incident to happen. But after all, it is a universal fact that time only decides everything.

The policemen were very tired after doing the investigation continuously, without taking a break for a single second. They had searched every nook and corner of the auditorium, including the CCTV footage, but were unable to find any evidence which could relate to the mystery of the tech billionaire's death. *What a bad thing! The day on which he became the most powerful person on Earth, he died. Happiness, in exchange for sadness,* thought Abner as he opened his bottle cap to sip in water. He had not eaten anything except a few potato chips at about 3 PM. But he still hadn't touched food yet. But there was nothing surprising as he had the experience of staying hungry during such complex cases. And this one was a very great one, not just for him or a few groups of people, but for the whole planet.

He had a very competitive personality, always loved challenges, and had the ambition of winning. But the case was getting so complex that he feared he lost the challenge with Anderson.

As he, along with a bunch of other policemen, had just settled down on the chairs of the auditorium, his phone buzzed suddenly, and he received a message.

Keeping the water bottle aside, he immediately saw what the message was and who had sent it.

His junior, who was seated beside him, asked in a tired voice, "Who's the message is there, Sir?"

But without answering the question, Abner got up from his seat, fully excited and enthused. There was a ray of hope and happiness visible on his face clearly.

The other policemen present there were surprised to see him becoming so happy amidst such severe turmoil and tension.

One of them asked with surprise, "What did you see in your mobile phone that suddenly made you so happy, Sir?"

Giving a broad smile, Abner replied with a voice full of courage and confidence, "Guys! You won't believe it, but this message was from Dr. Nathan Bell. He immediately called us to the Forensic department, for they had found something that would directly help us in finding the person who killed Brown Sir! So, without wasting time in discussion, let's move."

All the police officers felt that they were near the winning of the first step- of recognising the criminal. They became motivated and moved towards the Forensic department in their respective police cars. COP Abner was really, very, very happy.

The guard and Director Garcia were totally exhausted after searching Brown's whole house. They searched each and every corner, from the bathroom, toilet, and bedroom to the storeroom, study room, and living room, including other places. But they failed to find anything which related to Albert Einstein's last words. They were now thinking that the information was definitely not available in the house. With his tired limbs and painting arms, Garcia spread himself on the sofa in the living room and opened up a can of coke, which he drank within just 10 seconds. Canned cokes were his healing and stress-reducing things. So, it was a must for him to drink one at that time.

He could feel his mind somewhat relaxed as he lay on the sofa after finishing the can. But even then, his mind was constantly exploding with the thoughts of the mystery, which had kept the majority of the people around the world awake and impatient. **What were the last words of the genius scientist, and what special thing they signified that Brown Sir had not informed anyone, including his dearest friend Mr Davis?**

As the questions kept coming into his mind, the guard came from Brown's study room, his face totally disappointed and shattered. He was also looking very tired.

"Did you find anything?" asked Garcia.

"No! Nothing except this tiny poster on which there is the same quote written which Brown Sir loved very much and which we found written on his cupboard and many other things."

"Yeah! The answer to the Ultimate Question of Life, Universe, and

Everything is 42. Because The Hitchhiker's Guide to The Galaxy was his

favourite book of all the ones which he had read in his lifetime."

CHAPTER TWENTY-ONE

Lana sat in the balcony of her office on the ninth floor of NSRA. She was not at all in the mood of speaking with anyone. That night's devastating incident had created a dark place in her soft heart. She was weeping constantly.

Just as she was observing the night sky, she heard a familiar voice from behind.

The voice said, "Why are you crying so much, ma'am? Please smile a little bit. You should be able to understand the situation and control your emotions according to that. An emotionally weak person always runs into problems!"

"But how can I control my emotions, Z?! The person who was working so hard to change the world was killed so secretly! Does this mean the one who was doing a lot for the world got nothing but death? What type of justice is this? If God really exists, why did he take away such a kind person? Why not that fucking criminal who killed him?" Her tone increased, followed by annoyance.

Z11 could clearly see the burning fire inside her eyes for the person who had killed Brown.

"But now it's time for you to focus on finding and punishing the criminal! You have to stop getting disappointed now" replied the robot.

Wiping her tears and reducing her anger, she said, "You are right, Z. I should concentrate on the future instead of regretting the past."

Z11 was about to say something, but before that, a man's strong voice said, "May I come inside, Lana, if you don't mind?"

Both of them turned behind.

They saw a tall, white young man who was in his thirties. He spoke well, with a slight British accent. His hair was dark black and well-groomed, which made him look attractive. He was the Chief Marketing Officer of Virtual Eye.

Lana was very astonished to see him coming at that time. Standing up from her lavish chair, she asked with a tight smile, "Mr. Robin! Why did you come here at this time? You must sleep."

"Wow! The person who is not sleeping herself is telling me to sleep! Please come with me. I have arrived here to take you to my house to take a rest. Because I don't know why, but you are the one who is crying so much after Brown Sir's death."

Robin truly cared for Lana and wanted to calm her.

"No, Robin! I am totally alright. Don't take any tension and just go. I will sleep peacefully."

"No! I don't trust you. I am sure that you will not be comfortable. You have to come with me; otherwise, I'll not go from here."

Now Lana was stunned. First time in her lifetime, she was not able to make a quick decision. She was hesitating to go to his house, but was not able to say no.

Before she made her decision, Z11 as usual poked his nose in between, "I think he is right Ms. Lana! You are not in a state to sleep tonight. You must go with him to relax."

Robin was overjoyed after seeing that Z11 was convincing her to come and stay at his house for the next few hours.

Robin walked closer towards her and held her delicate and soft palms with his hands. She got extremely nervous at that time. She was unable to understand what was happening, but she was feeling very good.

A cool and crispy wind blew into the office from the balcony. Holding her palms, Robin kept staring into her black and attractive eyes. She was also doing the same. It was like both of them were peeping into each other's souls. Her brown chestnut hair was flowing due to the wind.

Staring unblinkingly into her attractive eyes, he said softly, "Lana! Please come to my house. I'll be very happy if you do so because I will not be able to sleep the whole night if one of my brightest colleagues is in tension. Please, will you come?"

Lana was speechless at that moment. Even if she was willing to, she was unable to say no. Robin's caring and loving nature impressed her a lot. The relentless force that was driving her to say no vanished instantly at that moment. She knew what to say further.

"Yes, Robin! I will come to your house. Let's go."

Robin was very happy. He had the opportunity to help Lana in her almost depressed situation.

Saying goodbye to Z11, both of them went downstairs, sat in Robin's car and headed towards his house.

Z11 was getting confused due to Lana's behaviour. *She is a very emotionally strong person. But why is she getting so broken after Brown Sir's death? There is some mystery.*

Leaving that matter, he decided to go to the back of the agency where Dr. Johnson, Jonathan and Anderson were solving the mystery of the meteorite.

Robin lived in an expensive house which was very close to the NSRA. In addition to his mesmerising and cool personality, he was very intelligent and sharp-witted.

The car stopped beside his house and both of them walked inside. Lana felt a bit nervous as she walked inside his lavish house. But she was not at all happy after looking at such an expensive and lavish house. Because she hated materialism.

Robin guided her to one of his bedrooms.

As they entered, Lana felt the air and environment of the room both inspiring and peaceful. At that moment, she forgot all the stress and tension and sat on the soft and large bed.

Robin offered her to eat some food and drink some water, but she rejected the offer by saying that she wanted to sleep.

"Lana, now I am going to sleep. You also sleep. If you need any help, wake me up. Goodnight."

"Goodnight."

And she slept after turning off the lights in the room.

On the other hand, Robin shut the door of his bedroom but forgot to lock it. Silently, he went and sat on his desk where he worked.

Silently and with a startled expression, he said to himself, "I think that I have to inform COP Abner about this. I am 90 per cent sure that he is only the mastermind behind the murder of Brown Sir. None will believe that, but after all, reality is always harsh."

CHAPTER TWENTY-TWO

Anderson went near to examine the meteorite. It was about the size of a bed but was spherical in shape.

As the 3 men walked near it, they saw that it was covered with a thick layer of mud and soil. It was due to its hard landing. Mr. Davis had already moved inside the agency, inside his office to get a few hours of sleep on the request of the 3. He was really broken after the death of his dear friend.

"Guys! We have to first clear the mud and thick layer of soil immediately. Otherwise, we will not be able to find anything," exclaimed Dr. Johnson with sadness.

Jonathan agreed. He suggested that they should call a team of robots to do that task quickly. But to everyone's surprise, Anderson rejected that idea and explained, "I feel that we should do this work on our own, manually. Yeah, I know that it is time-consuming, but we should not be dependent on robots and machines. Otherwise, one day, we will become so weak and lazy that AI will surpass and take over the world. And I would not like it at all, even if some people say that AI surpassing humanity will be the next step in evolution, for I love humanity very much. Human consciousness should be preserved forever. That's the reason why we did this Mars mission, so that mankind becomes a multiplanetary species, extending consciousness beyond Earth."

Jonathan found his argument logical. *It will definitely not be good to see these crappy and emotionless robots ruling the Earth.*

As Anderson finished speaking, Dr. Johnson came and extended the debate.

"You are right, Dr. Jacob, but it all depends on the situation."

Jonathan and Anderson became attentive.

"You know what, AI needs some regulation. Its use must be limited; otherwise, we will end up becoming weaklings and lazy. But now we have

a great and terrible situation in front of us, so we have to use AI and robots

only in order to save our time and energy. Because we have to solve

3 mysteries- Meteorite, Einstein's last words and Brown Sir's killer.

In order to work fast, we need the help of artificial intelligence, guys.

Because we have created them to provide us with the help of work and

speed."

Anderson's eyes went numb after hearing that. He realised that for the first time in his career, someone had won with him in a debate. It was really an amazing experience for him.

"You are right, Sir! We should call a team of robots to do this task."

But before they performed any action, someone yelled from behind, "You don't have to bring any team of robots. I have arrived."

As they turned behind to see who had spoken, they saw the boyish Z11 robot in front of them. He was approaching them, walking on his metallic legs and giving an artificial sheepish smile.

"Don't worry about the meteorite! I will clean it within 5 minutes!"

Anderson looked puzzled and gave an astonished look.

"You can clean it up so quickly?" asked Anderson with surprise.

"Yes! I can do it as I am a multi-purpose robot. I can do anything, literally anything."

"I feel that Brown Sir has coded that flaunting characteristic very well in Z!" exclaimed Dr Johnson with a cunning smile. He had taunted Z11.

Z11 motioned near him and said, "What did I flaunt, Sir? Can you please tell me?"

"Everyone knows that you always flaunt and irritate everyone."

"No! I don't! I just tell people my capabilities. I don't boast about my knowledge."

Anderson was puzzled after seeing the argument between a robot and a human. *Is Dr. Johnson going nuts? Why will Z11 boast his skills, as he is just a robot and doesn't have any emotions?*

"Whatever it is, but you are really very irritating!" shouted Dr. Johnson angrily.

But before the argument increased, Jonathan came in between and convinced Dr. Johnson to cool down.

The useless argument was surprising for Anderson but not for Jonathan. He knew that Dr Johnson hated him very much. He actually didn't know the exact reason, but it was believed that the robot once threw away the books written by Johnson on cosmology from his office, arguing that they were rubbish and didn't provide good knowledge to the population. The robot loved perfection. So, from that time onwards, Dr. Johnson hated him.

On Anderson's advice, Dr. Johnson went straight into his office.

Z11 gave a sad look. Anderson was baffled to see it. *The robot is giving the same expressions as human beings. What an amazing invention!*

Jonathan ordered the robot to clean the mud as fast as possible. Following the commands, the robot started his work enthusiastically.

Meanwhile, Anderson went near Jonathan. He looked very puzzled.

"I have one important query."

"What?" asked Jonathan.

"Just now, I observed that after the nonsense argument, Z11 gave a sad expression that looked exactly like the expression given by a human being. I am very shocked to see that."

Jonathan quickly sensed what was going on in Anderson's mind.

"I mean to just say that...."

"Does Z11 have emotions?" replied Jonathan instantly before Anderson completed his sentence.

Anderson felt his pulse tighten. He thought that Jonathan had the power to read and understand people's emotions.

He laughed and said, "Don't worry, Sir! Z11 doesn't have any feelings or emotions. He has been coded such that he can give expressions and converse like humans and nothing more. Brown Sir had actually envisioned a completely humanoid robot. But the project seemed far away from the current time."

Anderson suddenly began recalling all the books he had read about artificial intelligence and robotics, as he was one of the researchers in this field. *One day, AI will surpass human beings and rule over the planet Earth. Some people often forget to think about the future impact of AI on mankind, simply believing that it will be just the next step of evolution. But will these crappy machines be able to handle the whole planet after the extinction of humans? However intelligent or fast AI may become, it will always be considered less smart than humans because, after all, we have created it. Machines can't and will never replace the real intelligence of humans.*

"Whole work is completed! The meteorite is totally cleaned now."

Suddenly, Anderson came back from his world of thoughts. He felt as if he had suddenly teleported to reality from the world of the Matrix in which he lived.

Z11 cleaned up the ugly and shabby meteorite. But before it could say anything, a dark red light started blinking on its small screen attached near the neck. The robot was trying to say something but was unable to due to his low-level of energy.

"This indicates that Z11 is running out of battery. I think I have to recharge it now, as we will need his help in our research and investigation. You start the work, and I'll return within some time."

And saying so, Jonathan pressed a button on the backside of Z11's hard metallic body, and the robot became totally silent. It seemed as if his consciousness had faded away, and he died. But factually, he was a robot and not a human being.

Telling Jonathan to come back whenever he wished, Anderson looked high up towards the full Moon that was shining brightly. He suddenly could feel something as if it was not materialistic but totally spiritual. The hardest questions of human existence suddenly started occupying his mind. He was completely lost and immersed in those beautiful and mankind's favourite questions and started dreaming like an innocent and curious child.

A strong and chilly wind blew there, making Anderson shiver and stopping him from going into his own world again.

Rubbing his hands to get some warmth, he said to himself, "If I keep thinking about those questions, I will definitely run out of time. I have to start work immediately. I hope that Director Garcia gets some clue about Einstein's mysterious last words."

Leaving all that away, he slowly walked towards the meteorite. It was 11:45 PM.

But suddenly, a miraculous thing happened. As Anderson went near the meteorite, he could feel his reality getting distorted. His body started sweating profusely even in that cold weather. His eyes were gone off the track and he felt adrenaline pumping through his body.

Looking down towards it, he said anxiously, "Now I understand what Z11 was trying to tell us."

CHAPTER TWENTY-THREE

Faraway from the NSRA, the auditorium where the traumatising incident had happened was left completely silent. The decoration and design that was done at the intersection of art and technology became worthless. There was nothing that could have been done to save Brown, for he was destined to go.

Among all the halls and rooms of the auditorium, there was a tiny room that didn't make its presence felt to anyone, but it was the most important one of the whole auditoria. It was a small room, completely designed with advanced technology.

Inside it, large high-tech digital screens and computers could be seen and nothing else. They all displayed common things like the outside area of the auditorium, the main event hall and all the other rooms and halls. That small room was specially designed and produced to keep an eye on all the affairs going on inside and outside of the auditorium.

Technician Marina sat on her small and shabby desk, drinking her favourite strawberry juice, which was very sour as she liked it very much. She was the only person in charge of looking at the huge screens and keeping an eye on all the affairs of the auditorium. She always regretted that her whole life had been ruined due to such duty.

So, in order to enjoy and experience something good, she joined an association of dieticians who had the aim of making all people fit and attractive.

Marina earned a good income from there. But the main thing was that the association had helped her develop a beautiful and charming personality. She looked so pretty that even an old man of 70 years of age would easily fall in love with her. Her charming personality, slender figure and attractive eyes and face had made her famous among youngsters.

Staring at the wild screens in front, she said to herself, "Oh my God! I have to check everything that has happened before and after today's event. Maybe I can get some clues about the criminal from this."

Thinking for a while, she decided to check the waiters and servants of the auditorium. *Even someone close to us can be a betrayer.*

As she started checking the current locations of all the waiters, she became fully concentrated on her work. She always remembered her father's advice. Enjoy life very much, for we have only one. But work with your full dedication and heart at the time of work.

Checking the locations of the waiters could help her find the suspect. Because all the waiters who had been present lived in Los Angeles.

It is a great thing that our auditorium has this great policy of giving our workers special clothes, and a tiny in-built GPS system is built. Wherever they were, their locations could be traced easily. She appreciated the wise policy of the auditorium.

But suddenly, a very strange thing happened. What she saw on her computer screen left her utterly speechless. Immediately, she picked up her list of all the waiters who were present at the event. But as she flipped the pages, her heart began pounding faster than it really should. Her pretty and juicy lips dried up instantly.

She picked up her smartphone from the desk and started dialling a number as fast as possible. She was so frightened that she forgot that the person's number that she was dialling was already saved in her call log!

The ring started.

What the hell have I done? Was I smoking weed during that time?

The call started.

Marina said in a fearful voice, "Hello, Director Garcia! I have breaking news for you."

CHAPTER TWENTY-FOUR

Dr. Bell drank his glass of water for the third time, in just about 5 minutes. However much he drank, there was no way that his night would go easy.

After he looked at the whole stuff, which was present in front of his eyes, he realised that he should take more and more risks then onwards.

The neuroscientist asked, "Sir! Is this discovery enough for the investigation?"

Looking at him with his watery eyes, Dr. Bell replied, "Yeah. According to my thinking, I feel that this will be enough to locate the criminal. Let COP Abner come fast."

Just as he spoke about those smart police officer, he suddenly appeared in front of them as he came from the door of the lab which was open. Few police officers were following him.

With curiosity overflowing his mind, he asked, "What happened, Nathan? Please tell me quickly."

Quickly, catching his eye, Dr. Bell began explaining to Abner what they had found inside Brown's body.

"Sir, you know what? First, my team sent a tiny nanobot inside Brown Sir's body to investigate what had happened."

COP Abner was staring into his eyes without blinking. The sheer intensity of solving the case was clearly visible inside his eyes.

He continued with excitement, "As soon as it entered the body, it started to find the substance that led to Brown Sir's death. And soon after that, it detected such a thing which is unbelievable."

He paused and pointed his finger towards the digital board attached to the wall.

Abner could see strange biological sketches in front of his eyes, which were far beyond his understanding. It didn't make any sense to him.

With a feeling of shame, he asked, "Can you please explain this whole stuff to me?"

Biology was my worst subject in school. The fear of that subject in school has left a great impression on my life till now.

Pulling a deep breath inside his lungs, Bell stated, "So basically, the nanobot has found that the reason behind Brown Sir's death is a mysterious chemical that has the capacity to kill a person within a few minutes after consumption without leaving any trace or without impacting any organ and part."

Suddenly, Abner felt his eyes and knees tighten. He felt as if the acoustics of the room were turning different for him. With every passing moment, he was becoming madder and crazier.

"What did you just say now? The chemical kills a person without impacting any organ or body part?"

"Yes!"

"But how is this possible? I know that I am very poor at biology and chemistry, but I surely have this much knowledge to say that such a chemical doesn't exist!"

There was a long and unexpected silence in the laboratory.

"Yes, Sir, I actually don't know about the substance. But it clearly shows that the chemical entered Brown Sir's body and then quickly diffused inside and killed him. But the exact reason for which chemical it is still unknown."

COP Abner's mind was becoming crazy. Never in his whole career had he got so confused.

Clearing his throat and making his dry lips wet with his tongue, he said, "That is the exact reason you can definitely find by research. But how can we find the criminal from this clue of this invisible chemical? I am not able to understand anything.

"See, Sir," Bell began in a soft voice, "According to our research, we have found a very, very small substance inside the dead body. Just see here."

He told Abner to observe something under the laboratory's highly powered electron microscope to see the substance that was found.

Just after observing that, Abner's reaction seemed as if he had seen something very toxic and bizarre.

"What the hell is this? I have never seen this substance!" he blurted with irritation.

"Exactly. That's what we are trying to tell you. This substance is unknown to us, and how it came inside Brown Sir's body we don't know."

COP Abner gave an odd expression. It was becoming more difficult for him.

Dr Bell started speaking a bit faster this time, "You know what, Sir, this whole thing has led us to the conclusion that the criminal had definitely mixed it in Brown Sir's food or water. And when he consumed it, he died immediately. Thank God that this substance remained inside his stomach. Otherwise, we would have never come to know what had happened."

"The cold coffee that he was drinking in his favourite Einstein cup!" shouted Samuel hyperactively.

COP Abner recalled the scene of the death as he himself was watching it live from his luxurious bungalow. Brown was drinking cold coffee in his favourite cup during the time when he was telling the world about Einstein's last words. Now COP Abner was able to connect the dots.

Moving closer towards Dr. Bell, he said, "Nice job, Nathan! I think the criminal is not an ordinary person."

He walked away, looking dead serious.

"He is definitely a great scientist, biologist, researcher or something.

Either he created this mysterious substance or found it with the help of unknown sources or resources. Now, we have to quickly catch the criminal. I have to move immediately to the auditorium. I have clearly understood who the criminal might be."

Dr. Bell gave a surprising look. *COP Abner understood who the criminal is.*

Who? While leaving, Abner turned back and said with a smile, "Don't worry, Nathan! I have not understood exactly who the criminal is, but I have understood." And he left.

On the other hand, Dr. Bell ordered his researchers to start discovering the truth and properties of that mysterious substance.

CHAPTER TWENTY-FIVE

"Are you speaking the truth? What the hell are you saying!" exclaimed Director Garcia, getting up instantly from the sofa. Marina's voice was becoming more and more tense as she was

speaking.

"Yes, director! My news is totally correct. One of the waiters in our auditorium is on a flight which is going from Los Angeles to the Pyramids of Giza, Egypt. I am extremely sorry that I didn't note his details, like his name or phone number, when he joined us this evening. I thought that he would provide a bit more help, so I directly assigned him his job. After

all, I was also very excited for the speech." *Overexcitement sometimes leads to tough situations, thought Marina and regretted with a sombre heart.*

Now, Garcia did not have that much time to scold Marina.

So immediately, he cut the call and told the whole story to the guard who was standing in front of him.

"Oh my God! This clearly shows that the waiter is a suspect," he blurted.

"Yeah! Now, I think I should immediately inform COP Abner and Dr. Anderson about this. If Marina's news is one hundred per cent accurate, it will become very easy for us to catch the killer."

But as Garcia was dialling Anderson's number, he became a bit puzzled.

But is it real that the waiter has only killed Brown Sir? But why would an ordinary waiter do it?

Far away from Los Angeles, as the aeroplane was heading towards the great pyramids of Giza, the master and Joseph were watching the latest news on their smartphones. And the whole media was blasting and exploding with the news of Brown's death and his last mysterious speech.

Global Mysteries.com

'Who has that much guts to kill Sir James Brown? And what is the criminal seeking from the murder? But the most mysterious thing is what the genius Albert Einstein's last words were,

which Sir Brown was going to announce before his death. And what mystery did they contain? Do they contain valuable information that can change the world? Another shocking thing is that the spaceship of 12 crew members that was launched this morning has returned back because the leader of the members, Ms Lana, has vowed not to do any mission unless the killer is found. Well, time will only tell everything. Please stay active on our channel as we will keep informing you about the situation.'

As they both watched the news, the master said to Joseph, "We don't have to worry as I have worn my heavy coat above the clothes of the waiter. None will get to know that I am one of the waiters who worked at the auditorium of Los Angeles where we created havoc today."

But both of them were astonished to hear that the spacecraft abandoned the mission and returned back.

The aeroplane now began to fly faster but in a very comfortable way. Looking down at the beautiful world from the window, the master said seriously, "Now, in just one and a half hours, we will reach our destination to perform our final task."

CHAPTER TWENTY-SIX

Anderson's jaw dropped as he heard about the mysterious waiter from Garcia. He could sense something relative to the case but was unable to express it.

On the other hand, he also found something very interesting about the meteorite lying in front of his eyes on the barren land behind the NSRA. *Simultaneously, 2 shocks? What is happening today?* He thought with a happy but astonished mood.

"Sir, I think that we immediately have to inform COP Abner and the local authorities about that waiter. Unfortunately, we don't have his name or any other personal details, but with our new technology, which was actually made by Virtual Eye, we can constantly trace his location due to the clothes he is wearing."

"Okay, then you immediately inform COP Abner about this so he can take further strict actions. But be careful that you don't let this information go public. Otherwise, the waiter can do endless things to hide his location," replied Anderson, his voice growing anxious.

"Okay, Sir! Bye-bye!"and Garcia cut the call.

As the call ended, Anderson gazed at the sky above. It was his favourite thing- looking and staring at the dark sky and thinking about endless scientific and philosophical questions. *But now I don't have time for this.*

There are several mysteries lying in front of me. But I am sure that what Garcia and I have discovered now that it is going to be of great help. As he thought about that, he turned and decided to run towards theagency to inform Jonathan and Dr. Johnson about what he had justdiscovered.

But as he looked behind, to his surprise and happiness, he saw Jonathan coming nearer, bringing a cup along with him, on which the name and logo of the NSRA were glowing elegantly.

Just as Jonathan came near him, Anderson shouted with joy, "Come here and quickly learn what I have discovered about this meteorite!"

Jonathan felt a wave of excitement hitting the beach of his intelligent and curious mind. He immediately hurried towards Anderson and handed him the cup in which he had brought hot black coffee.

"Look at this meteorite, Sir! See."

As Jonathan glanced at the meteorite in front of him, his whole body suddenly froze. He wasn't blinking his eyes at that moment, becoming completely steady. When he strained his eyes towards it to observe it carefully, his brain lost signal. His face seemed as if he had seen a ghost or something.

Without looking or paying attention to him, Anderson began his explanation excitedly, "I have just carefully examined it and found out that it is not the sort of traditional meteorites that we often come across with, that is, rocks, stones or pieces of an asteroid," his voice became more tense and deep, "This is not a rock or any sort of that meteorite. But it is actually a heavy piece of metal that has fallen from an unknown source."

He paused in between and started thinking about that whole stuff.

After a while, he continued, his voice filled with fear and simultaneously surprise, "Actually, this whole thing leads us to just one point. That this piece of metal has fallen down from a spaceship, satellite or, speaking like fantasy, a UFO."

But suddenly, Anderson stopped speaking, noticing something strange.

He unexpectedly observed that Jonathan was not interacting with him at all. He hadn't spoken a single word during that time. *How can it be that he is not interacting with me despite knowing that this meteorite must have fallen from a spaceship, satellite or an alien UFO?*

Before he spoke anything, the frozen and stationary Jonathan flickered back in the state of motion and silently moved towards the meteorite, or we can say the piece of unknown metal.

Anderson sensed that something wrong had happened. He could feel the fear and shock in Jonathan's scary eyes.

Motioning towards the bed-sized piece of metal, Jonathan bent down to examine and study it properly. His mind was exploding with some very strange and unimaginable thoughts.

Becoming more nervous, Anderson asked in a very low voice, "W...What has happened? Why are you looking so astonished and puzzled?"

"My doubt was absolutely correct! I knew that was the case!" exclaimed Jonathan, again, is standing erect and becoming normal again.

Anderson gave a puzzled look and stared at him for a long time, eager to know what Jonathan had found.

Walking on the barren land and moving away from the metal, Jonathan said with a smile, "Dr. Jacob Anderson! Sorry to say, but you are totally wrong about this."

Anderson felt unusual. *None had ever said sorry to me before proving me wrong.*

He continued with his heavy voice, "This metallic thing has not fallen from any unknown spacecraft, satellite or an extraterrestrial UFO!"

"Then from where?" fired back Anderson.

"This is just a small part of the spacecraft named XYZ-001 that was sent 2 months ago in space along with 5 crew members, and which unfortunately lost contact with us and eventually disappeared in the vastness of the mysterious space!"

The cup of hot black coffee fell from Anderson's hand after hearing

Jonathan. He was staring widely at him with utter disbelief and shock. The night, which he had thought of enjoying, had really turned into one full of strange mysteries and shocking incidents.

CHAPTER TWENTY-SEVEN

Exactly as the environment became colder, Lana suddenly woke up from her peaceful sleep. The young and handsome Robin had given her a treatment like that of a very close relative or friend. She was not able to express her happiness in words.

But her thirsty throat had disturbed her silent and peaceful sleep. Now she was awake. She would again recall the sad memories of her past moments. Death of her beloved boss, his Einstein mystery, and the meteorite. It seemed as if she was again coming back to live her normal but stressful life after waking from sleep.

Slowly, pulling the warm and fluffy blanket aside, she got down from the comfortable bed and turned on the lights of the room, just pressing a tiny button located on the wall beside her bed.

Even at midnight, she was looking as beautiful as a model. Her long, silky hair made her personality more attractive. She had worn shorts, and her long legs gave her a slight actress-like look. Her pretty face was still glowing at that time.

Motioning towards the door, she opened it and headed towards the kitchen in order to quench her thirst. *Not keeping water near while sleeping is a bad habit of mine and is extremely difficult to get rid of.*

But as she walked towards the kitchen, suddenly she saw something that astonished her.

She saw that the lights in Robin's room were still on at that time.

Unable to understand why he had not yet slept, she decided to ask him.

But as she went near, she saw that the door was open. *Would it be nice if I just walked inside without informing him? Because it is wrong to enter someone's bedroom without letting the person know about it.*

Thinking about the basic ethics of life, she was just about to knock on the

door when suddenly she heard Robin's voice from inside. So, she put her ear on the door to know what was happening inside.

Several miles away, COP Abner sat inside his Ford Police Interceptor along with his bunch of policemen accompanying him, when suddenly, his Samsung Galaxy Note 10 rang with an unusual ringtone.

As he removed the elegant phone from his pocket, he saw that the caller was Robin. The number of Robin was saved in his call log as they both had become good friends after meeting at a party.

Even though he was on an important investigation, he decided to receive the call.

"Hello! Are you COP Abner speaking?"

"Yes! I am COP Abner Ardolf."

Robin's voice sounded tense. He said, "Sir! Sorry to disturb you, but I have called you because I want to speak about something very important to you."

Abner became a bit startled to hear that Robin wanted to speak something important with him.

"How important are you willing to speak?" he asked anxiously.

"Sir, actually it is very important because," he started speaking fast, "I suspect one famous person who might be the mastermind behind this secret plan."

COP Abner sat still on his front seat beside the driver as he heard Robin.

His mind was again moving toward the path of craziness.

"And you would not believe it, but I think that the criminal is none other than Dr. Jacob Anderson!"

Now the expensive mobile phone was about to fall from Abner's hand.

"What did you just say now?"

"I said that I think Dr. Anderson is the one who has planned to kill Sir Brown, because he wants to bury the secret of him."

Growing more tense, Abner asked, "What the hell are you speaking?! Why would Dr. Anderson want to kill Brown Sir?"

In short, he explained the whole Forensic department to Robin. Simultaneously, the policeman sitting next to him showed him a message sent by Director Garcia stating that the mysterious waiter was heading towards Giza. Now, Abner's doubt turned real. And he told Robin about it.

Hearing it all, Robin fired back, in a polite manner, "But Sir, I think that because just a few minutes before Brown Sir's death, Dr. Anderson was behaving strangely. He was sweating profusely and was completely immersed in his own world of stressful thoughts. And when I asked him what had happened, he simply diverted the topic by saying something.

But by looking at his behaviour and way of speaking, I am one hundred percent sure that he was hiding something which he didn't want to tell. And after a few minutes, Brown Sir collapsed on the stage.

Whatever you say, Sir, I feel that we have to capture Dr. Anderson as early as possible because he might have some connection with the waiter.

Because the person who can mix something in the coffee can be none other than a waiter. Please try to believe me. You are clearly aware that whenever I find someone suspicious in any type of case, he/she is found to be the criminal. Now, everything depends upon you."

COP Abner was stunned. Literally, he was stuck in a great problem. *How is it possible that the person behind all this is Mr. Anderson? I have no guts to capture and take him in custody. But it is the truth that whenever Robin has suspected anybody, he/she has turned out to be the criminal. And after all, his doubts are correct. Why was Dr. Anderson scared just before the death of Brown Sir? This means he knew that Brown was going to die.*

So finally, COP Abner agreed with Robin in desperation. Their next plan was to go directly to the NSRA and take the intelligent Anderson in custody.

"Thank you, Sir! I will gather more news about the waiter stuff from technician Marina. And you gather information from Anderson. If he speaks

the truth and it relates to the waiter, we will immediately tell the waiter to

surrender himself from the aeroplane itself and also punish Dr Anderson. Bye-bye."

Without going into over-thinking again, COP Abner asked the driver to

speed up the car towards NSRA.

He then thought, "I wish that this time Robin would turn out wrong."

Lana's pulse tightened, and her heart throbbed fast as she heard the whole

conversation between Robin and COP Abner. It was a jaw-dropping moment for her.

Robin feels that the mastermind behind this whole catastrophe is Dr. Anderson?

Her heart strongly urged her that everything would go wrong if they captured Anderson. Because according to her, the authorities should immediately catch the mysterious waiter and not Anderson. Because she thought that the waiter was only the killer as a mysterious substance had been mixed in the cold coffee of Brown Sir. And none can do that except waiters. She was thinking that they should find the waiter as soon as possible before he could create more havoc.

I should immediately inform Mr Anderson about this. He must quickly move, not just from Los Angeles, but from the whole United States!

Because now I have to catch the waiter as soon as possible. And Dr. Anderson will be my best companion of all, a highly clever man who will provide great help in catching that waiter, who would then reveal all the secrets about the tumultuous events happening tonight. Dr. Anderson's rest of the night should not go with the police but with me to catch the waiter and finally reveal the mystery of Brown Sir's death and the last words of Einstein.

Then, without straining her mind further, she silently moved towards the living room took a small key from a hanger which was attached to the wall, opened the main door and walked outside without informing Robin.

Unlocking the door of the BMW that was owned by Robin, she quickly sat inside, inserted the key, started the car and headed towards the NSRA.

Hearing the noise, Robin came outside rushing. He was astonished to see his amazing BMW being stolen!

"Hey, you bloody fool! Stop!" he shouted at the top of his voice.

But the poor Lana was not in the state of stopping. She had to reach the NSRA before COP Abner. While accelerating the BMW, she sadly thought, *Sorry Robin, but I have to do this. Even though you have been so kind and helpful to me tonight, I have betrayed you. But I have to do this in order to give justice to our Brown Sir and, after all, reveal the mystery of his favourite scientist, Albert Einstein's last unknown words.*

CHAPTER TWENTY-EIGHT

Anderson was so shocked by Jonathan's words that he didn't care to even just take a look at the cup of coffee that fell down from his hand at that moment.

"Are....are.....you kidding?" asked the science lover with a slightly odd look.

"No, I am not! This metallic part is none other than one of the parts of the spacecraft XYZ-001. We have at least found one part. But the rest of the spacecraft and our 5 beloved astronauts....."

Jonathan suddenly became emotional. His fierce eyes suddenly turned upset. Because the 5 astronauts were the most intelligent ones and everybody's favourite. Unfortunately, what everyone had not expected happened. Now, another mystery remained: where did all the 5 go?

"I think that just wondering about this will not help us in any way. We must quickly work on this crappy metal, as we can find something totally extraordinary that can prove excellent for us," declared Anderson, full of enthusiasm and confidence. His gestures and mood represented his curiosity and eagerness to research the meteorite. (Metallic piece)

But Jonathan's mind was taking another road. He was not at all interested in running a serious or any sort of research on that spacecraft's part. He just wanted it to get away from his eyes due to the emotional sadness and several other strange reasons.

But Anderson kept explaining to him the importance of doing research on it. "No, Sir! Don't give up easily. Maybe we can find something useful here."

"You first focus on searching for Albert Einstein's last words! Then think about this spacecraft part," he fired back, his voice mixed with irritation and annoyance.

Anderson didn't feel bad about that. He was very good at understanding people's feelings and emotions. He understood that Jonathan was in emotional distress at that time, so he tried to cool him.

But before he spoke, Jonathan came near and put his rough but strong and muscular hand on Anderson's shoulder.

Giving a normal but happy smile, he said politely, "Sorry, Sir! I hurt your feelings. But I am not in the state of speaking, discussing or researching on any topic related to that spacecraft. So so sorry, but I can't do it."

And saying so, he motioned silently towards the sleeping rooms of the NSRA.

Anderson, even if he was willing, was unable to stop Jonathan. He knew that at such times, people should be left all alone to get a few moments of peace.

Now it was twelve-thirty. Anderson was all alone in that cold weather on the barren land behind the NSRA. The thing that he, including everyone, had thought of as a normal meteorite turned out to be a part of the XYZ-001 spacecraft.

But he sensed that something special was there about that metallic part.

If the spacecraft has disappeared for 2 months, how could possibly one of its parts disintegrate from it and come down and land exactly here? There must be some reason behind it.

A sudden idea flashed in Anderson's brain. He quickly pulled out his iPhone and started surfing through the internet by twitching on the keypad.

Then, by clicking on a website, he began reading something very dedicatedly.

As he kept reading the information, he became happier with every passing moment.

Suddenly, turning his phone off, he screamed, "Oh my God! I was correct. My doubt was correct."

The spacecraft had lost contact with Earth when it went very far away.

This means it turns out that the astronauts had a very big problem. Maybe they knew that they were going to die. So intentionally, by using the great in-built target technology of the spacecraft, they pushed this part so that it would come and land here. First, they must have cut this whole piece of the spacecraft with extremely sharp laser technology and then sent it here. So, it finally turns out that this metallic part of the lost high-tech spacecraft contains something very important that the crew members wanted us to find. But what is it?

To seek the answers, he began looking for something that he could find on that metallic part, which was entirely made up of aluminium.

CHAPTER TWENTY-NINE

Anderson glanced at the part as if he was staring at God, the creator of the Universe is according to religion, not science.

He was touching it at each and every spot to examine and check to find some important clue or thing which he thought the 5 lost astronauts wanted them to know about it.

But even after examining it closely, he was not able to find anything special.

Then he decided to take a walk around to relax for some time, still thinking about the breathtaking mysteries of that night.

But just as he started walking, lost in his own world, he accidentally stepped on a stone and fell down. The falling didn't hurt him much.

But instead of paying attention towards that, his eyes kept staring at the

bottom side of the bed-sized metallic part of the XYZ-001 spacecraft. He

was continuously staring at a particular place as if something

extremely antique was happening there.

Swift, as an eagle, immediately rolled his body toward the circular metallic part and started pulling out something with his hand from its bottom. The circular part of the lost spacecraft was glowing brightly,

After all, it was cleaned by the smart and intelligent but irritating Z11.

Anderson was at the peak of his happiness at that precise moment. As he pulled that thing, he became more enthralled and excited.

And to his joy and extreme happiness, he finally pulled out the thing! And

just after that, he got up and stood erect on his legs. His dark black suit had got a bit dirty due to the dust from the ground.

With the glowing happiness on his face, he was holding the thing which he had just now pulled from the bottom of the metallic part. The thing was glowing brightly, its silver light emanating with an amazing look, but not much. *I have finally found out what the 5 crew members wanted us to find.*

But just as he was about to examine it closely, he saw a nice BMW coming near to him. The driver was driving it so fast that Anderson thought he was going to be killed by that.

But nothing happened like that. The BMW stopped suddenly. The door opened, and a tall, pretty girl with brown chestnut hair and long, slender legs hurried towards Anderson.

Who is this American beauty wearing shorts in such cold weather and heading directly towards me?

But as she came closer, he quickly recognised who she was within a fraction of a second.

"Ms. Lana Wilson! What are you doing here at this time? The kind-hearted Robin had taken you to his house to rest, so why did you come here?"

Suddenly, Lana became stunned. *What will Dr. Anderson feel when I tell him that the person to whom he is referring politely and kind-heartedly has turned against him?*

Now, both of them were face-to-face. They kept staring into each other's eyes for a long time.

Then suddenly, Lana began, "Dr. Anderson! You won't believe it, but you and I have to move out of the USA as soon as possible."

Anderson gave a puzzled look and replied, "Move out of the USA? What the hell have we both done? But the main thing is that we both haven't spoken much and stayed together this whole evening!"

But now we will for countless upcoming hours, thought Lana and become hyper.

"You are right! But Robin has told COP Abner to catch you as quickly as possible and hold you in police custody, for he feels that you are the mastermind behind today's devastating incident."

Anderson suddenly felt all his reality getting distorted. He was unable to digest what Lana was saying. Inside his heart, he was swallowing the little anger that he had suddenly developed for Robin.

"What the hell on this Earth does Robin think that I have planned to kill

Sir Brown?"

Now Lana thinks it to be the best time to explain to Anderson what she listened to in Robin's house.

She narrated the whole story to him seriously about the waiter, which he already knew all the other things.

"What? I was just getting some intuition as I sat there to witness the event! Actually, I have some extraordinary power to experience the future.

How could he think that I am the criminal?" his voice mixed with anger and sadness.

"Yeah! I know that, Sir. Therefore, I immediately ran away and came here to inform you about this so that you would be safe. Now, we both should quickly fly to the Pyramids of Giza to catch that waiter. Time is running up; let's move early, as COP Abner might come in just a few minutes to capture you."

Now Anderson was lost somewhere for a moment. There was no other option for him than to escape the United States and fly to Africa to catch that waiter who had dared to kill James Brown.

But after a while, he said, "But just now, I have found this small chip which was attached at the lower end of this metallic part of the XYZ-001 spacecraft. I am willing to do research on it, but I can't due to this growing tense situation."

A swirl of storms hit Lana. She felt that her ears had gone nuts.

"What the hell did you say right now? This circular thing, which we thought was a normal meteorite, is a metallic part of the XYZ-001 spacecraft?"

"Yes!" replied Anderson with an odd expression. And then he explained his theory to her, which he had developed about that part after learning deeply about the lost spacecraft from a website.

Lana watched the part in utter disbelief and shock. She became very anxious after learning that the meteorite was not a meteorite but a part of the XYZ-001 spacecraft that was lost in space 2 months ago.

Slowly and gradually, she walked near it and said, her voice filled with dark bands of emotions and sadness, "We all were extremely unhappy after losing our 5 astronauts. But after all, time is the one that changes our whole life. None can fight or control it."

Now Anderson felt the need to motivate her as they had to perform very important tasks.

He put his soft and heavy arm on her shoulder and said, "Ms. Lana! Now it's not the time of regretting or panicking, but of moving and catching the waiter. We haven't found those intelligent and brave crew members, but we will find the killer of Brown Sir and finally reveal the secret of Einstein's last words that he was going to declare tonight."

He then pulled out the small silver chip which he had got from the part of the spacecraft from his pocket and said, "You please immediately start preparing for our flight, and I will go and give this chip to Jonathan, who will later do research on it."

"Yeah!" replied Lana, her tone becoming more confident, "I know the plane that will personally take us to the Pyramids of Giza for our next journey. Now come on, move quickly."

Without wasting time further, Anderson ran like a sprinter towards the sleeping rooms of the NSRA, where Jonathan had gone a few minutes before.

The NSRA's sleeping rooms were very large and simple. There were hundreds of beds on which the workers slept during overtime or during any other complex projects or missions. Even though he looked very simple and innocent, Mr. Davis was extremely tough on his employees, just like his other 2 business partners- Elon Musk and James Brown.

That night, only one person was sleeping there- Jonathan. As Anderson walked the floors, he decided to avoid making any noise as Jonathan would get disturbed.

Silently, he motioned towards the bed where Jonathan was asleep. But his face still looked very sad and pale.

Grabbing the right opportunity, Anderson, without making any noise, kept the chip right next to a small table near the bed, along with a small chit of paper, written by himself.

Before leaving, he looked at the asleep Jonathan and said to himself, "Dear! Don't worry. Lana and I will definitely give justice to Brown Sir."

Then he turned his full attention towards Jonathan and thought, *when you wake up, immediately read the chit and start doing research on the chip.*

Maybe it can prove very helpful to us.

And then he left and hurried towards the barren land near the spacecraft the part where Lana was waiting for him.

Lana waved her hand to Anderson, telling him to hurry up. He just ran like a great athlete.

But when he went near, he was astonished to see the pretty young astronaut's look.

A few moments ago, she was wearing shorts and a plain t-shirt. But now she wore tight black jeans with a soft white top with a nice pink muffler around her neck and heels in the legs.

Extremely beautiful, thought Anderson as he motioned towards her.

When they both were ready to leave, she said, "Now we have to use your Tesla Model Y will proceed towards our destination. I think COP Abner will be coming."

But just as they talked about that, they could hear the sound of a few cars approaching them. Lana sensed who was coming. *COP Abner has arrived to capture Dr. Anderson. We have to leave now.*

Without informing him anything, she pulled him inside the Model Y and started driving it. Anderson became a bit startled.

Does Ms. Lana know how to drive?

But just as they were about to leave, COP Abner's Ford Police Interceptor arrived there. He walked outside with some police officers and took out his small pistol.

But before he could do anything, Lana accelerated the Tesla Model Y and both of them left the NSRA.

COP Abner shouted at the top of his voice from behind, "I order you to stop, Dr. Anderson! Otherwise, you will be given a harsh punishment."

But to everybody's surprise, a beautiful girl peeped out from the window of the driver seat and fired back, "We will not stop until we find the killer and the mystery of Einstein's last words, COP Abner!" COP Abner stood frozen there.

Ms. Lana has run away along with Dr. Anderson to catch the killer of Brown Sir? Is she trying to save Anderson? I think now we have to chase them before they do anything. I am now sure that both of them are involved with that waiter. We have to catch them.

But after all, he was astonished to see that the spacecraft which had left for Mars in the morning and returned back.

Outside the NSRA, as she was driving the Tesla, Lana asked Anderson to dial a number on his iPhone without asking any questions. And he did as she told him, becoming totally blank and confused.

When the receiver received the call, Lana said seriously, "Listen! We have to go on an exhilarating journey. Please be ready!"

CHAPTER THIRTY

Pilot Dylan Carter looked so shocked as if he had seen a ghost, while he was seated on his bed. The mobile phone in his hand was shaking due to his hand.

What the hell has happened? Ms. Lana has given the order to stand ready near Brown Sir's private jet, but why? What has happened?

Dylan immediately pulled away his blanket and got down from the bed.

His peaceful and silent sleep had just evaporated in a few moments after the call. He turned on the lights and confusingly wore the professional clothes that he always wore when on duty.

Before leaving the house, he checked the time on his latest Fastrack watch. It was 1 AM.

Faraway from the NSRA, Lana kept increasing the speed of the Tesla Model Y. The silent electric engine of the car was really a great thing. *Ms. Lana drives very well,* thought Anderson.

But his mind was all puzzled. He was not able to understand where they we're going.

"Where are we going, Ms. Lana?"

"Just call me Lana. Because you are now my companion. I will also call you Jacob, if you don't mind."

and she smiled.

Anderson was all okay with that. He never required any respect for his name or surname or post.

Turning his head towards her, he asked with a startled look, "Can you please tell me where we are going?"

"We are heading towards Brown's private jet, Sir, Jacob." Anderson gave a puzzled look.

"Brown has a personal jet? I thought that he didn't have any."

Turning the Tesla Model Y towards the left, Lana replied, "Yes, of course he has! Because he was very much interested in flying among the skies and clouds. He was also a great lover of travelling."

But the curious mind of Anderson was exploding with several questions and doubts.

Leaning towards her face, he asked, "What would you think would be Einstein's last words were that Brown Sir decided not to tell anyone, including his dear friend Mr. Davis?"

Lana suddenly looked stunned and became silent. She was also constantly thinking about that matter only.

"I can't imagine or guess what Einstein's last words were," her tone sounded tense, "But I can certainly tell that they hold some very valuable information which has the capability of changing the history of the whole planet. Because they were Einstein's, a genius scientist's last words, so they must definitely contain some scientific or technological mystery."

"I am really extremely excited to know what they are and what the information they contain."

"Yes, but for that, we have to capture the evil waiter. I am one hundred percent sure that he is the only assassin. And if he is the assassin, it is obviously clear that he just wants to bury the genius's last words. So, when he understood that Brown Sir was going to announce the information, he killed him so that the information would remain a mystery for the whole population. This shows that the killer also knows about the secret, that's why he wants to bury it."

Anderson's heartbeat suddenly increased. Sweat flowed down from his forehead.

Accelerating the car towards the east, Lana asked him surprisingly, "What happened Jacob? Why are you becoming so hyper suddenly?"

Wiping the sweat with his handkerchief, which was of the design of space, he said, "I am worried and simultaneously shocked by one thing."

Lana was eager to hear what he was worried about.

"Brown Sir knew about the mystery of Einstein's last words. But he is not alive now."

He then turned his attention outside the window.

Staring at the dark sky above, he said in an extremely serious voice, "Now, only one person on this whole planet knows about the mystery. The waiter who is moving towards Giza."

CHAPTER THIRTY-ONE

Jonathan's sleep suddenly broke as he saw a very scary and fierce nightmare. Taking a deep breath and becoming less tense, he thought *it was a very bad dream. Sir Brown's killer is never found, and he kills Mr Davis too.*

Then Jonathan recalled that the object which they thought of as a meteorite was actually a part of the XYZ-001 spacecraft. He then, still sad, decided to return back to the place where he thought that Anderson was working.

But as he stepped down, he was startled to see a shiny silver object was glowing on the tiny table beside his bed, under which a small chit of fresh paper was kept.

Who kept this here when I was sleeping?

Becoming more confused, he silently grabbed the tiny silver object and began to read the chit.

But his surprise and confusion reached the apex level as he read that. His palms started sweating profusely as he reread the note written by Anderson. He was stunned after reading about the mysterious waiter who was heading towards Giza and learnt that Anderson and Lana had gone on a journey to catch him. But his greatest interest lay in that chip that was founded by Anderson from that part of the XYZ-001 spacecraft.

Without thinking anything, he hurried directly towards a small research laboratory of the agency to quickly run research on that chip that he was holding in his hand.

Some distance above the ground, on the second floor of the NSRA, Dr. Johnson was tired of reading the biography of Einstein by the famous and bestselling author Walter Isaacson, who had also written great biographies of famous people like Steve Jobs, Benjamin Franklin, Leonardo da Vinci, Henry Kissinger and also that of Elon Musk.

Keeping the book aside and removing his round spectacles, he said to himself, 'Actually, I don't know why, but I always get angry on Z11. He is really a very helpful robot with a broad and extensive knowledge of several topics. But sometimes, he is so irritating that I feel like demolishing it. But why did he throw the books I authored into the dustbin, considering them rubbish? Either he is not very smart, or I am not a great author. But considering it, I prefer that the former option is correct.'

Forgetting that dumb matter, Dr. Johnson decided to walk down and see what Anderson and Jonathan would have discovered. But as he walked down the stairs instead of using the elevator, he sensed something strange and unusual.

As he turned his eyes to his left side, he was astonished to see the lights of a research laboratory turned on. He sensed that something was going on inside the lab.

Due to his growing curiosity, he decided to walk inside the lab and experience what was happening inside.

As he motioned inside the lab, he could only hear the stamping of his feet in the environment and nothing else. The air inside the lab felt thin as he gazed deeper.

Before him, he saw that his rival Z11 was put on charging in one corner of the vast lab. The robot's human-like eyes were completely lifeless, and his cute face was stationary.

How cute he looks when not active. But once he comes back to life, he leaves not a single chance or opportunity to trouble me.

But as Dr. Johnson looked around, to his astonishment, he saw that Jonathan was standing, bent towards a huge desk and observing some the shiny metal thing with fully concentrated eyes.

What is he looking for now? Have he and Anderson found something from the meteorite?

Immediately, he hurried to the desk where Jonathan was studying the silver chip carefully.

"Hey! What are you examining with so much attention at this moment?" he exclaimed in some accentless English.

Hearing his voice, the laser-focused Jonathan turned his head and stared at Dr. Johnson with a serious face.

"Sir, you would be amazed to know what Anderson and I have discovered and what is happening currently in the world. I want you to listen to me carefully."

Dr. Johnson's pulse quickened as he heard the ongoing chaos and unbelievable incidents taking place that night, around the world and also at the NSRA itself.

"What? What did you say right now?! A waiter has killed Brown Sir by mixing a mysterious chemical inside his cold coffee?" Johnson blurted in total shock and surprise.

Motioning a bit near him, Jonathan ventured, "No, we cannot actually say that he is only the killer. However, the conditions prevailing now directly lead us to the point that he is only our main suspect, as reported by the Forensic department and COP Abner. But on Robin's insistence, they are now chasing Dr. Jacob, doubting him as the mastermind behind this whole chaos."

Dr. Johnson was stammering at that moment. His heart raced rapidly as he heard more about the secret chip that Anderson had found from the part of the lost spaceship. He was also totally shocked to learn about the reality of the meteorite. *I can't believe that it is a part of the XYZ-001 spacecraft.*

"Please give me the chip, Jonathan." Dr Johnson was curious to have a look at the silver chip.

As Jonathan handed him the tiny chip, Dr. Johnson began examining it closely. He glanced at the chip with such concentration as if he was looking at the Mona Lisa painting.

Jonathan was thinking that Johnson might get some clue or hint about the chip as he had an extremely vast knowledge of materials due to his love for chemistry.

However, as time passed, Dr. Johnson's face started becoming less stressed. By looking at his expressions and gestures, it seemed as if he had solved the mystery of that chip!

"I have found it! I have found it!" screamed Johnson at the top of his voice.

Jonathan, who was standing beside him, was very shocked to see that Johnson had so quickly found out the secret of the silver chip.

"What have you found, Sir? Please tell me!"

Johnson began happily, "Dear Jonathan! This chip is none other than the one manufactured and created by Dr. Serena Hawthorne!"

Jonathan's jaw dropped as he heard the intelligent female scientist's name. She was one of the 5 lost crew members in XYZ-001.

"What?! Did Hawthorne manufacture this chip? And I don't know about this. How can that be possible?"

Now, Dr. Johnson was in a situation where he had to explain the whole matter to the confused engineer in front of him.

Leaning at his puzzled face, he began the explanation, "You must be well aware that Dr. Serena Hawthorne was one of the major members of the team that was working on the creation and production of Z11."

Now, blood started flowing inside Jonathan's body at a faster pace. The nerves of the hands felt uneasy as he heard Dr. Johnson mention Z11.

"Z11? What's the connection between this chip and the small robot?"

"That's what the main connection is!" replied Johnson with a broad smile.

Turning more closely, he said, "Dear Jonathan, this chip was produced by Dr. Hawthorne in order to keep Z11 secure."

Secure?

Johnson spoke fast, "Dr Hawthorne always feared that if anybody ever takes advantage of Z11 by sharing with it a secret and telling him not to reveal, it could literally prove harmful for humankind if the intentions of the person are evil and cruel. Therefore, she smartly made this tiny chip to insert inside Z11 so that his programme would get restructured in such a way that the robot would suddenly spit out all the things which were told to him not to reveal! But I don't know the place where this chip can be inserted."

Jonathan became alarmed and impressed by the information. *How smart and intelligent Dr. Serena Hawthorne was,* he thought.

Now, they both quickly understood the reason why the crew members had cut part of the spaceship before dying. They just wanted to give this chip back for humankind's safe and secure future.

"But why did they cut out and send this whole part where this chip was located, instead of just sending this chip by the advanced targeting technology of the spacecraft?" asked Jonathan with a question mark clearly visible on his face.

However, the smart engineer Johnson also had the answer to this question.

"Because they must have feared that this chip would get burnt due to the extreme heat and friction or any other problem. After all, it is definitely not safe to send such a tiny chip, considering the fears and risks of the vast cosmos."

Dr. Johnson is also very smart and logical.

But as their conversation was going on, a completely robotic voice echoed inside the whole laboratory.

'Fully charged! Fully charged! Fully charged!'

Both the engineers realised that Z11 was fully charged. Now it was the time to remove the charger and reactivate the boyish robot.

Dr Johnson ran quickly at him and turned the charger off. He was not able to tolerate the buzzy and irritating sound.

As soon as he removed the charger, Z11 again came back to life and started shouting rapidly, "It is not a meteorite! It is a part of the XYZ-001 spacecraft!"

Johnson silenced him by telling him that they already knew about that.

But the boyish-looking Z11 continued speaking and irritating him, "Okay! You know that I am very happy. It shows that you really know something."

Now, Dr. Johnson's face started turning red with anger. He was boiling with rage more and more as Z11 insulted him.

"What the hell did you say?! I know something? You, sheepish-looking robot! I am the author of 5 books!"

Z11 fired back, "Yes, I am well aware of that. But according to my knowledge, those all are worthless and useless."

Jonathan's body was sweating profusely as he sensed that something terrible was going to happen between the robot and the man.

Dr. Johnson's face turned red like a ripe and juicy tomato. By behaviour, he was actually a very short-tempered and arrogant person.

Clutching the tiny silver chip in his right palm, he shouted with extreme anger, "You bloody robot! How dare you insult me again! I have been tolerating your nonsense for many months, but I will not tolerate it anymore now."

Saying so, he stretched his right hand backwards.

Jonathan immediately sensed what his next action would be. He was looking very scared and frightened.

"No, Dr Johnson! No! Don't do that!"

And he ran towards him. But soon, he realised that he was too late.

On the terrace of the eleven-storey building of NSRA, Mr Davis gazed at the full Moon with his whole focus. He recalled the sad incident that happened a few hours ago at the auditorium. *Whatever everyone had thought of, nothing happened like that. Everything has changed.*

Jonathan, Dr. Johnson and Anderson had felt that he had slept inside his office. But on the other hand, he was staring at the Moon by standing on his terrace all alone. It clearly seemed that he was waiting for something.

After a few minutes, a chopper suddenly emerged through the dark sky and headed towards Mr Davis. *It has finally arrived.*

Quickly, he jumped inside it and sat on the comfortable seat.

The pilot asked in confusion, "Where do you want to go at this time?"

Mr. Davis told him the location where he was willing to go.

As the chopper lifted from the terrace and started flying towards the location where Mr Davis was willing to go, he said to himself very seriously,

"I am going where I must go."

· 177 ·

CHAPTER THIRTY-TWO

Pilot Dylan Carter stood awaited near the personal jet of James Brown.

Each and every passing moment was becoming like a mysterious riddle for him. *Why has Ms. Lana asked me to be ready with Brown Sir's personal jet? He is dead now.*

But after all, he didn't dare to deny the orders of the great astronaut and scientist. So, he kept waiting for her in the cold environment, the air of the surroundings smelling nice and fresh.

On the other hand, Lana was accelerating the Tesla Model Y as fast as possible. The confused Anderson was seated beside her, immersed in his own world of thoughts.

What would be Albert Einstein's last words that Brown considered them to hide from everyone, including his close and dear friend? Whatever they are, they carry information that would be definitely incomparable with anything in this whole world.

"Oh my God! I have to accelerate the car more!" groaned Lana.

Anderson suddenly became normal, returning back from his thoughts. He asked Lana what had happened.

She was so busy driving that she simply asked him to take a look behind their car from the rearview mirror.

As Anderson looked behind from the rearview mirror of his car, his teeth clenched with vibrations. *COP Abner is chasing us?*

Anderson's mind's bulb suddenly lit up at that moment. He understood that COP Abner had traced their location to the iPhone he carried with him.

"Hurry up, Lana! If they catch us, time will slip from everybody's hand, and the waiter will do what he wants to."

"Yes, sure, Jacob!" and she increased the car's speed. Some 15-20 metres behind them, COP Abner, urged his driver to accelerate

his Ford Police Interceptor. "We have to capture Dr. Anderson at any cost now. His running away from us clearly states that he is the only one who had planned today's horrifying act. But the situation also compels us to say that Ms. Lana is also involved with him."

Accelerating the Ford, the driver replied, "But Sir, Ms. Lana told us that she and Dr. Anderson are going to find and hold the waiter hostage and reveal the Einstein death mystery. So how could they both be criminals?"

Taking a deep breath and filling his strong and healthy lungs with oxygen,

Abner said, "Innocent chap! You don't know that this emotional drama is in the blood of criminals and killers! She told us that so that we would think that they were really going to catch the waiter. But in reality, they would go and help the waiter to complete their further tasks."

The driver felt that COP Abner was really a very smart police officer.

Forgetting all that stuff, the driver turned the car towards left from a sharp corner and chased Anderson's Model Y.

As Pilot Carter was scrolling his phone, watching the news about the conspiracy theories developing about the mysterious words of Einstein, which he had spoken about before his death, he saw a shiny Tesla Model Y coming fast towards him. He quickly understood that it was Anderson's car as he saw the number plate. The number 369 was carved stylishly on the plate.

Everybody who recognised Anderson also knew that he was one of the greatest fans of the Serbian-American inventor Nikola Tesla, who, with his inventions and discoveries have made the 21st century look as it should look like.

Now, as he shifted his gaze from the number plate to the driver's seat, he was astonished.

Ms. Lana is coming along with Dr. Anderson?! But for what?

Anderson could see the nice view before him. There were tall trees all around. He immediately understood that they were a few metres behind Brown's house because Lana told him. In between those tall and green trees, there was a small runway over which a beautiful, but not much longer, big jet was located. Anderson sensed that it was the private jet of Brown Sir.

Sir Brown's compact yet sleek private jet is reminiscent of the renowned Dassault Falcon 8X took out an elegant persona under the night sky. Its compact size resembled the streamlined and sophisticated design of the Falcon 8X, which had its maiden flight on 6 February 2015.

Anderson's eyes were unable to move from the beautiful architecture in front of his eyes.

The jet's exterior, coated in a deep, midnight white, glistened under the moonlight. Its modest length allowed it to blend seamlessly with the dark backdrop, making it a discreet presence on the tarmac. The subtle curves and aerodynamic lines of the fuselage mirrored the iconic design of the Falcon 8X, evoking a sense of speed and precision.

Inside, the cabin exuded an intimate and exclusive atmosphere. The interior featured plush leather seats and fine technological accents. While the windows were smaller due to the jet's size, they still offered a glimpse of the starry night.

The Ford Police Interceptor drew closer as time passed. Inside it, COP Abner was very serious, and it seemed from his behaviour that he had the ultimate goal in his life: catching Lana and Anderson. Many other police cars were following it.

Now, finally, they both reached the jet. Lana immediately commanded Anderson to get out.

As they moved outside the Model Y, Pilot Carter gave a puzzled look and started peppering them with questions.

"What happened? Why have you called me at this time, ma'am?" His voice sounded quite tense.

Looking anxiously towards him, Lana responded fastly, "Dylan! We don't have time now to discuss all these things! Please start the jet quickly as we both sit inside. And for your information, please fly towards Giza."

Fly towards Giza? Africa? But for what? thought Carter with a startled mind.

But he clearly knew that if he asked more questions, he would definitely get scolded by Lana. So, without thinking further, he directly hurried inside the jet and began to start it.

Lana and Anderson immediately decided to flee from the place and sit inside the comfortable jet of Brown.

But as both of them were about to move inside a harsh and deep voice yelled from behind so loudly that a sleeping dog suddenly got frightened and started to bark.

"Dr Jacob Anderson and Ms Lana Wilson! Please stop. You both are under arrest!" The voice of COP Abner clearly resembled his bad and intense mood at that time.

Motioning a few steps ahead, Lana replied annoyingly, "Mr. Ardolf! You are doing a totally wrong thing. Dr. Anderson is not a criminal! But the waiter who is flying towards Giza is. You should catch him, not us!"

Clutching his right hand at his back, he fired back, "But according to Robin's observation, Dr. Jacob was sweating profusely and behaving in a very strange and cowardly manner just a few moments before Brown Sir's death! And now he is running away with you without making any statement.

And after all, it seems that you are also involved in this whole nuisance."

Lana swallowed the anger inside her. At that moment, she felt like stabbing COP Abner. Anderson was very frightened and was willing to speak. His heart raced rapidly by looking at the gang of police officers in front of him. But before he opened his mouth, Lana erupted angrily at the COP, "Do what you want, but we will stop only when we catch that bloody waiter and crack this

whole case!"

And saying so, she held Anderson's right hand as tightly as possible and both of them rushed inside the private jet.

Looking at both of them, COP Abner commanded his police to catch them. Following his commands, the policemen started running behind the 2.

And silently, COP Abner pulled his pistol and aimed it at the leg of Anderson. His fingers were dying to pull the trigger at that moment, but he felt that it would be too much if he did that. So, finally, he abandoned his dangerous decision and ran behind them.

Pilot Carter was very puzzled and confused as he seated and was ready to start the jet. But he was not able to hear Anderson or Lana's orders or any of their voices.

But just as he thought about it, he heard Lana's voice commanding him inside his high-tech headset, "Please start the jet quickly, Carter! Otherwise, we would get stuck in a great problem! Fly towards Giza."

Listening to her orders, within a fraction of a second, he started the jet.

The electric motor inside the jet spun the main shaft until there was enough air blowing through the compressor and the combustion chamber to light the engine. Fuel then started flowing, and an igniter ignited it.

Then, the fuel flow was increased to spin the engine up to its operating speed.

Before COP Abner or any other police officers reached to catch them, the jet taxied along the runway and eventually took off from the ground!

Lana kept the small device aside through which she had ordered Carter to start the jet. Along with the handsome but shy Anderson, she peeped down at the receding ground towards COP Abner from the window.

Several metres below, the annoyed and irritated COP Abner said to his policemen, "We must not regret now! We have the important task of catching them. So, without wasting time, let's proceed on our journey of chasing and catching them."

And saying so, he sat inside his Ford Interceptor.

Several metres above the ground, the aircraft was accelerating towards Africa.

The skilled and smart pilot Dylan Carter was baffled, thinking about what was happening at that time. How the whole night was ruined and disturbed.

But amidst his confusing thoughts, his headset suddenly vibrated, and a familiar voice emanated from it.

"Hello, Carter! I am very thankful towards you that you literally saved us

today," Lana exclaimed at the top of her voice. Her tone seemed happy.

"Welcome, ma'am! But I request you to please explain to me what is happening. My brain is really going off track!"

Clearing her throat, Lana relayed all the information to Carter. As he learnt about all the mind-boggling incidents which had happened that night, he was totally in a puzzled state.

"What?! The waiter, part of the XYZ-001 spacecraft, Dr. Anderson, is a suspect. What is happening? Firstly, I was baffled by Brown Sir's death and what he said about Einstein's last words. And now this."

There was a temporary and unexpected silence.

Then Lana concluded, "Please fly the aircraft as fast as possible as we have to reach Giza's airport. I know you can do it."

"Yes, ma'am! Don't worry! Just enjoy the journey."

As Lana kept the device aside, she saw that Anderson was gazing at her continuously.

"What happened, Jacob? Am I looking so pretty?" and she gave a sweet laugh.

Anderson suddenly felt unusual as he sat face-to-face with her on a comfortable seat near a window.

But without hesitation, he admired Lana's bravery and confidence, "You are really a very courageous lady. And I am highly impressed by your love towards your boss."

They both exchanged happy looks.

But suddenly, Anderson asked, "Can you please tell me what is the name of this private jet of Brown Sir?"

Lana gave a broad smile and replied, "AE-0761! "

Anderson realised that there might be something special about that name.

A genius entrepreneur like Brown would definitely keep a unique name for his aircraft.

Observing his thinking, she said, "Are you able to decode the name Dr. Anderson? Or should I tell you?"

Anderson was not in the mood to involve his brain in thinking about another mystery. That night, his mind was already engaged with many other mysteries.

"So, see, hear Jacob ',' her tone increased, "If you look carefully at the name, you will see AE at the beginning. And tell me who Brown Sir's favourite scientist was?"

"AE for Albert Einstein!" exclaimed Anderson with amazement.

She continued, "Yes, and if you add the numbers succeeding it, you will get 7+6+1= 14. And recall what the genius scientist's birth date is?"

"It's 14th March 1879! The number 14 represents his birthday, which is celebrated worldwide as World Genius Day."

Anderson realised that Brown really had great love and respect towards Einstein.

But in between that, he saw that Lana suddenly became sad and distressed.

Keeping his left hand on her delicate shoulder, he asked, "What happened? What are you wondering about?"

As he kept his hand on her shoulder, Lana could feel the warmth and care in his hand. She was sure that he was a very kind-hearted person.

Lana shot an anxious glance at Anderson and replied, "Jacob, I am constantly thinking about what Einstein would have spoken before his death, and what information his words carry which Sir considered so important that he didn't tell anybody?"

Anderson stared at her in disbelief. He had also been thinking about the same thing that night.

Leaning at her face, he whispered, "Don't worry much about that, Lana! Once we catch that waiter, we will definitely find the answers to all of our questions. I hope we reach Giza airport as soon as possible."

Lana felt somewhat better after hearing him. *A ray of hope is there before us,* she thought with some satisfaction. But for that, there was only one thing that they had to do- catch that mysterious and unknown waiter. *But who could be that waiter who dared to kill Sir? What does he seek from the murder? Does he want to bury the secret of the last words? But why?*

Amidst that, Lana noted a strange thing. She saw that Anderson was totally immersed in his own Universe. But he looked extremely puzzled and shocked.

"What happened, Jacob? Why are you looking so startled?" her voice was low.

The aircraft accelerated at a rapid speed.

Sensing something confusing, Anderson exclaimed, "Lana, I want you to answer my one question!"

"Sure, Jacob!"

He now bent very close towards her and spoke in a very serious tone, "

Most of the help of this Mars mission was provided by AI scientists, as robots were first sent to the red planet to build the research laboratory there! And all the top researchers and AI scientists from around the world were working with Virtual Eye, SpaceX and NSRA for the mission, right?"

Lana stared at him in utter disbelief, trying to process his words. The intelligent researcher had just asked her a very normal question.

"Yes! You are right. The top AI scientists from around the globe worked with us for this mission."

Now Anderson gave a smile and got up from the comfortable seat of the AE-0761 jet. His face was glowing with sudden happiness.

Lana was very baffled by his strange behaviour. Getting up, she exclaimed surprisingly, "What has happened to you suddenly? What is all going on inside your head at this instant?"

Becoming normal again, Anderson replied with great happiness and excitement, "You won't believe Lana! But I have understood who that mysterious waiter is who is heading towards Giza."

CHAPTER THIRTY-THREE

Jonathan was too late to stop the angry Johnson. Before he could do anything, Dr Johnson had already thrown the silver chip annoyingly towards the robot.

But to both of their surprise, an extremely unbelievable and shocking thing happened. The 2 brilliant engineers' eyes widened, and they were unable to trust what was happening.

Dr. Johnson threw the tiny silver chip straight at the forehead of the small, boyish robot Z11. But just as the tiny chip dashed at his forehead, a very strange and mysterious thing happened, which left both of them speechless. The reality was distorted for them, and it seemed as if they had seen a very horrible nightmare.

As the chip dashed Z11's forehead, unimaginably, it entered inside it! The silver chip disappeared inside his forehead like a soul or spirit! The scene was amazing and unbelievable!

"Dr. Serena Hawthorne had created the spot in the robot's forehead for inserting that chip! How smart! None can figure it out easily! Amazing!" exclaimed Jonathan with an astonished look.

But between that, one more strange incident occurred. Jonathan observed that Dr. Johnson was gazing at the robot in a very unusual and puzzled way. So, in great confusion, Jonathan asked, "What happened, Sir? Why are you looking so uncomfortable?"

But without uttering a single word from his mouth, he directly and silently pointed his hand towards Z11.

As Jonathan shifted his gaze at Z11, he was totally baffled after looking at what was all happening.

The boyish and irritating Z11 was vibrating and buzzing in a strange manner. It looked as if he was literally dancing.

And during that, he was screaming in a completely synthetic voice, "Code restructuring! Code restructuring! Reveal all the secrets! Reveal all the secrets!"

And shouting unusually, the robot motioned towards a wall. Surprisingly, a projector-like device was raised from its right metallic shoulder, and it started projecting a video on the wall of the research laboratory.

Johnson and Jonathan motioned towards the robot and stood beside it.

Now, their eyes were just on the video that was playing on the wall.

About 2 minutes later, the video ended, and Z11 became normal but silent.

Both the engineers were looking at each other as if they were going to die.

After a while, Johnson exclaimed, "Holy shit! Holy shit! It's unbelievable! I can't believe it."

Before Jonathan could reply, Z11 said, now in a human-like voice, "You believe it or not, but it is the truth."

Dr Johnson was so baffled after watching the video that he found it difficult to distinguish between happiness and shock. His heart was racing with every passing moment.

Jonathan came near him and said happily and excitedly, "We should quickly publish this video on the internet! As it goes viral, several mysteries will be solved."

"Yes! You are absolutely correct! Tell Z11 to project this amazing video again on the wall. I will shoot the whole scene on my mobile phone and publish it on the internet."

Following his commands, Jonathan did what needed to be done at that time.

Z11 started projecting the video again on the wall, and Dr. Johnson began shooting it using his smartphone.

Looking at all that, Jonathan said very joyously to himself, 'Now finally the world will come to know what were the last words of the genius Albert Einstein.'

CHAPTER THIRTY-FOUR

Lana stared anxiously into Anderson's eyes. The throbbing of her heart suddenly increased, and her nerves began to vibrate.

"What?! You have really understood who that waiter is, who is heading towards Africa?"

"Yes! I have," replied Anderson with a broad smile.

Now, Lana's tension was increasing rapidly. The curiosity of knowing the identity of the waiter made her uneasy and uncomfortable.

"Please quickly tell Jacob, I can't wait any longer. I want to know who is that evil soul who has killed our beloved Brown Sir by mixing that mysterious chemical into his cold coffee!"

Anderson requested Lana to sit on the seat in order to listen to him carefully. She did what he told her.

Now, their faces were closer towards each other. Lana was staring at him continuously. She was so curious that her eyes were also not blinking.

"Listen to me carefully," his voice sounded serious, "The top AI scientists of the world were working together for this Mars mission. And if I am not wrong, the scientists who worked are ranked among the top 100 in the world. If we run a Google search, we will find their names in the top list. Right?"

Lana nodded in agreement.

"Okay! So, if I am accurate, Professor Victor Malachai was also working with you, was he?"

"Yes! There is definitely no doubt that he wasn't working. Everybody knows that he is the best and the most genius scientist and expert of artificial intelligence alive on Earth now." Lana stared in utter disbelief and shock towards him.

"Exactly! That's what my point is! You know what? Lana, the waiter flying towards Giza is none other than Professor Victor Malachai!"

Lana's jaw dropped instantly. It seemed as if her heart stopped beating at that moment. Her mouth was left speechless.

With a puzzled look, she got up from the seat as fast as light.

Leaning down towards the smiling Anderson, she shouted, "What the hell are you saying, Jacob!? Are you aware of the words you just spoke now? Professor Victor is the killer of Brown Sir? How dare you say that! They were both very good companions and Brown always highly appreciated him. What made you think that Professor Victor is the murderer?"

Silencing her and calming her mind, Anderson spoke, "Just relax, Lana! I am explaining to you the reason why I think Professor Victor is only the killer."

Lana was really very annoyed with Anderson. She was swallowing her anger as she always believed in first listening to what the person is trying to tell.

"The whole world knew that today was a great speech and celebration organised by Brown Sir and Mr. Davis," he began silently, "All the top senior executives and engineers of NSRA, Virtual Eye and SpaceX were attending the event. Also, most of the AI researchers and experts were present there including me, except Professor Victor."

Now Lana's memory flashed with the thought that they had invited Professor Victor and his beloved friend, assistant and employee, Joseph, for the event. But everyone was baffled as they didn't receive any message from the 2. None of the 2 had received the call nor sent any type of message. James Brown told her this information himself. But he also assumed that the intelligent scientist would have been stuck in a personal problem or something else.

In a very low voice, Lana said, "Yes.... He didn't come to the event. But this doesn't mean that he is the killer! He and his beloved employee Joseph must have got stuck in some sort of problem."

"What you are thinking is completely wrong, Lana!"

"Why do you say that?"

Anderson took a deep breath and replied, "You know what, when I entered the auditorium during the event, a strange waiter suddenly dashed me who was wearing a mask which covered his face. I kept staring at him because my inner voice was telling me that I had seen him somewhere as he was a famous personality. But he simply rejected my notion by saying

that he was an ordinary waiter."

The AE-0761 jet was accelerating rapidly towards Giza. Pilot Carter was a well-experienced and skilled pilot.

"But the main thing is that, when I asked him his name, he replied 'Nexus'. And it clearly is a name someone gives to a robot. And he also told me that he has a great love for AI and robots."

There was a long silence inside the flying jet. A cool and fresh breeze blew inside from the window.

Anderson concluded his explanation, "We all know clearly that Professor Victor is really very mad about robots and AI. He had also decided to launch a company in cyborg engineering but was not able to do so, as people, including the government, opposed it. By looking at all this, I am sure that the waiter is none other than him. He could have given any other name and reason when he met me in the auditorium, but he simply told me everything related to AI. A person who loves something extremely doesn't think of hiding it even in times of danger related to that. And after all, we know that he has been missing since the afternoon."

Now, Lana also sensed that the intelligent Professor Victor was only the criminal. But she was unable to believe it. Her sensitive heart became extremely sad after hearing that.

She was so disheartened that she sat on the seat and started looking outside the window with a sombre heart. Her beautiful and charming eyes were filled with tears of sadness.

Anderson silently went near her and kindly handed his space handkerchief to her. She felt a deep feeling of kindness and generosity in him.

"Why are you looking so mournful?" asked Anderson.

The disappointed Lana replied in an extremely low and sad voice, "Why should I be happy, Jacob? The person who worked so closely with Brown has mercilessly killed him? Did he not think a single time before performing this cruel act? But why did Professor Victor do that?"

Anderson became emotional after feeling the sad vibes in her voice. He was a very sensitive person like her.

Motioning away from her, he said seriously, "Lana! This whole thing clearly leads us to the conclusion that Professor Victor wants to bury the secret of Einstein's mysterious last words. Means that he knew about it, so he killed Brown Sir before he could announce its secret."

But Anderson suddenly stopped in between. He felt that time was suddenly frozen due to some strange things.

This means except Brown Sir, Professor Victor knows about the mystery of Einstein's last words. But how is that possible? Brown Sir himself, claimed that he didn't share that information with anybody on this Earth, including his friend Mr. Davis. So, how come Professor Victor knows about this?

When he told Lana about his doubts, she was also very baffled and confused.

But just as both of them were going to start discussing that matter, Anderson's iPhone buzzed. Someone was calling him.

As he pulled it out of the pocket of his black coat, he was surprised to see Garcia's call.

On Lana's insistence, he put the call on speaker.

A surprised and startled director, Garcia spoke, "Hello, Dr. Anderson!" Hello! What happened, Ethan? Why did you call at this time? Is everything fine? And you know what, now I am with......"

"I know that whole story, Sir! COP Abner told me that. But leave that. I have great breaking news for you! Please open the **Global Mysteries.com** website and see what's happening. A small video uploaded by Dr. Johnson is attracting a huge amount of viewers all across the world. The video is going extremely viral."

Anderson found it difficult to digest his words.

"But what is there in that video which is attracting the population so much and you want me to see that?"

Director Garcia took a deep breath to become a bit stressless and replied in a very mysterious and serious voice, "You won't believe it, Sir, but the video uploaded by Dr. Johnson contains the last words of Einstein."

CHAPTER THIRTY-FIVE

Inventor and neurologist Harrison Drake gazed at the moonlit sky above him as he was walking all alone on the silent street of Santa Monica, the city close to Los Angeles.

A few days ago, the news of Drake's suicide plan went viral on the internet. Everyone was sure that he was going to take away his own life because great investors, including the government, had opposed and refused to fund his dangerous project. His behaviour clearly showed that he had great ambitions and dreams towards inventing a groundbreaking device that was going to change the history of mankind itself. He was extremely passionate towards his work.

But even after everybody had refused to fund his project, there was one man who came like an angel and helped him. Drake was not able to express his happiness towards the middle-aged man. But there was one strange thing: the man refused to inform anybody about it unless he told him. Drake accepted his offer as he just wanted money for his project. So, after that, he put off his plan of suicide and started working happily on his project.

After walking for a few minutes, he came to his lab, where he had spent sleepless nights to invent his great device.

But at that time, he was looking highly puzzled and surprised. His face had suddenly lost the glow and interest that it contained. It seemed as if he had completely lost the battle with his life and was almost on the verge of giving up. This is not a surprising thing about him. Even though he was a very intelligent and genius inventor who had contributed highly to various types of big government projects, he was not at all happy and satisfied.

But that night, the person who had funded his project had called him suddenly and asked him to wait outside his lab.

Drake looked at his watch. It was 1:30 AM.

Why did Sir call me at this time? What the hell does he want to talk about with me?

Just as the tall and very thin young man glanced again at the sky, he suddenly could see a chopper coming towards him. Firstly, that night's devastating incidents had taken a toll on his mind. Brown's mysterious death, Einstein's last words, etc. When he watched that video uploaded by Dr. Johnson, which contained the last words of Einstein, he was very, very confused.

As the chopper descended and landed smoothly beside his lab, a tall and thin man like him came walking near him. Their body structures were similar. Only the difference was between their ages. The man who was coming near him was a middle-aged man who looked like he was in his fifties.

As he approached near, Drake started throwing questions at him.

"What happened, Sir? Why did you call me at this time?"

The man looked very upset and replied seriously, "Dear Drake, I want to tell you something very important today. I know that you will not believe a single word that I am going to speak. But after all, you have to accept the truth."

Drake's face became pale after hearing the man speak like that.

"Please listen to me carefully."

And then the middle-aged thin man started telling a whole story to the neurologist.

As he told everything, Drake stood frozen before him. The weather was very cold at that time, but still, he was sweating profusely. He was really unable to believe a single word or alphabet that the man had spoken. He could suddenly feel that his whole world had changed just within a few minutes. Actually, the rest of his life had changed.

"Hey! What has happened? I am not able to understand anything." His eyes were red with anger and also filled with tears of sadness.

The man came near and tried to motivate him.

"Don't get upset and broken so easily."

He then urged Drake to sit inside the chopper. Without realising anything, Drake silently motioned inside the chopper. His state was such that he felt a need for a partner or companion at that time.

The thin man ordered the pilot to fly to the next location, where he demanded to go.

Wiping his tears, Drake asked surprisingly, "But where are we actually going? And why?"

Giving a small smile and hiding the sadness, the man replied, "Drake! We are going to such a place where we must go now. No other place on this Earth will help us to get inspired, than this one where we are going."

CHAPTER THIRTY-SIX

"What!? Please repeat what you told me just now?"

Still, with a serious voice, Garcia said, "I said that please watch the video uploaded by Dr. Johnson, for it contains the last words of Einstein."

There was a pin-drop silence in the jet. Lana and Anderson exchanged startled looks. They felt as if they were watching an unbelievable dream.

Bending her head and face towards the iPhone, Lana asked in a low voice,

"The video contains Einstein's last words?"

"Yes, ma'am!" replied Garcia with a fearful tone. Anderson was unable to believe it.

"How is that possible, Ethan? How did Dr. Johnson come to know about it? What is going on?"

"No, Sir! The matter is quite different from what you are thinking. Don't waste time in this useless discussion, and please watch the video carefully. You will come to know everything and also get great help."

Immediately after that, Anderson put Garcia's call on hold and surfed Google to open the **Global Mysteries.com** website. With every passing second, both of them were getting hyper and excited. Garcia's words were hovering over their confused brains.

As Anderson opened the website, he could see headlines flashing in bold letters titled: -

Einstein's last words found! The secret for which the whole world

awaited these many hours has finally been revealed! Please watch the

video by clicking on the link below to learn about that breathtaking secret.

Current viewers: - 100 Million

Anderson clicked on the link provided below the headlines, and soon, a video started.

He told Lana to sit down on the seat of the jet, and he also did so.

Both of their eyes were on the iPhone on which the video was being played.

What must be the genius's last words? The viewership is 100 million. This clearly states that the secret is very amazing and mind-blowing; thought Lana.

And soon after that, the video started.

Dr. Johnson's face was clearly visible. He started speaking, "Hello, guys! I have uploaded this video in order to share with you all an unimaginable thing. You all won't believe what Jonathan and I found now."

The camera now turned to the small robot Z11. His face and whole body were visible, and he was facing a wall.

Z11? Why is Dr. Johnson showing him? thought Anderson, becoming more tense.

Dr. Johnson's voice spoke, "A news was going viral today that a meteorite had landed behind the NSRA. But to your surprise, I want to tell you that it is not a meteorite, but a cut-out part of the XYZ-001 spaceship, which was mysteriously lost in space 2 months ago!"

After a while, he continued, "But Dr. Jacob Anderson had found a small silver chip which was attached to that metallic part."

Anderson felt a bit proud as Johnson took his name.

"And when Jonathan and I ran research on it, we found that the chip is none other than the one manufactured by Dr. Serena Hawthorne!"

Anderson's eyes grew wide as he heard that. *Serena Hawthorne was one of the 5 crew members who got lost in that mission.*

Johnson then explained all about that chip, which made Lana and Anderson more puzzled. They were surprised as well as impressed to learn that Serena had made that chip in order to make Z11 reveal all the information that was told to him not to reveal.

"But today, a very strange incident occurred."

Johnson's voice sounded tense, "When I angrily threw this chip towards Z11, it got inserted miraculously inside his head and disappeared. But the most shocking thing came after that."

Lana and Anderson were totally immersed in the video.

And soon after that, Johnson pointed his camera towards the wall where Z11 was projecting another video.

To both of their astonishment, the video projected by Z11 started.

The scene was of the NSRA. The environment was normal, and it was night. The scene was constantly moving in the forward direction.

And suddenly, an unusual thing happened. James Brown was himself coming near the camera. His face was very dull, and the dark circles were clearly visible under his eyes. He was wearing normal clothes that he used to wear while doing engineering and design work.

He motioned for a while but suddenly stopped and said, "Hello, Z11!"

Anderson and Lana exchanged very puzzled looks. They were not able to digest that the person who was moving inside Z11's video was none other than Z11 himself. The robot's camera was shooting the video.

"Hello, Sir James Brown! What are you doing here at this time? You have worked tirelessly the whole day, so you should take a rest now," his human-like voice blurted.

Brown bent towards the robot's boyish face and said in an extremely low voice, "Dear Z! Please come inside my office right now. I want to talk about something very important with you."

And soon after that, Z11 followed Brown and walked inside his office at the NSRA. Brown had told Davis to construct an office for him inside the NSRA.

Now, the scene of Brown's office was visible. He was sitting on his chair, looking very silent and confused.

"What do you want to tell me, Sir?"

The startled-looking Brown leaned towards the robot and said very seriously, "Dear Z, I want to share with you my mysterious and unbelievable nightmare which I saw just now."

"Nice! I love nightmares. We robots don't see any, but we like to hear one. What was your nightmare?"

Now Brown got up from his chair and directly walked near a window.

Looking outside, he said, "Listen very carefully to what I am telling you. The scene completely focused on Brown, who was still staring outside his window.

In a serious and deep voice, he started telling his nightmare, "It was a chilly night. There was not a single noise. Birds were sleeping peacefully in their nests. Complete silence.

I was walking on a silent road all alone. Not a single person was visible anywhere. I was scared a bit but still kept walking. Walking nearly for 5 minutes, I suddenly got tired and decided to take shelter somewhere and sleep nicely.

But suddenly, a very mysterious and creepy thing happened. As I shifted my gaze towards my left side, I saw a little white bungalow which looked like a school in a village a few metres away. But it was constructed elegantly and painted beautifully. It was painted completely white, like my own house. I was really very happy after seeing it. I was sure that my night would go easily there. Actually, I didn't have a mobile phone or any other device.

Without wasting any time, I went directly there.

But as I came near the bungalow, I could see a beautiful garden before me.

It was completely covered with grass, and there was not a single flower anywhere. Medium-sized trees were also visible. It was a beautiful and nice environment. The air smelled sweet and fresh.

But when I went to knock on the main door, I was astonished to see that it was already open. So, developing some courage, I entered inside as there was not any other option.

But the most surprising thing was that all the lights in all the rooms were on. I found it very puzzling. I was calling if there was anybody inside and also searched for any person inside the room. But there was none. I found it very shocking, but I was still very happy when I found a place to sleep at night.

Before going to sleep, I decided to just take a walk in the garden. But after a few moments, it seemed as if my life had changed completely. What I saw and experienced led me to wonder deeply.

As I was motioning towards the garden, suddenly, a man's voice came from behind. He was calling me by my name. His voice led me to think that he was an old man.

So, I turned behind with astonishment to see who was calling me. But when I gazed at the old man, I was totally speechless. It seemed as if I was in heaven or somewhere else in the Universe."

Brown walked very silently with his head bent down and, coming near his desk, sat on the chair. His head was still down as if he was looking very strange.

The camera of Z11 turned towards him, and the robot asked, "What? Who was that old man?"

Lana and Anderson glanced very excitedly at the video. They were highly curious to know who the old man was.

Brown continued in an extremely serious voice, "When I turned back, I was not able to believe what I was looking at. The old man before my eyes was none other than the most influential and greatest scientist of all time

and my real hero and my God, Albert Einstein."

Lana and Anderson's body felt a sudden and unusual vibration. It was like some type of invisible energy suddenly entered inside them as they heard Einstein's name.

"I was extremely happy and also very startled. But still, I walked towards him. He looked very old, and it seemed as if he was very ill. He was wearing his sweater and was sitting on a huge throne-like chair. I was unable to believe that.

As I came near him, he threw a happy smile towards me. I also smiled. I was very happy at that moment because I was meeting my God face-to-face.

But before I could speak anything, Einstein began in a poor voice, 'Dear James! I want to tell you something very important.'

I nodded in silence.

He then leaned towards me and said, 'You are well aware that I died at 1:15 AM in a hospital in Princeton. But before my death, I spoke something in German. And the nurse who came there didn't understand anything as she didn't know German. So, for everyone, my last words were lost.'

I glanced anxiously at him.

He again leaned backwards into his throne-like chair. His face suddenly lost its glow and happiness, and he looked a bit upset.

At last, he said very seriously, 'But today I am going to tell you what I said before taking my last breath. In other words, I am going to tell you what my last words are.'

Anderson's forehead was flowing with a river of sweat. His hands and fingers shook as he looked at the video.

'Dear James! Please listen to my final words, which I spoke on 18 April 1955 at 1:15 AM.'

And after that, the camera showed Brown, who again walked near the window. And looking outside, he told Z11 what were the last words of Einstein.

'Before my death, I suddenly felt something very different and unusual. It seemed as if I was experiencing some intuition. And then, before dying, I spoke: -

Go under the ground near the Great Pyramid of Giza which was built by the Pharaoh Khufu. Under it, you will find the answers to the ultimate questions which have startled humankind for hundreds and thousands of years.

"How was the Universe created?"

"What is the meaning of Life?"

And remember one thing, James. Please don't share this information with anybody until you announce it to the public. But Z11 is the exception. Tell him only before you tell the public.'

I was highly confused. It was very difficult for me to process his words and understand them. I was very puzzled to hear that he told me to share this information with only you and no one else. But before I could ask him why, he suddenly evaporated like water, and my dream broke."

CHAPTER THIRTY-SEVEN

Lana and Anderson stared at each other as the breathtaking video ended. They were exchanging totally startling looks with each other. What they had just seen was extremely complex and difficult to believe for them.

Their mind was completely changed after hearing that.

Anderson turned the hold option off on his iPhone. Now, Garcia's voice said, "Did you watch the video? How was it?"

Anderson's mouth and lips were dying to scream and express the feelings of his heart. But he was so shocked that he was unable to open his mouth to speak.

Before he could say anything, Lana took the phone and exclaimed, "Director Garcia! What we saw just now was unimaginable. We had never thought that this would be the whole matter. I am really very, very confused."

Talking for some time, Garcia thought that he should not disturb the 2.

They should focus on catching Professor Victor, he felt. He was very

puzzled after learning that the waiter was none other than the popular and controversial AI expert from Lana.

At last, he said, "I am cutting the call now. Hope that both of you catch him as soon as possible. But there is no need to worry, as I think that Professor Malachai will be caught. I have informed the local authorities of Giza to quickly capture him at the airport."

Anderson and Lana felt adrenaline rushing faster through their bodies. It seemed as if the acoustics of the AE-0761 were not working for them. Both of them stood stationary.

"What?! What did you just say right now?" asked Anderson with astonishment.

"I said that I have informed the local authorities of Giza to capture the waiter, that is, Professor Malachai, as soon as the aeroplane lands. Policemen must be waiting at the airport."

Lana chuckled and replied, "Thank God that you informed them, director!

Extremely thanks from us for that. Now, it would be very easy for us to catch them."

"Thanks, ma'am! But it is my duty to do so. Bye-bye, and have a safe journey."

And Garcia cut the call.

Now, the aircraft was rapidly flying towards its destination.

She could see that Anderson was sitting on the seat, totally frozen like a cube of ice and completely immersed in his own world of thoughts. She knew what was going on inside his smart brain.

Leaning towards his face and smiling, she said politely, "Jacob! Now it is clear that Professor Victor wants to bury the secret that contains the answers to the 2 most fundamental questions of human existence."

As the aeroplane was just a few kilometres away from the airport of Giza, senior and skilled Pilot Griffin was controlling the aircraft in utter shock and disbelief. He was very shocked to see what was happening to him.

He could clearly feel the presence of the technologically advanced robotic gun which was pointed at his head. His whole body was shaking with fear.

Beside his seat stood a tall and handsome man wearing the clothes of a waiter with a dark and heavy suit above it. His face was covered with a mask. He looked very upset but tried to hide it in place of cruelty.

Pointing his robotic gun at Griffin's head, which was his own invention, Professor Victor Malachai said very seriously, "Do what I am telling you and don't try to act too smart. Fly this aeroplane directly towards the Pyramids of Giza, where my assistant and I will jump out using our parachute. Then you fly wherever you want."

Pilot Griffin was compelled to fly the aircraft towards the great pyramids of Giza. He had no other option as the lives of the handful of passengers in the aeroplane, including his, were at stake. He had never imagined that the aircraft which he was controlling would get hijacked. But his mind was filled with strange thoughts.

Why do this evil soul and his assistant want to go to the great pyramids of Giza? Why are they behaving so cruelly with us?

Pointing the gun closer at his head, Professor Victor said in a very harsh and annoying voice, "Don't keep thinking about both our purpose of going to the Great Pyramids. You just do what I have ordered you to do. Otherwise, the results would be devastating."

CHAPTER THIRTY-EIGHT

Global Mysteries.com

Breaking news! Breaking news! A recent video uploaded by Dr. Johnson of the NSRA has caught widespread attention worldwide. More than 100 million people have watched the video. It is becoming impossible to digest the information which is present in that video.

• James Brown saw a nightmare where Albert Einstein himself spoke with him and told him what his last words were.

• But surprisingly, the genius told Brown to share that information with none except Z11, the young and boyish-looking intelligent robot. But why?

• Einstein's last words have been finally revealed. But they contain information that is definitely going to change the world. The science prodigy's last words directly relate to the ancient, mysterious great pyramids of Giza.

• His last words state that under the Great Pyramid built by the Pharaoh Khufu, there are answers to the 2 most important and fundamental questions to which humankind has been struggling for thousands of years to find the answer.

• "How was the Universe created?" What is the meaning of life?" If we find the answers, it will be the greatest leap in the achievements of humankind. We would finally find the answers for which we, including our ancestors, have been struggling for thousands of years. To remain updated about the latest news about it, please stay active on our channel.

• 215 •

CHAPTER THIRTY-NINE

COP Abner was flying very fast towards Giza in a great aeroplane provided by the government. With the help of GPS technology, he was able to trace the exact location of Anderson and Lana. But after watching the breathtaking and unbelievable video, he was completely silent, immersed in a very different world of his own. But after all, his main goal was to catch both of them as soon as possible.

And unless he would accomplish that, he would not eat a single grain of food. He was extremely passionate about his work and always performed his duty sincerely. The rest of the night was going to be extremely tough for him. In between that, he also thinks about the mysterious waiter who is flying towards Giza. *Anderson, Lana and the waiter might be the main criminals of today's chaos*, he thought.

He told the pilot to chase Brown's AE-0761 jet as fast as possible.

Technician Marina was looking very upset. She felt very guilty

about why she had assigned the unknown waiter a job without noting down

his personal details and address. That night, she realised that overexcitement was really very bad. But still, she was able to trace the killer's location, thanks to the technology of the clothes.

As she kept regretting herself, suddenly, the small room's door opened, and Director Garcia walked inside and motioned near her.

She turned her attention towards him and exclaimed with disappointment,

"Sorry, Sir! I really feel very guilty about this matter. But now....."

"Don't get demotivated so easily, Marina!" Garcia's voice sounded inspiring, "We still have access to Professor Victor's location. So, it will be easy for us to provide the information to Dr. Anderson and Ms. Lana. And after that, they will catch him and crack this case and, in addition to that, find the answers to those 2 fundamental questions."

Marina stared anxiously at him as if she had seen something very creepy.

What all Garcia spoke was beyond her understanding.

And when he explained all the stuff to her, she was unable to grasp and believe it. Her already ruined night was getting more complex and confusing.

But suddenly, a very strange thing happened. As Marina and Garcia glanced at the huge screen in front of them where the location of Professor Victor was visible, and both of them were stunned and became emotionless.

They could see that the aeroplane which was supposed to land at the Giza airport was miraculously heading towards the place where the 3 great pyramids of Giza were located.

Breaking the silence of the room, Garcia spoke fearfully, "I think we have to inform Dr. Anderson about this."

CHAPTER FORTY

Lana and Anderson were constantly staring into each other's eyes.

The incidents which they had witnessed a few moments ago had left a

deep impact on their brains and hearts.

"I am really not able to believe that the Great Pyramid of Giza was built by the Pharaoh Khufu and contains underneath it the great answers to the fundamental questions," said Lana with an expression of astonishment.

Anderson cleared his throat and replied, "You can't imagine how excited I am to find the answers to these questions. Since childhood, I have always been fascinated by these questions. Every day I think about these questions and start developing my own theories."

The weather was becoming cold and exciting with every passing moment.

The jet was not very far from Giza.

Throwing a sweet smile at Anderson, Lana asked, "Jacob, what do you think about these questions? What are your views on this topic?"

Anderson's brain released a tiny amount of dopamine. He was always excited to find the answers to these questions. Whenever anybody asked him those questions or started discussing such extraordinary topics with him, he was always ready to have a discussion and debate.

"You know what, Lana, there are 2 conflicting views for the first

question," he said very enthusiastically, "Religion says that God created the Universe, while science says that the Universe was created due to the big bang explosion."

Lana felt enthralled as he spoke further.

"There are various stories in different religions which state the creation of the Universe."

He spoke faster now.

"For Hindus, the Universe was created by Brahma, the creator who made the Universe out of himself. After he created the world, the power of Vishnu preserves the world and human beings. As part of the cycle of birth, life and death, it is lord Shiva who will ultimately destroy the Universe.

According to Islam, Allah created the heavens and the Earth, and all that is between them in 6 days.

If you look at Christianity, it shares a story similar to the Quran.

According to the book of Genesis, God created the Universe- and all the heavenly bodies, the Sun, the Moon, and the stars - in 6 days.

There are similar stories in various religions which put forward the argument that it is God only who created this whole Universe and everything. On the other hand, Buddhists believe that this Universe is eternal, which means it has neither beginning nor end."

Now, there was utter silence inside the jet. Lana was getting very excited

as their philosophical conversation continued.

"Even though there are various stories about the creation of the Universe

in religion, science has entirely different answers.

According to the most famous and currently accepted model, the Big Bang theory explains how the Universe was created.

Billions of years ago, everything present in the Universe was contained in a tiny ball that exploded. The tiny ball is known as singularity. It contains all the forces, matter, density, temperature, pressure, etc. And when it finally exploded, the Universe was created."

"But actually, I don't believe in the Big Bang theory much!" Lana suddenly erupted, "Because I feel that the Universe must have come into existence due to something entirely different."

"Does it mean you think that some supernatural entity created everything?" replied Anderson with a laugh.

"No! I don't mean to say that, Jacob. I simply believe that something very different had happened at that time, which is beyond our senses and understanding. I cannot express my feelings and cannot tell you what I feel."

Anderson nodded silently.

"But you laughed when you asked whether I believed that some supernatural entity created the Universe. Means, are you an atheist?"

Anderson smiled and replied intellectually, "Actually, many people ask me about it, Lana. It is a very difficult question for me. But speaking simply, I am an agnostic. This means I am not sure whether God does exist or not. I don't oppose religion and God, and I also don't favour it. I am highly attracted to science and believe that by studying nature's laws, we can find the answers to the ultimate questions."

Lana agreed with him as she also claimed to be an agnostic.

Now, as the jet accelerated and came nearer to Giza, both of them jumped on to the second question. What is the meaning of life?

"Actually, this second question is more startling and complex," said

Anderson, as he gazed outside the window of the jet, "Because we don't understand why we are living, why we are here and what the purpose of consciousness and survival is. You know what? I am a great fan of one of the famous quotes from the author of *The Hitchhiker's Guide To The Galaxy*, Douglas Adams."

"Which quote?"

Staring at her charming face, he replied philosophically, "There is a theory which states that if ever anyone discovers exactly what the Universe is for and why it is here, it will instantly disappear and be replaced by something even more bizarre and inexplicable. There is another theory which states that this has already happened."

"Oh, really great! This means there might be a possibility that life was dwelling long before we thought, and during that time, a person found the ultimate answers, and then everything was replaced by more puzzling things, which we now think of and experience."

Anderson has now started shedding his knowledge about various philosophers.

"As you know, many philosophers in world history spent their entire lives to find the answer to this question."

The air inside the jet felt wonderful.

"Socrates, the founder of Western philosophy, laid the foundation for the future generation of philosophers. His philosophy focused more on how to live our lives rather than why we live. His death is one of the well-documented events in ancient history."

Suddenly, Lana recalled the emotional and heart-touching death of the great philosopher.

"The Athenian government charged Socrates as they thought that he was corrupting the youth of Athens with his teachings. As per the law, he was given 2 options. Either to stop teaching or embrace death by drinking the cup of hemlock. He politely replied to bring the cup of hemlock and drank it."

Anderson said, "Salute to him as he was so serious and loyal towards his principles."

Lana nodded and extended the conversation.

"Aristotle, for instance, believed that the purpose of life is to achieve eudaimonia, which refers to happiness or flourishing. He said that this state could be achieved through virtuous living and the cultivation of moral and ethical values. After all, there is some truth to his philosophy as we all work, struggle and live to be happy and satisfied."

"Schopenhauer, on the other hand, had a pessimistic view. He believed that life is filled with suffering and that we are the ones who have to find meaning in the suffering, end the pain, and bring happiness."

The jet was moving with great acceleration.

Anderson continued, "Voltaire, a prominent figure of the Enlightenment who was known for his sharp wit, valued reason and critical thinking. For him, life's meaning was in the pursuit of knowledge, freedom of thought and speech and the improvement of society through education. Ultimately, it means happiness."

Lana leaned closer towards him and said, "Kabir das, the mystic poet and philosopher from India focused on the spiritual aspect of existence. He focused on the unity of all beings and the importance of love, devotion and selflessness in attaining spiritual enlightenment and liberation from the cycle of birth and death."

"By the way, who is your favourite philosopher?"

Anderson smiled as Lana asked that question.

"My favourite philosophers are Socrates and Friedrich Nietzsche. Nietzsche, I really love him."

"Yeah! He is known for his concept of the 'Will to Power'. He saw life as a constant struggle for power and self-overcoming. He emphasised the importance of embracing challenges and hardships for personal growth and self-realisation. He argued that we should become God by developing such virtues and ethics like him."

Lana noticed that Anderson was looking upset. He was thinking about something.

"What happened, Jacob?"

Anderson came back from his own world and said, "I was wondering that we just have different views and opinions on the meaning of life. But I want to know what the absolute truth is, the absolute meaning of life. I hope that the absolute answer is hidden under the Great Pyramid."

Without letting the conversation head towards sadness and depression, Lana asked one more question.

"Do you believe in the afterlife?"

Anderson was amazed to hear that. He loved that topic very much.

He folded his hands and said with a philosophical expression, "You know what, you can say that I almost believe in the afterlife. Almost because these questions are such that none can support a site fully. Even God himself doesn't know who he is or how he came into existence."

Lana was impressed.

He continued, "According to me, life after death is possible because information is never lost in the Universe. When we die, our feelings, emotions and memories merge with the vast cosmos, forming an afterlife."

Lana agreed with that theory.

As they were getting involved deeply in their philosophical conversation,

Director Garcia once again called Anderson.

As he picked it up, Garcia exclaimed with shock, "Sir! Ma'am! You won't believe what I am going to tell you. There is a great twist."

Lana and Anderson asked in chorus, "What twist?"

Taking a deep breath, he answered, "According to our GPS systems and all that, the aeroplane in which Professor Malachai is present is directly heading towards the Great Pyramids instead of going to the airport! I am going to report it to the local authorities of that place, but you should directly go near the Great Pyramids."

And saying so, he cut the call.

Without wasting time in thinking, Lana quickly activated the communications device of the jet and started speaking with Pilot Carter who was flying the AE-0761 very nicely.

"Hello, Carter! Please tell me how much time we require to reach Giza?"

The pilot replied politely, "About half an hour."

"Okay! So please do one thing: instead of landing anywhere, please fly directly towards the Great Pyramids."

"But why?" asked Carter in astonishment.

"You will come to know about it in a few hours, and also the whole world."

And she turned off the device.

Now, both of them were stuck in another great problem.

"The aeroplane was hijacked, Jacob! Professor Victor is on a journey to destroy the secret. He will now go to the Pyramid of Khufu and destroy the answers to the ultimate questions. "Her charming and attractive face suddenly turned pale and tasteless.

Anderson groaned, "But why does he want to destroy the secret? What profit will he gain from that? We humans have come across the answer to the greatest mysteries, and he is trying to destroy the secret! But why?"

Now, the 2 intellectuals clearly knew what they had to do. Their goals and actions were very clear to them.

With his hands kept inside his pockets, Anderson walked away from the seat and said, "Lana! Humanity has finally found out the location of the ultimate answers to life and the Universe. The doors of the profound and greatest truths have finally opened. And we cannot miss this golden opportunity which is bestowed upon us by nature and the Universe."

He paused in between and thought something.

Then he continued, "We have to stop Professor Victor from destroying that secret which has been buried for many years. At this juncture in history, humanity stands poised on the precipice of discovery, where the elusive Ultimate Truth may, at long last, be unveiled."

CHAPTER FORTY-ONE

On a cold night at the Great Pyramids of Giza, a surreal and mystical atmosphere envelopes the ancient structures. The Moon's gentle glow casts an ethereal silver light and shadow. The chilly desert breeze rustles through the surrounding palm trees, carrying a faint whisper of history.

Stars twinkle in the clear, dark sky, adding a celestial backdrop to this iconic setting. The Pyramids stand in silent grandeur, their ancient secrets hidden within the cold desert night.

The desert was completely silent. The bright Moon was shining elegantly in the dark sky. Nobody could be seen around the Pyramids. The mystery of the Great Pyramids surrounded it on all sides.

The massive structures were built about some 4,500 years ago. They were constructed in such an era when humans had not invented wheels or other advanced technologies. The most puzzling thing about the structures is the technique of construction that was used at that time.

Scientists and archaeologists are unable to find out how the Pyramids were constructed. But by observing all this, we should not think that our ancestors were not as intelligent as we are. They were also highly advanced in technology, maybe more advanced than us. Another great question that is startling everybody is what the purpose of building the Pyramids was. There are various theories for this question. It is said that these 3 Pyramids, constructed during the Old Kingdom period, stand as monumental tributes to the pharaohs they were built for.

The Great Pyramid of Khufu, the largest of the trio, was built for the Pharaoh Khufu around 2580-2560 BC. Rising to a height of 146.6 metres, it is a colossal structure made from massive limestone and granite blocks, with the exact construction techniques which are still subject to debate. Its primary purpose was as a tomb, and it is accompanied by a complex of structures, including a mortuary temple and a causeway.

The Pyramid of Khafre is the second largest of the 3, built for the Pharaoh Khafre, who was the son of Khufu. It appears taller due to its elevated position on the Giza plateau. It features a distinctive Tura limestone casing and a tomb with an associated Great Sphinx, a mortuary temple, and others.

The smallest is the Pyramid of Menkaure, which was constructed for Pharaoh Menkaure stands approximately 65 metres in height. Like the others, it was also built as a royal tomb and comes with its own mortuary temple and valley temple.

On that chilly and peaceful night, 3 dark figures were mysteriously walking towards the 3 Pyramids. They were wearing their special non-reflecting black coats and night-vision goggles. None could see them due to their scientific strategy of making themselves almost invisible. The dark environment and sky were already helping them. And those 3 non-detectable figures were none other than the 3 famous Egyptian archaeologists- Benjamin, Lucas and Adrian.

With their special strategy, they deceived security as they were totally invisible. And to their good luck, that day, the security was extremely weak for some unknown reason. The 3 of them were also wondering about that only. But when the news of that mysterious secret was revealed before the world, it was sure that the security around the Great Pyramids would get very tight. So, before that, the 3 dark figures had to complete their task.

As the 3 prominent and famous archaeologists motioned fastly near the Great Pyramids, various thoughts were vacuuming inside their brains.

They looked happy but had a tinge of stress on their shoulders.

As they got close, their footprints were leaving their mark behind on the sand of the desert. Actually, this is a very ordinary thing as thousands of tourists walk on that sand, leaving their footprints. But it was not the same case at that time. The 3 researchers' footprints were going to make history. They were on the journey of doing such a thing, which, if completed successfully, would transform the whole life and future of humanity.

"Now we are just a few metres away from our destination. Once we reach near Khufu's Pyramid, everything will be changed," said Adrian, who looked very excited as his other 2 companions.

Agreeing with his point, the old and the most experienced of the 3, Benjamin exclaimed, "Guys! I had never imagined in my whole life or career that the answer to the ultimate questions might be hidden under these Great Pyramids. Now we just have to search for it and reveal the truth before the whole world."

"Yes! Because now, I am sure that the Egyptian government will not allow anyone to reveal the secret. And maybe, unfortunately, something might happen in the future, leading to the destruction of this mind-blowing Ultimate Truth. So, before anything happens, we should reveal this secret for which everyone has been waiting for thousands of years," said Lucas.

All 3 of them reached the massive and beautiful ancient structures.

Bathed in the soft, silvery glow of the Moon, the 3 archaeologists stood side by side at the base of the 3 Great Pyramids of Giza. The desert sand stretched out around them, vast and serene, as a gentle breeze carried the ancient whispers of history. The night was clear, and the stars above twinkled like diamonds in the ebony sky, casting a mystical aura over the ancient structures.

Benjamin, his eyes sparkling with anticipation behind the night-vision goggles pointed to the tallest of the 3 Pyramids, the Great Pyramid of Khufu spoke with reverence, "Look at the marvel of human achievement, the precision, and the mystery it holds."

Lucas, with a torch in his hand, nodded in agreement. He shone his flashlight on the hieroglyphics that adorned the massive stones, capturing the intricate details with great interest. Inhaling the fresh and enthralling air, he said, "It's astounding, the symbols and stories etched into the very heart of these colossal monuments."

Adrian, the youngest and the geologist of the trio, was engrossed in examining the composition of the stones. As he immersed himself in its beauty, he exclaimed with joy, "The incredible engineering techniques they employed are awe-inspiring."

As they stood there, a deep sense of enthusiasm and respect for the history and mystery of the Pyramids enveloped them. The stillness of the night allowed them to soak in the majesty of these structures, igniting their passion to uncover the secrets of the ancient world. But after all, they knew what the great secret was that was waiting for them to be unveiled before the world.

Moving a few footsteps ahead and towards the Pyramid of Khufu, Benjamin walked in pride, pointed his index finger towards the greatest Pyramid, and said in a soft and satisfying voice, "Now, finally, the time has arrived. Let's start our journey, guys. We are standing in front of the structure under which the Ultimate Truth has been lying for thousands of years."

Lucas was feeling proud of himself. His heart was turning into a river of enthusiasm and excitement. Like his other 2 companions, he was highly curious to find the answers to the Ultimate Truth.

But Andrian was totally lost in his own world of thoughts. He was continuously staring at the sky above as an aeroplane drifted away, not making any noise.

But as he glanced with more focus, he could see something very puzzling and strange. His brain was suddenly going off track. What he was looking at was totally startling and shocking for him.

As Lucas began following Benjamin near the Pyramid of Khufu, he observed that Adrian was constantly staring at the sky as if he were looking at extraterrestrials.

"Hey, Adrian! Don't waste time. We already have very little."

And motioning near him, he dragged him, and both of them followed Benjamin.

But Adrian was continuously thinking about something but was unable to express it in front of the 2.

Now, the 3 of them stood very close to Khufu's Pyramid. They had all the high-tech equipment and tools needed for the excavation, thanks to the development in the technology of archaeology and excavations. But the 3 of them were startled as they didn't know where the secret might be hidden.

But after a small discussion, they finally decided to enter the Great Pyramid for their further search.

But at that moment, a very strange incident happened. As the 3 genius and brave archaeologists began to enter inside, a familiar voice shouted from behind.

"My dear curious archaeologists, follow my commands and stop where you are."

The 3 of them stood frozen where they were. It seemed as if a sudden fear had entered mysteriously inside their bodies. For the first time in their lives, they got frightened to such an extent.

But as they turned behind and saw the origin of the voice, they were speechless.

Two tall and slender figures approached. Their faces were very familiar, and it was clear that one of them was a well-known famous personality.

As both of them walked near them, the 3 archaeologists stared at them with utter disbelief and shock.

Lifting his bony hand and pointing it shakingly towards the 2 strange men, Benjamin asked, "Are.... are you Professor...."

"Victor Malachai! Yes, I am the world-renowned AI expert, Victor Malachai and he is my assistant and colleague, Joseph."

The 3 archaeologists exchanged surprising and shocking looks.

Adrian realised that his doubt was correct.

CHAPTER FORTY-TWO

Dr. Johnson and Jonathan were expected to relax a bit after all that chaos. But no, they were very confused after coming across the last words of Albert Einstein.

Both of them were sitting, with the thoughts of the 2 questions hovering over their heads, including that of most of the people around the world. They were having a serious discussion on those 2 ultimate questions that have been startling humankind for several years.

Seated in the office of Dr. Johnson, both of them sat on a luxurious sofa and were emptying bottles of coke.

"What do you think? Is Brown Sir's dream real? Because I am still unable to imagine that the answer to the 2 ultimate questions is buried under the Great Pyramid of Khufu."

Taking a sip of cold coke, Jonathan replied, "If we consider his dream real, then it clearly states that the Great Pyramids were built just for the sake of storing the answers to the ultimate questions of life and the Universe! Amazing!"

Loosening his tie, Johnson replied, "But how is this possible? Means somebody in that era discovered the answers to those ultimate questions! But how can we believe that?"

"You know what, I am very much interested in dreams and nightmares. If we don't consider physics and space, so my favourite subject is dreams and neuroscience."

"But what do you want to convey to me?!"exclaimed Johnson with astonishment.

Throwing the can in a faraway dustbin that was situated in a corner of the office, Jonathan replied with interest, "Some people believe that dreams can serve as a bridge between the living and the spiritual realm.

And in this case, seeing a deceased person alive might be a message or a sign. The deceased person, as Einstein in Brown Sir's case, might be trying to convey something very important.

As Brown Sir always considered Einstein to be a God, the genius scientist shared his last words with him. And eventually, the whole world came to know what the words were."

Johnson nodded in agreement. But still, inside his heart, he was not able to believe that the truth was real. What Jonathan was saying seemed like a bit of a fantasy.

"I have always felt that the most mysterious thing that comes from the same list of life, the creation of the Universe, time travel, black holes, etc., is dreams. Because till now, scientists and researchers are unable to solve the mystery of dreams and their purpose of existence."

"Some people say that nightmares are nothing but merely the mixture of what we see and think in the whole day," added Johnson.

"But I reject that notion. Because I strongly feel that nightmares are definitely the messages of the future. And my theory is that the dreams we remember exactly as we have seen them are one hundred percent the messages for the future as many people have experienced that, including me also."

Dr Johnson agreed with him. He was also now feeling somewhat that Brown Sir's dream really carried the precise information. However, both of them were unable to figure out why Einstein had told Brown to share that information with none except Z11. *What is the connection between the Ultimate Truth and Z11?* Thought both of them.

Looking a bit afraid, he said, "If the dream is correct, it means that humanity has finally found the location where the Ultimate Truth is buried by our ancestors. Unbelievably, the place is none other than the ancient, elegant and massive structures, the Great Pyramids of Giza. The truth lies under the largest one of them, the Pyramid of Khufu."

As the night was getting more and more complex, their excitement was also very increasing.

Suddenly, Jonathan got up from the sofa and said, "Let's go inside Davis Sir's office and see what he is doing. I think that he might be sleeping or wondering about Brown Sir. Let's motivate and inspire him by filling his brain with powerful thoughts and quotes and also by sharing this groundbreaking information with him."

Johnson agreed, and both of them left for the eleventh floor, which is the highest floor of the agency, where Mr. Davis's office was situated.

As the elevator descended, the 2 of them motioned towards the office of their CEO, acting to look happy as if they were willing to inspire him. Even though that night Brown became the richest person in the world, the shares of Virtual Eye were continuously dropping as their founder and CEO died.

As they came near the door of the office, they were surprised to see that it was open.

Exchanging, puzzled looks, they entered inside. But to their surprise, they found that Mr. Davis was nowhere! He had suddenly disappeared.

"How is that possible? Before leaving, he helped us extract the meteorite with his secret invention of that cylinder, and he told us that he was going inside his office. And he was also unable to be seen inside the sleeping headquarters. So where has he suddenly disappeared?" exclaimed Jonathan with an expression of utter astonishment.

"You go and check the terrace. I will check the rest of the agency."

Jonathan hurried towards the terrace and Johnson toward the elevator.

But as the elevator opened, Johnson was startled to see Z11 in front of him. He stared at the robot's boyish face with surprise.

"What are you doing here now?" asked Johnson with irritation.

"Mr. Davis is not anywhere inside the agency. Using my special detection feature, I searched every nook and corner, but he was not able to be seen anywhere."

"That's crazy! Let's proceed on the terrace."

Johnson understood that Z11 was also trying to reach Mr Davis to tell him the breathtaking information.

Now both of them reached the terrace, just to see Jonathan holding and staring at something in his hand.

As both of them hurried towards him, they found that the thing at which Jonathan was staring at none other than a smartphone.

"Whose smartphone is this?" asked Z11 before Johnson could open his mouth to ask anything.

With a highly shocked look, Jonathan replied in a low voice, "This smartphone is none other than that of Mr. Davis!"

Dr. Johnson and Z11 gazed at each other in utter disbelief. The robot was giving surprised looks, which were purely artificial. But its little humanoid characteristics made him look like a real boy with emotions.

"What?! Davis Sir has mysteriously disappeared somewhere suddenly, leaving his mobile phone? But where has he gone?"

Glancing at Davis's phone, Jonathan replied seriously, "Now we can come to know where he has suddenly gone, only if we find the password of his mobile phone and then check his call history and trace his location."

CHAPTER FORTY-THREE

Benjamin, Lucas and Adrian were stunned as they saw the world renowned and most prominent AI scientist and expert in front of their eyes.

Their expressions were similar to that of an astrobiologist who has suddenly come face-to-face with alien species. Neither of the 3 was able to believe what was happening with them.

Turning his whole attention towards the unexpected people, Benjamin said with hesitation, "Professor Malachai and Joseph.... Why have you both come here?"

The genius AI scientist's face glowed under the moonlight. His dark hair and French beard made his personality charming, helping him to look smart.

His blue eyes looked like 2 small blue diamonds.

There was an unexpected silence. The blowing cool and crispy wind made its chilly presence felt.

Throwing a cunning smile, Professor Victor replied in a heavy voice, "Dear Benjamin! I am sure that you have come for a very important task here.

Just remember that I have come here to do the complete opposite of the task that you have come here to do."

The 3 archaeologists exchanged startled looks. Their brains were getting irritated and puzzled with every passing moment. They had very little time for the task which they had come to do.

Becoming a bit annoyed, Benjamin said, "Professor! Finally, I will tell you why the 3 of us have come here. We 3 have been on a journey to find the Ultimate Truth that has been hidden under this Great Pyramid of Khufu for thousands of years. Our main goal is to unveil that mind-blowing secret for which everybody till now was waiting to know as the government can stop us from finding it or some other bad incident can happen, leading to the destruction of it."

Victor and Joseph looked at each other and laughed heartily.

Still in a laughing mood, Victor said, "You guys don't know anything, dear Benjamin," his voice became more comfortable, "We both are here to destroy that Ultimate Truth! And you are saying that the government can stop it or something else can happen in the future?"

"Before all that, we are the ones who will be destroying that ultimate truth," exclaimed Joseph, his voice filled with stress.

Coming forward near Benjamin, Lucas fired back angrily, "What the hell are you doing?! Humankind is standing on the cliff, where it is going to find the answers to the most fundamental questions of its existence, and you are shamelessly planning to destroy it? You are destroying the precious information that God wants us to find? But why?"

Becoming a bit annoyed, Professor Victor replied, "Why are you including God in between? What is the proof that God wants us to find and learn the Ultimate

Truth?"

Clearing his throat and moving towards him, Benjamin said, "It is just God's wish, Professor! Because if it wasn't, then why did Einstein come into Brown Sir's dream and tell him all this? And you are well aware that it is a widespread belief that if a dead person comes alive in our dream and tells us something, it is a message or warning for the future. And in this case of Brown Sir's dream was a great message given by God through Albert Einstein."

Victor's mind was boiling with rage as Benjamin spoke more about God.

He was not an atheist but a believer in God. But he hated it extremely when people included God in anything and any situation.

"You are totally wrong! In this case, God wanted us to warn about this information."

"How?!!"shouted Benjamin and Lucas in chorus.

"That is not necessary for you to know. You just do what I am telling you to. Please keep your mouths shut and let us do our work. Come on, Joseph."

But before they started walking, Lucas exclaimed in astonishment, "Hey! Wait one minute. You both suddenly disappeared somewhere this morning and didn't receive any call or reply to any message. Your phone was also dead, right?"

Both the master and Joseph stood silent at that moment. They didn't move a step either and remained frozen at the specific place where they were standing.

"Please say something, Professor! What was the reason for your sudden disappearance? I want an answer from you!" said Lucas with great annoyance and irritation.

Pulling the fresh and cool air of the peaceful desert, Victor started speaking, with some fear included in his voice, "Actually if I speak the truth...."

"Wait, Sir! What are you doing? Don't tell them!" shouted Joseph, trying to stop him from saying anything.

As he approached near, Victor replied politely, "No, Joseph! We finally reached our destination. Now it's time to tell the truth."

"But Sir!"

Victor urged Joseph to keep quiet. The loyal assistant silently followed his master's orders and shut his mouth.

Victor started walking with his hands kept at the back. He was now going to speak the truth about his and Joseph's sudden disappearance.

"You know what, guys?" he began in a deep voice. The weather and surroundings were perfect to hear the truth. The 3 giant Pyramids added a feel of thrill.

The 3 archaeologists were staring at him without blinking their eyes.

They were very eager to hear the truth about his disappearance.

"Long before the world came to know about this secret, Joseph and I knew it only before."

The 3 men were not able to trust their ears.

Increasing his speed of speaking, he continued, "I had been anonymously messaged by somebody and told to destroy the Ultimate Truth. And the sender also said that Sir James Brown knows about this secret. So, I feared that he would announce it before the whole world."

He paused in between. A sudden feeling of guilt filled his heart. His face turned sad, and he didn't feel like speaking.

But the intelligent and experienced Benjamin understood what he was trying to tell.

In a frightened and extremely shocked voice, he asked, "Means... if I am not wrong, you are the one who killed Brown Sir?"

Victor nodded in agreement.

Benjamin's body suddenly seemed lifeless. He frowned and suddenly jerked backwards as if he was falling down. But Lucas and Adrian held the sixty-three-year-old archaeologist and tried to calm his mind.

Motioning a bit closer towards the stationary AI scientist, Lucas shouted very annoyingly, "Are you really mad and insane, Professor?! Just to bury the Ultimate Truth, you killed a great and innocent tech billionaire who was constantly trying to change our lifestyle and push the bounds of science and innovation? You are really a villain, not a hero. Shame on you!"

"But I am compelled to do it, Lucas! You can't understand my situation. I am just doing this to prevent a huge catastrophe from happening! And I can't explain the reason to you."

Benjamin became normal and, pulling Lucas a few steps behind came face-to-face with Victor.

He swallowed a fraction of his anger and fired, "Now your game is over Professor! You have become one of the greatest criminals of today's time.

And now it is the time for you to face a serious punishment. First, you killed Brown Sir, and now you are on the way to destroying this breathtaking truth. But your wish will remain a wish only. I am now informing the local authorities to catch you!"

And immediately, he pulled out his phone and started dialling a few numbers. Simultaneously, he commanded Lucas and Adrian to catch both of them.

But as the 2 archaeologists, who were raging with anger, hurried towards Victor, their eyes widened suddenly, and they stopped instantly where they were.

"I will get a strict punishment, and the Ultimate Truth will be unveiled before the whole world only if you 3 remain alive."

And silently, Victor pulled out his technologically advanced robotic gun and directly pointed it towards Benjamin.

"But the Ultimate Truth will never be revealed before the world as you 3 will not be there to find it and unveil it."

The 3 archaeologists breathed heavily as he pointed his gun at Benjamin's forehead. Now, just pressing a button would end Benjamin's life.

"Please don't do anything, Professor! Keep that gun inside!" shouted Adrian with fear.

Walking near Benjamin, Victor said, "Sorry, friends, but I have to do this in order to avoid a huge catastrophe from happening."

The 3 archaeologists started sweating profusely. Their hearts thundered with a sudden shock.

Walking away from Benjamin, Victor again pointed his gun at his forehead. His dark hair was flowing due to the cold wind. And his dark black coat was also flowing.

Becoming serious, he announced, "Dear friends! I love humanity very much. My main goal is to always make people happy so that they can live peacefully. I can do anything for humankind's happiness."

Before pressing the button and shooting Benjamin dead, he said confidently, with a mixture of sadness, "If I have to kill 3 people to save the whole of humanity from darkness, I will do it elegantly."

And saying so, he pressed a small button on his robotic gun and a sharp and intense laser shot with a very great velocity towards old Benjamin and pierced into his forehead.

"Oh my God! Save me!" shrieked poor Benjamin in pain as he fell dead on the sand of the desert of Giza, before the 3 Great Pyramids.

Lucas ran as fast as possible towards him, but unfortunately, he was also shot in his heart and left the world instantly.

But before Victor could shoot the laser towards Adrian, the archaeologist suddenly fell down on the sand, pressing his heart tightly.

As Joseph and Victor went near his body, they checked his heartbeat and pulse. But nothing could be felt.

Sweat flowing down from his forehead, Joseph said in a low voice, "Before we could kill him, he died from a heart attack."

Victor's hands were shaking with fear, and his heart sank in a river of disappointment. He had never imagined that he would one day kill 4 innocent people. But after all, happiness and contentment of humankind was his ultimate goal. So, he had to do it as he had no other option.

Dropping his robotic gun in disappointment near the corpse of Adrian, he said to Joseph very seriously, "Now all the thorns are eliminated from our path. Please take out the great device so that we can finally finish the task for which we have been murdering great personalities since the evening."

But after all, Professor Victor finally understood who was sending him all the messages and who had told him all the secrets.

CHAPTER FORTY-FOUR

The aeroplane which was heading towards the Giza airport had suddenly changed its direction. It was now flying away over the Great Pyramids but was now changing its direction constantly. Its trajectory seemed very strange and unusual.

Commissioner Garza and a few policemen were waiting near the Giza airport. His sleep had been ruined when Director Garcia called the authorities and requested them to be ready at the airport and immediately catch the person who was dressed as a waiter. Therefore, he had to arrive there as he felt a great need, and everybody thought that the waiter was only the killer of Brown Sir. Garza was astonished to learn that COP Abner felt that Anderson was the criminal. Garza was a tall and muscular officer who was very well-known for his great fighting skills and unbelievable strength. He became a famous personality when he managed to defeat a strong judo player at a public event.

But suddenly, there was huge chaos at Giza's airport. Everybody,

Commissioner Garza was especially baffled after learning that the aeroplane, which was destined to arrive at the airport of Giza from Los Angeles, was suddenly flying over the Great Pyramids of Giza at a very high velocity, larger than the aeroplane's usual velocity

Garza was motioning here and there, unable to understand what was happening. Nobody had imagined that such an incident could occur.

"Please keep continuously checking the direction in which the plane is

flying! And try to communicate with Pilot Griffin," shouted Garza at one of the policemen, ordering him to do what was needed.

The airport's air traffic control was unable to connect with Griffin.

The officers were shocked to see that the pilot was not responding. But the strangest thing was that the aeroplane was flying perfectly, and now it was approaching the airport as fast as possible from the Great Pyramids. But still, its strange behaviour was beyond anybody's understanding. Pilot Griffin was still out of contact.

Commissioner Garza was staring at the sky, still the thoughts of the strange motion of the aeroplane exploding inside his brain. But as he gazed with high focus at the sky, he could see such a thing that he became very happy and excited. His heart thundered suddenly.

The aeroplane was heading with constant velocity towards the runway where it was going to land safely.

"The aeroplane is gonna land! Come here!" screamed Garza with a sense of excitement and happiness.

All the policemen rushed with excitement towards the approaching aircraft. They just wanted to solve the mystery of the absence of communication with Griffin and catch that suspicious waiter.

Under cover of darkness, the aeroplane descended, its navigation lights piercing through the night sky like beacons. The runway lights guided its path, casting a soft, eerie glow on the asphalt. As the aircraft got closer, the landing lights pierced the darkness, revealing the runway with a sharp contrast.

The landing gear extended, and the wheels touched down on the illuminated runway, creating a subtle, ghostly mist as they made contact. The aircraft glided silently, save for the distant hum of the engines, as it gradually slowed down. The midnight landing was a symphony of subtle contrasts and dimly lit details, creating an atmosphere of tranquillity in the midst of the night.

Commissioner Garza and the other policemen hurried towards the aeroplane that had just landed smoothly on the runway.

The doors opened with a sound, and passengers started walking out rapidly. Their faces clearly resembled those of astonished and extremely frightened people.

Garza ordered his policemen to examine all the passengers very carefully and catch the one who was wearing the clothes of a waiter. There were just 12 passengers in all, and to everyone's surprise, none of them had worn the clothes of a waiter!

Garza was startled to see that. He was getting crazier with every passing moment. The person for whom he had been waiting for so long was not there inside the aeroplane!

He quickly rushed inside the huge aeroplane and started searching every nook and corner of the aircraft. The other police officers followed him.

But they didn't find anybody who was wearing the dress of a waiter inside the long and vast plane.

Garza remembered at that instant and hurried towards the pilot's cabin in the front. His mind was making theories about the pilot, Griffin, who had been totally out of contact for the last few hours.

Just as Commissioner Garza entered the cabin, he was astonished to see that Griffin was sitting on the floor of the cabin instead of sitting on the main seat.

He ran towards him, pulled him upwards and shouted angrily, "Hey! What the hell were you doing? We tried to contact you, but you did not reply to us! Why?! And what on this Earth made you fly this plane over the Pyramids?"

Pilot Griffin was shaking with fear. His face went white as if he had suddenly seen a ghost in front of his eyes. He opened his mouth to speak, but a sudden fear was stopping him.

Keeping both hands on his shoulder, Garza shook his body with irritation and screamed annoyingly, "I want an answer, Griffin! Why did you fly this plane over the Pyramids? And where is the waiter? According to the location traced by technician Marina and told by Director Garcia, the waiter was surely inside this plane only. So, where the hell did he go?"

"He jumped off the plane along with his assistant using a parachute!

The other 12 passengers' lives were in danger, including mine. The waiter was pointing his robotic gun at me, and his assistant was threatening the passengers. He demanded that if I didn't fly the plane over the Pyramids, he would kill me and jump out using the parachute. And if I would have died, then you can think what would have happened. I was really very frightened and was compelled to follow his orders."

Griffin's eyes went numb. They also turned red with anger.

Commissioner Garza felt the whole world going nuts. His lips dried, including his throat. A sudden and unknown feeling entered inside him. He was baffled after hearing all that and immediately pulled out his mobile phone and dialled a number.

"Whom are you calling?" asked Griffin, still the sadness and fear in his voice.

"COP Abner Ardolf," replied the Commissioner.

"What are you saying, Sir?!"COP Abner jerked forward from the comfortable seat of the jet in which he was flying. He clutched his Samsung Galaxy Note 10 tightly and spoke.

"Yes, Abner! The waiter also has an assistant with him, and they are now near the Pyramids of Giza! I am sending local authorities there now. You catch Anderson and Lana as soon as possible! Now we have to make the security tight around the Pyramids."

He cut the call and proceeded towards his car, where he ordered the policemen to follow him. Now, it was time to make the security around the Great Pyramids very tight.

COP Abner was totally startled. He now began thinking that the whole stuff of the 3 Pyramids was related to the secret of the Ultimate Truth.

In addition to that, he was very baffled after learning that Lana and Anderson were heading towards the Great Pyramids. He ordered the pilot to accelerate the jet and chase the AE-0671 jet as fast as possible.

The case was getting more and more complex with every passing second.

Lana and Anderson were lost in their own universes of thoughts.

The weather was turning more chilly and cool. And into that weather, the mystery of the Ultimate Truth and Professor Victor was enthralling the 2 of them.

The AE-0671 jet was pacing rapidly towards the Pyramids. Pilot Carter was putting as much effort as he could to reach the destination as early as possible.

Anderson studied the silent and beautiful Lana for a few moments. Her pink lips had turned completely dry, and her face wasn't looking as attractive as it always was. But still, she looked pretty, and she wore that soft white top with a pink muffler around her neck.

Anderson broke the silence and said, "The Great Pyramids of Giza are one of the mysterious things which have fascinated me the most since my childhood."

Lana suddenly came back from her thoughts. She turned her gaze towards the smiling Anderson and replied, "Oh really?"

"Yes!" he replied with sudden and unexpected enthusiasm. "Because those complex and massive structures hold great unsolved mysteries within themselves."

It seemed as if he was now lecturing Lana as he used to his friends and very close ones.

"The 3 Great Pyramids were built and constructed some 4700 to Five thousand years ago in Giza. These structures were designed and made with such extraordinary and complex engineering and skill that today's archaeologists and researchers are still not able to understand how they were made. This is the greatest mystery about these elegant structures."

"There are many conspiracy and mind-blowing theories that provide different views on how these Great Pyramids were constructed. Right?" interrupted Lana in between.

"Yes! There are several theories about it. Some dumb people believe that these structures were made by the ancient Egyptians with the help of advanced extraterrestrials."

"Dumb people? Does this mean you are wholly against the Pyramids being constructed with the involvement of an ancient, advanced alien civilisation? Why?"

Anderson turned serious and replied, "The Pyramids were constructed a very long time ago from now. Looking at the great design and engineering marvel of these structures, we have to consider that the ancient Egyptians were very advanced in terms of technology and knowledge. Even 5000 years from now, our future generation will look at the great and enormous things built for us, like the Burj Khalifa, Opera house, etc. So, they can also think that we, meaning their ancestors, built these unbelievable things by taking help from some advanced extraterrestrial civilisation. But is it true? Absolutely not."

He paused in between and then continued, "Similarly, the ancient

Egyptians were highly advanced and intelligent beings, so they built these Pyramids using their skills. We cannot say that they were being helped by shitty aliens."

Lana was very impressed by his logic and different thinking.

Drinking a glass of water, he said, "Even our greatest and most controversial tech entrepreneur, Elon Musk, has said in a Ted Talk that technology doesn't automatically improve. It only improves if a lot of people work very hard to improve it. The ancient Romans built the aqueducts, but they forgot to build them. The ancient Egyptians built the Great Pyramids, but they forgot how to do it.

So, the ancient Egyptians built the Pyramids by themselves. There is no need to involve aliens in between. I often get angry when people involve aliens or some highly advanced extraterrestrials in anything."

Professor Victor gets very annoyed when people involve God in anything and anywhere, thought Lana.

Anderson looked a bit irritated and said, "People are involving aliens everywhere nowadays, and after some days, they will say that rain occurs because an alien urinates from the sky!" And he gave a huge laugh.

But he noticed that Lana stared at him uncomfortably as he cracked his joke. *I forgot that I am talking with a respected astronaut cum scientist and, after all, a girl.*

"Sorry, Lana, if I said something wrong...."

Lana laughed heartily and replied, "No, Jacob! It was really a very funny joke. And correct also."

And they laughed in chorus.

After that, they returned back to their Pyramids conversation.

Leaning towards Anderson, she asked, "Leaving this theory, there are several other theories which make a bit of sense."

Anderson seemed very interested.

"According to the most famous theory, which everyone believes to be right is that the Pyramids were constructed as the tombs for the pharaohs."

Anderson poked in between, "Yeah! It is a widely accepted belief. But the most intriguing and strange thing is that we haven't yet found a single tomb inside any Pyramid, leave the 3 Great Pyramids aside."

Lana nodded in agreement and became silent as Anderson wanted to speak. She felt and sensed that he was really very interested in Pyramids.

"One more theory is there, which is really very logical, and I also somewhat believe in it."

"Which one?"

"The great inventor Nikola Tesla thought that the Pyramids were the centres of power generation. He believed that ancient Egyptians had invented electricity already and used these Great Pyramids to supply electricity to the Egyptian empire. He thought that the Pyramids were built to be used as giant power plants to generate electricity and run machines."

He suddenly became a bit serious and continued, "Tesla even believed that the Pyramids were somehow linked to cosmic energy, which could be used for spiritual enlightenment and healing."

Lana suddenly felt a change in Anderson. He was talking with great interest with her but suddenly became strange. It seemed as if he was thinking about something very deeply.

"Wh..What happened, Jacob? Why have you suddenly turned serious and a bit sad, too?" asked Lana with astonishment.

Anderson pulled a deep breath. He returned back from his own world of thoughts and replied, "You know what, Lana, I am one of the greatest fans of Nikola Tesla, as everyone who knows me knows."

"Your Model Y's number plate also contains the number 369! And if I am not wrong, this is the Tesla code as Nikola Tesla believed that these 3 numbers hold the key to the mystery of the Universe."

Anderson ignored her and said, "Nikola Tesla was such a scientist who changed the whole world with his groundbreaking inventions and discoveries. He is regarded now as the pioneer of modern electricity supply.

He pioneered the generation, transmission and use of alternating current electricity, which can be transmitted over much greater distances than direct current. Without his contribution, we would not have the radio, AC electricity, power grids, television, Tesla coils, neon lighting, fluorescent lighting, radio-controlled devices, robotics, X-rays, radar, microwaves and many other inventions applicable to our daily lives."

Lana was again very impressed with the electricity wizard's talent and intellect. *Without him, our world would not have looked as it is looking.*

Suddenly, Anderson became extremely emotional. His eyes flashed red with a bit of anger, but the anger was hidden behind the layer of extreme sadness.

In a low and disappointed voice, he said, "But even though he worked so hard for humanity, he didn't receive any fame or respect in his life. Nobody understood his futuristic vision and his extraordinary mindset. He was very weak in terms of financial manners. He was not at all interested in money or fame and also didn't like to give interviews. But his weakest thing was

that he gave his inventions for free."

Lana felt as if she was watching a very emotional movie where the main hero was Anderson.

Anderson turned more sensitive and emotional and continued further, "The investors of that era showed little interest in Tesla's ideas for new types of alternating current motors and electrical transmission equipment.

They decided that the manufacturing side of the business was too competitive and opted to simply run an electric utility.

Tesla was the only one who led the foundation for today's radio. But his rival Guglielmo Marconi got all the patents for that. But after the death of

Tesla, the US Supreme Court ruled that all of Marconi's radio patents were invalid and awarded the patents for radio to Tesla."

Anderson's eyes began watering a little as he recalled the last days and humiliation of Tesla.

"He was never happy in his whole life," his voice sounding extremely disappointed, "All the years of his life, till his last breath when he was 86, he continuously worked hard to provide free and wireless energy to the world. He also never married, just to focus on his inventions and avoid distraction. According to one incident, Tesla continuously worked for 84 hours in his laboratory without taking any rest. His sleeping hours were between 1.5 - 2 hours daily.

He spent the last years of his life all alone in a very poor condition at a hotel, with a huge amount of debt over his head. His last letter to his mother is highly shocking. It brings tears to the eyes of the person who reads it. I was so disappointed after reading it on the internet that my brain memorised its main and emotional lines automatically."

Now Anderson recalled Tesla's last letter to his mother in utter sadness and shock.

"I wish I could be beside you, Mother, to bring you the glass of water. All these years which I have spent in the service of mankind brought me nothing but insults and humiliation."

"Why does kind always suffer? Even though Tesla has gained an enormous amount of fame and respect today, he could not have experienced it in his life. After all, he had to die in poverty with utter sadness and tears, all alone inside a hotel. The man who sacrificed his sleep, food, personal life and family got nothing in his life except insults and criticism. All the people know Newton, Edison, Einstein, and Darwin, but very few know the genius Tesla."

At last, he said seriously, "If we travel through time and bring Tesla into our present-day modern world, he will definitely be unable to control his tears."

Anderson's charming eyes filled with tears of sadness. Lana offered her soft and pink handkerchief to him, showing a sign of kindness.

She gave a smile to refresh his mood and said in a soft and kind voice, "Don't feel too sad, Jacob. Nikola Tesla must be very proud today, considering the progress mankind has made. He might have been happy at the time of his death, thinking that he made the future of our civilisation look great and comfortable. I also feel very sad recalling that the man who made our future bright got nothing in his life except sadness and criticism.

The founders of Tesla, the greatest electric car company in the world, Martin Eberhard and Marc Tarpenning named the company after the surname of the intellectual, giving a tribute to him. His name is now becoming famous worldwide, as it should be. The name Nikola Tesla will be remembered forever." Suddenly, the communications device buzzed, and Lana talked with the Pilot Carter.

"Ms. Lana and Dr. Anderson!" His voice sounded happy, "We will reach near the Great Pyramids in just 20 minutes."

"Nice work, Dylan!" replied Lana and kept the device aside.

Now, turning her attention to Anderson, she said, "Now we have to quickly stop Professor Victor from destroying the Ultimate Truth. Humanity has finally come across the breathtaking secret for which it was waiting for hundreds and thousands of years."

CHAPTER FORTY-SIX

Professor Victor was in a world of his own. The strange and unimaginable incidents that were happening to him that night had created a great storm inside his mind. He was unable to understand what was happening to him.

"Sir! Now, I will take out the gadget, and then we should quickly start the work. We don't have much time as now the security will get extremely tight near these Pyramids. The news about the mystery of Einstein's last words has gone viral all over the whole world."

Professor Victor's mind was vacuuming with very different thoughts. Motioning a bit closer towards Joseph, he said in a very deep voice, "Don't worry, my dear! Now I have finally understood who the anonymous messenger who has been sending us this whole stuff is."

Joseph was also trying to connect the dots. With each passing second, he was coming closer towards the answer. And he was now sure about the anonymous messenger who had been sending them everything.

"And he is the only one like us who also wants this truth to remain buried. That's why he told us everything so that the truth remains always buried."

Joseph tried to speak something, but seeing his master continuing, he stopped instantly.

"And now I am one hundred per cent sure that he is the only one who can help us in this situation. We have to quickly text him and tell him to somehow stop the security guards and police officers from coming here so that we can finish our whole mission and save the world from a huge apocalypse."

Professor Victor walked away from the 3 corpses of the archaeologists. A very cold wind suddenly blew through the whole desert.

However cold the weather would have been, Professor Victor's body was sweating with stress, tension and the guilt of killing 4 famous personalities.

He ordered Joseph to pull out their special gadget in order to excavate the ground fast and in an easy way.

Simultaneously, he pulled out his smartphone to text the anonymous sender, whose identity was now clear to him, including to Joseph. *It is all fine for me if I have to kill a few more people today in order to destroy the Ultimate Truth.*

Commissioner Garza was constantly irritating his driver to accelerate the car. The other policemen were following him.

Garza quickly informed all the security guards to tighten the security at the Great Pyramids. Now, it was clear that the killer was trying to do something near the elegant ancient structures.

As they were accelerating towards the desert, the driver suddenly peppered Garza with some questions.

"I have one doubt, Sir. Can I please ask you?" asked the middle-aged driver in fluent English.

"Ask only if it makes sense to me or is important."

The driver nodded and made an odd look. Garza gave him the permission to ask.

"Why is there no security around the Great Pyramids? Because there is always very tight security around those massive ancient marvels to prevent any misuse or damage."

Garza tried to ignore it but still answered.

"You know what, Sir Brown was a great fan of ancient architecture and monuments. And in that, the great Pyramids of Giza were his favourite."

The driver slowed the car a bit, but Garza didn't notice it.

"2 years ago, he had announced that the day he would leave this world, the Pyramids should be kept open for everyone to explore them. He had

requested the government to pay tribute to him after his death by doing that just for 24 hours. That's why there is no security today."

The driver felt that the killer got a nice opportunity to do his task at the Great Pyramids by killing Brown Sir as all the security was removed from there. Garza noticed that the car's speed was low, and he angrily commanded the driver to speed up the car.

But amidst that, he immersed into his own world of strange and confusing thoughts.

The killer is around the Great Pyramids, which means he wants to do something there. And everybody knows that Brown Sir had declared the security to be removed around the great marvels after his death. What does he seek? What is his main mission? And is it so important that he dared to kill a personality like Sir Brown?

Professor Victor and his beloved assistant Joseph were sweating profusely. Even though the weather was very chilly all across the desert, both of them were wet with sweat. The air around them smelled strange to them. Speaking really, at that moment, everything seemed strange.

As the environment turned more enthralling and cold, Joseph walked a few steps ahead and reached near the Great Pyramid of Khufu.

He shifted his glance from the ground towards the massive structure that was in front of his eyes. Professor Victor was a few steps behind him. He was observing peacefully what was the mental state of Joseph at that time.

Pulling the crispy and chilly air of the desert inside his lungs, Joseph said in a loud voice, which was mixed with admiration, happiness and seriousness, "Never ever in my whole life have I thought that one day I would contribute to the destruction of a great thing. The whole of humankind has been seeking this answer for the past countless years. And today, we are on the journey of destroying that secret."

Cutting him in between, Professor Victor started walking and said in a deep tone, "Hundreds of genius scientists, philosophers, inventors took birth on this planet and became a part of our species."

His voice became more serious as he spoke.

"Sir Isaac Newton, Galileo Galilei, Albert Einstein, Nikola Tesla, Aristotle, Socrates, Stephen Hawking, and countless other intellectuals in our world history. These men were the ones who changed our understanding of the world with their smartness and curiosity towards understanding the nature of the Universe. They spent countless hours, days and nights developing theories, making great discoveries and inventing technology." He now stood completely erect near Joseph and kept his hand on his shoulder and gave a philosophical smile.

"These men were dying to find the meaning of life and how the Universe was created. But even though they were so brilliant and genius, they were unable to find the Ultimate Truth. And today, one of those masters, Albert Einstein gave an important and groundbreaking message to one of his greatest fans, Sir James Brown, in his nightmare, telling him the location where the final reality of everything is hidden. Really, Einstein was an extraordinary human."

Joseph's delicate eyes started watering. He was extremely sensitive since childhood. And as he turned his eyes around, he could see that his master was speaking as if he were a great saint or monk. Professor Victor was speaking with his heart and soul at that time.

He motioned away from Joseph and finally said what he was willing to say since the morning.

"Dear Joseph, now the time has finally arrived. We have to do what we need to do at this moment. We don't want to do this thing at all, but we must do it. There is a great difference between must and want. But people often flow into emotions and forget the so-called important 'must' part of life.

We should not do any work because we want to do it. But we should do it because we must do it. After all, everybody's ultimate goal should be the bright and happy and well-being future of humanity. Now forget everything, my dear Joseph, and start work as time goes by. We have to stop the invisible virus of sadness from affecting the whole of mankind."

Joseph felt motivated and fresh after hearing his master's powerful words. The fire of saving humanity from sadness ignited within his heart again. At that moment, he forgot all the emotional things.

His main focus was just to do the task that was lying in front of his eyes.

Without opening his mouth, he silently moved and pulled out a device about the size of a laptop from his bag.

He then kept the laptop-like device on the ground near the Great Pyramid

of Khufu, typed something on it, and pressed an extremely thin button

on its surface, which was almost invisible.

And within a few seconds, the device suddenly sprang to life and utilised laser ablation and sensors and its other digital features and started excavating the ground.

Joseph stared at the process with full determination. On the other hand, Professor Victor glanced at the Moon and said, "This is one of the greatest inventions of my life."

CHAPTER FORTY-SEVEN

Harrison Drake gazed in utter disbelief and shock at the scene down from the chopper. He didn't ever imagine that his Sir would bring him to this place in the middle of that strange night.

How's that possible? It is impossible to believe that such a person like him will come here!

Inventor Harrison Drake was unable to control his curiosity and confusion.

Staring wildly in his dark black eyes, he asked, puzzled, "Sir.... Are you sure that we are going to land here? Because I can't believe it."

Mr. Davis, Harrison's Sir who had come like an angel to fund his groundbreaking project, threw a smile and replied politely, "Dear Drake! You believe it or not, but I have finally decided that we are going to land here."

"But it is fine that I can land here, but you? Because you have an entirely different mindset than me in this matter!"

Mr. Davis again said politely, "Dear, now it is not a matter of mindset or anything. I just want to attain peace and learn such things that will guide my future life and make me free from all the evil stuff."

Before Drake could say anything, Mr. Davis ordered the pilot to descend the chopper as soon as possible.

I have finally reached the place where I must reach due to the current situation.

Under the cloak of night, Mr. Davis and Harrison's chopper descended towards Chimayo in New Mexico. The elegant and simple village lay beneath them. The silhouette of the surrounding mountains framed the

scene. The air smelled very fresh and peaceful. Stars twinkled overhead

and cast their radiance on the beautiful structures below. As they landed, the village's charm unfolded. But their chopper landed some distance away from the main village.

Both of them jumped out of the aircraft and smelled the mystical air of the environment.

Mr. Davis gazed at the pilot and said, "Do not go until we both return. We will spend some time together but stay here. It's my order to you."

Without any argument, the pilot shut up and pulled out his new smartphone began surfing through the latest news, especially through the conspiracy theories developing over the Ultimate Truth that was claimed to be buried under the ground near the Great Pyramid of Khufu. At that instant, he didn't dare to waste Davis's time in peppering him with questions as the innovator was not in the mood to speak at that time.

He just wants peace, for what sake God only knows, thought the pilot and turned his attention towards his new smartphone as both of his passengers walked away.

As both of them walked away from the chopper, Drake became totally unaware of his surroundings. He felt as if he had suddenly entered into a strange world.

But before he could speak anything, Mr. Davis exclaimed, "Are you not aware of this place, Harrison? Because you look so startled."

Pulling fresh air, Harrison replied, "No, Sir! I don't have much knowledge about this place, but I am well aware of it and what it is. If I am not wrong, we are walking inside Chimayo?"

Mr. Davis nodded in agreement.

Continuing further, Drake spoke, "I don't look puzzled because I don't have knowledge or information about this place. But because a person like you, who has entirely different views about the world and Universe, is walking at midnight, ruining his sleep, here."

Now, Mr. Liam Davis understood what Drake was thinking and feeling. It didn't take much time for him to understand.

Keeping his hand on his shoulder, he said in an extremely soft voice.

Harrison was surprised to see the sudden change in the NSRA CEO's behaviour overnight. He was a strict person who rarely spoke politely and softly. His dictionary was mostly filled with words and tones like rude, harsh, etc.

"You know what? The world is divided into people with different opinions and views." They were now entering the silent village and motioning towards the place where Mr. Davis was willing to go.

"Some people are the ones who strongly believe in a higher power, like a supreme being, whom they call God. According to their philosophy, God is the ultimate creator who has designed this vast cosmos and everything.

They are known as theists. Most people often grapple with the questions of morality, existence, etc. Some people, whom we call theists, find the answers through religious philosophy, drawing strength from the belief in a higher power that guides everyone. But on the other hand, some people like me find those complex answers without the presence of a divine force."

Now, Drake became interested in the conversation. He felt that the rest of the night was going to be filled with the clouds of philosophy.

"Theists are also divided into 2 parts - Monotheists and Polytheists." His tone became faster now.

"The individuals who believe in and worship multiple deities or Gods are known as polytheists. There are several ancient religions, such as Greek mythology and Hinduism, that have held belief in this part. On the other hand, the individuals who believe in and worship a single, supreme deity are categorised as monotheists. Religions like Judaism, Christianity, and Islam are examples of monotheistic faiths. They follow in one all-powerful God."

Now, Drake wanted to ask him a question.

"Means, Sir, if I am really correct, then you are in the category of atheists who believe that none directs the Universe and there is no God."

Mr. Davis smiled his polite smile and replied, "Here is where you are mistaken! And not just you, but there are many who are mistaken."

"Mistaken?! But how?"

Now, they were walking under the crystal-clear moonlight. The air of the village made a peaceful presence for them.

"You know what, I am an atheist, but still, I believe in a divine force. I am not in the category of those individuals who don't believe in divine force but am in the category of those who do not at all believe in a personal God whom people worship. And in addition to that, I am a great hater of religious people who fight amongst themselves for just the sake of proving that their God is great."

Harrison was a true believer in God, but still, he felt Mr. Davis's words were powerful. *Religious people just fight instead of cooperating with each other.*

Mr. Davis's voice turned a bit annoying, and it seemed as if his mind had suddenly hit with a small firecracker of anger.

"If religious people believe in God and hold a strong belief in following their religion, why do they not respect another's religion? Similar to their particular religion, another's religion also believes in God and tries to find meaning. So why this meaningless behaviour?"

A crispy and chilly wind blew towards them. But they were so immersed in their talks that they didn't feel cold.

"I hate religious people because they don't understand that despite being the followers of different religions and faiths, we all belong to the same species- Homo Sapiens. We all are, after all, humans, a common global community irrespective of any religion, faith, belief or even nationality.

According to my suggestion, instead \of just fighting, why can't we develop a single religion and live happily and peacefully? I am sure then we will make more progress."

Harrison Drake was not in the mood to listen to that. Instead, he was more interested in Mr. Davis's personal views on God.

"I agree with you on all this matter, Sir, but I want to ask you what your opinions on God are."

Now Mr. Davis turned into a serious mood.

"There were several genius minds in mankind's history who had different faiths and beliefs. Sir Isaac Newton was a deeply religious man and a great follower of Jesus Christ. He spent many years of his life deciphering the codes of the Bible."

Mr. Davis's idol was a religious person, and he was an atheist. It seems an odd combination, thought Drake.

"Galileo Galilei was also a religious man. However, the Catholic Church opposed him when he came up with the idea of the geocentric model because they believed that God would have put his most amazing creation at the centre of the Universe, meaning the Sun could revolve around the Earth. And when he started proving it wrong, they got highly mad and called the father of science a heretic! But after all, everyone now knows who was correct." And Mr Davis laughed.

Without pausing, he continued, "Stephen Hawking was a pure atheist and didn't believe in any God or so-called creator of everything."

Drake wanted to speak something in between, but he didn't after looking at the billionaire's seriousness as he spoke.

"Albert Einstein believed in Spinoza's God, who reveals himself in the orderly harmony of what exists, not in a God who cares about the individual fate of man."

Now, Drake finally blurted, "I don't want to hear the views of different scientists but want to hear yours!"

Taking a deep breath, Mr Davis replied in a soft and eerie voice, "Dear Harrison, actually, I believe in a supreme cosmic energy, which I think is present behind this vast Universe and everything. I am completely against any religious God like Jesus, Shiva, Vishnu, Allah, etc. I just believe in an energy that is the master of science and which runs everything. Cosmic

energy does not interfere with our daily lives as it won't take that much time, in my opinion. But concluding everything, I hate religious people and also religion."

Now Drake's brain was driving crazy. He was literally going nuts at that time.

Leaning closer towards Mr. Davis as they both walked, he exclaimed, "If you hate religion, then why are you here at this instant? This place is famous for its religious significance! It is a pilgrimage site and a place of worship. It is meaningless for you to be here!"

A wistful smile crossed across Mr Davis's face.

"Chimayo isn't just a place of religious significance and worship, but also a symbol of hope and renewal. We both have made terrible and unforgivable mistakes, so this journey here will give us a chance to confront our pasts, seek forgiveness and rediscover our life."

"But how?!"asked Drake in bewilderment.

"That you will come to know once we reach inside."

But Drake was still startled.

"But why are you entering a religious place despite being an atheist?"

Mr. Davis replied passionately, "Because in difficult times, even an atheist forgets about atheism and everything and recalls the name of God. And the same case is with me now."

Harrison Drake was unable to believe his ears.

"Even though the interpretation of religion is not good for mankind's

progress and never has been, in my opinion, there is still no other thing in this whole world that can highly inspire us and provide solace than it. Even science cannot."

CHAPTER FORTY-EIGHT

Professor Victor was unable to believe his eyes. The incidents that were happening in front of him were beyond his senses. A few steps ahead of him, his beloved assistant who was more of a friend, also stood frozen in the middle of the cold night in the Giza desert, just in front of the Great Pyramid of Khufu.

As both of them shifted their gaze downwards, they could see that the device they operated did its work extremely well.

Before them, from beneath the excavated ground, the device's mechanical arms extended, delicately probing the unearthed soil. Precision sensors detected the anomalies, and the device carefully extracted something and came out of the ground, handing the thing which it had found hidden into the soft hands of Joseph.

"Sir! It is unbelievable! The Ultimate Truth has at last been found! We have achieved such a feat that no one has ever believed or imagined! I am now fully sure that God is with us. Please come here. I will wipe it neatly as it is completely filled with mud. But as I am holding it in my hands, it seems that it is somewhat like a stone or a clay tablet."

And then pulling out his rough and thick handkerchief and also using his hands, Joseph started cleaning it to see what exactly was the mysterious object that was in his hands.

On the other hand, Professor Victor suddenly departed into his own world of thoughts. His eyes were dying to see what they had found. But still, he was unable to return to his thoughts. Standing stationary in the middle of the cool desert at night, he suddenly recalled the strange and surprising evening of 5 days back.

It was 6 PM. The weather was very mesmerising and amazing. It was a perfect time for doing anything that one liked and loved.

And exactly like that, Professor Victor was doing his favourite thing apart from all the work and stuff which he was constantly doing at Virtual Eye with James Brown. And that thing was none other than reading books. He had actually been an avid reader since his teens and devoured various books ranging from artificial intelligence, politics and astronomy to religion, theology and philosophy.

Professor Victor was sitting comfortably, wearing shorts and a half sweater over his nice t-shirt, which had been gifted to him by Elon Musk which was black in colour and bore the title 'Occupy Mars.'

And we are going to take our first step within 5 days.

Becoming happy and excited for an amazing future for humanity, Professor Victor picked up Dan Brown's Origin. He was going to read the book for the sixth time.

How many times have you read it and you aren't satisfied? Because Dan Brown mixes philosophy, science and mystery so well that it becomes impossible to put down the book, and it really becomes unforgettable.

He got very excited to reread that book.

But amidst that, a very strange thing happened.

Just as Professor Victor picked up the book and sat down on his luxurious sofa inside his bungalow, suddenly, his mobile phone buzzed. He had forgotten to keep his phone on silent mode.

So, he picked it up and decided to make it silent. But when he took it in his hands, he saw that he had received a message from an unknown number.

Unlocking the password, he saw that someone was willing to chat with him on his Gmail.

But when he opened it, his heart thundered, and he got up from the sofa as if he had seen a monster in front of his eyes. His eyes were fixed on the screen, and his whole body was shaking in a very strange manner.

What the hell in this world?

As he read the message, his jaw clenched, and his limbs pained. A mysterious energy had entered his mind and soul.

'Hello, Professor Victor Malachai! I have texted you in order to tell you about an extremely important thing which you won't believe at all. The thing which I am going to tell you will be groundbreaking. Please reply immediately.'

Without thinking a shit about anything, Professor Victor started chatting with the anonymous contact.

'Yeah, I am here! What are you gonna tell me?"

Instantly, the reply came back.

'The thing that you are now going to listen to is a secret, which if revealed will completely shatter the whole world.'

'What's the secret?! Please tell me what it is and by the way, also tell me who you are.'

'Knowing my name is not important now. I will reveal my identity later. Now just listen to the secret carefully.'

Professor Victor was in utter bewilderment. But he didn't think of trusting the sender.

'How can I believe an anonymous sender whom I don't know also!'

'Dear Professor, I don't have much time to discuss these things with you. I just have the aim of saving the whole world from a great apocalypse.'

'Great apocalypse?!! What the hell are you saying? Did you not get another person to do a hopeless prank?'

Professor Victor was getting irritated with every passing moment. His peaceful and charming evening had been ruined by a stranger. He didn't even know whether the sender was a male or a female.

'That's what I said, Professor! You will not believe what I will tell you. Please listen to me. Humanity is going to face a great threat and danger.' Finally getting irritated and a bit worried, Professor Victor decided to listen to the sender.

'I know a great secret which, if revealed to the whole world, will cause a great apocalypse.'

'But what's the secret?! Please tell me, as I am getting irritated by typing.'

And soon after that, the anonymous sender told the secret to the Professor Victor.

As soon as he learnt about the secret, Professor Victor jerked backwards but somehow managed to avoid falling. There was complete silence in his hall. Just the ticking of the clock, which was attached to the wall, was audible and nothing else.

Professor Victor felt as if he had suddenly entered a parallel Universe.

Time seemed frozen for him at that instant. What he had heard was unbelievable.

'Are you kidding? Or have you gone mad? Am I a fool to believe what you are saying? This seems something like a legend that you have just created.'

'Don't forget, Professor, that sometimes legends also are true. And why will I do such a great prank on you? It's my kind request to you to please follow my orders. You are the only genius and brave scientist who can save humanity from danger. Please, Professor! And if you don't believe me, you can directly talk with Him!'

'If you.....are telling the truth, what danger can this secret have on the world?'

'Many, Professor! Listen to me.'

As the anonymous sender explained some reasons why the secret could be harmful to human civilisation, Professor Victor's whole world suddenly changed. Now, he was in such a position where he was unable to resist the request. He was very well aware of the problems.

'You are right! The unveiling of the secret can be a great risk for civilisation.' But still, Professor Victor was unable to believe that the secret was real.

'Great! Now, after 5 days, if the Mars mission is successful, Sir Brown and Mr. Davis are going to hold a great event. And none except me knows that Sir Brown is going to reveal the secret before the whole world.'

'Beg my pardon? What did you say just now? What is the relation of Sir Brown to this whole thing?'

As the sender told Victor about Sir Brown's strange nightmare, he was totally astonished. His jaw dropped instantly, and he felt his reality completely reshaped.

'I will follow your every order and do what you tell me. Please guide me.

The Ultimate Truth will definitely get destroyed. I promise. I can do anything for humanity! Even if it risks my life.'

'Really? You can do anything to save humanity from an apocalypse by destroying the Ultimate Truth?'

'Yes! Anything.'

'Okay. So do what I tell you. Follow my steps and act bravely.'

'Definitely! Tell me the first step.'

Without any pause or anything, the sender calmly texted back.

'Go and kill Sir James Brown.'

The mobile phone fell down from his hand.

Now, as those memories faded away, Professor Victor returned to the present.

The greatest truth of humankind lay a few steps ahead of him. He had never ever imagined that humanity would finally find the Ultimate Truth and that also in his lifetime.

But unfortunately, he was compelled to destroy the greatest gift bestowed upon humans by the Universe.

On the other hand, he was not at all worried about the police officers or security guards as the anonymous sender was handling the situation nicely.

Professor Victor had smartly told him what to do.

But now the truth is going to be extinct forever. None will find it.

And he finally turned his attention ahead.

But in the middle of that, a very strange thing happened.

Just as he was speaking to himself, the object that Joseph was holding in his hands suddenly fell down from his hands with a metallic sound.

Professor Victor sprinted towards him with astonishment.

"Hey! What happened?"

Joseph was trying to speak, but something was stopping him or pulling him back from speaking.

Without opening his mouth, he straightly pointed his finger towards the object that was lying near his feet.

With utter confusion, Professor Victor bent down and examined the object closely. He kept in mind that he was looking at the greatest truth ever.

But as he saw, his eyes went numb. Suddenly, his eyes forgot to blink, and his heart raced rapidly.

"No!! This can't be real! Am I watching a nightmare?" With his whole body shaking, Joseph replied in a very fearful voice, "No Sir! It is not a nightmare but a reality. I am also wondering how this is possible. It is impossible for this device to exist 5000 years ago!"

CHAPTER FORTY-NINE

Commissioner Garza was baffled in the middle of the night. His car was racing as if it was F1. The other cars followed him, and many police officers were seated.

He was in a hurry and also in great stress at that time. It seemed as if the rest of the night was going to be tense.

Hope we catch the 2 mysterious people as soon as possible. Otherwise, the Great Pyramids can be in danger as we don't know the waiter and his assistant's mindset and further plans.

But suddenly, as he was wondering to himself, his mobile phone buzzed.

As he pulled it out from his pocket, he saw an unknown number. He was not at all in the mood to receive it. But as they had more time to reach their destination, he finally picked up and spoke.

"Hello! Commissioner Garza here! Who is speaking?"

"Hello, Garza! Head of security and Chief of Antiquities for the Pyramids, Tarek Mansour here."

Garza suddenly jerked forward from his seat and became serious.

"Ye...Yes Sir! What happened? And why are you calling from another number? And what happened to your voice? It appears to be somewhat different."

The line went for a pause for a few seconds.

"Actually, my phone unfortunately got broken, and I have a severe sore throat. But leave all that and listen to me carefully."

"Yes, Sir! Listening."

Captain Tarek Monsour's voice sounded uniform without any change.

"Commissioner Garza! Please stop your car right now as you don't have to come here. The case is resolved, and the situation is under control. There's no need for further intervention. Your cooperation is highly appreciated."

"What?! Is the situation under control?"

"Yes! We caught those 2 people. One is a waiter, and the other is his assistant. Now, we are going to extract the truth of the whole situation from them. Bye."

Before Garza could speak anything, the line went dead. Captain Tarek Mansour cut the call instantly.

Seated inside the fast-moving car, Garza immediately ordered the driver to stop. And so, to all the drivers of the cars that were following him.

Everybody got crazy after hearing that the captain and head of the security of the Pyramids had ordered them to stop as the situation was under control, and the 2 suspects were finally caught.

There was a sudden environment of happiness and contentment among the police officers. They were delighted as now they could go home and relax.

But amidst that, Commissioner Garza was very astonished and puzzled.

He was unable to believe what had happened.

How can the security guards of the Pyramids reach there so fast, as everybody was on leave today following the death of Brown Sir? And we informed them only half an hour ago about this whole situation. How can this be possible?

Even though the case was claimed to be solved, Commissioner Garza

would not be able to sleep the whole night thinking about the situation. And he didn't have the guts to call the captain and enquire thoroughly as the captain would be extremely busy at that moment.

As the driver sped the car towards the Commissioner's house, Garza constantly kept thinking about the unusual situation.

But as he remembered, he immediately called COP Abner to give him the good, but startling news that the 2 suspects were now in custody.

On the terrace of the eleven-storey building of the NSRA, Jonathan came running and looked here and there as if he was searching for something.

As he shifted his gaze towards his left, he could see the boyish Z11, who was leaning against the wall of the terrace, immersed in his own synthetic world.

"Hey Z11! What are you doing there? Please come here and help us search for the password for Davis Sir's mobile phone! Dr. Johnson has already started the work."

The robot turned backwards and replied in a normal voice, "Yeah! Sorry for the inconvenience. I am coming."

And saying so, he followed Jonathan inside Mr. Davis's office.

But as he moved on, he said to himself in a synthetic voice, "Acting is really an art and a very beautiful and interesting thing."

CHAPTER FIFTY

Professor Victor stood in awe before the Great Pyramid of Khufu beside his dear friend and assistant Joseph as he glanced at the ancient object in front of his eyes. The 3 corpses of the world-famous archaeologists were lying a few feet away from him.

The moment Professor Victor had been waiting for 5 days had finally arrived. His body trembled with fascination and fear as he stared at the object lying on the ground in front of his eyes.

"If I am not wrong, is this object a ......"

"Yes! You are right, Sir."

Now, Professor Victor was experiencing a sudden change in his life. He had never ever wondered that he would one day come across such a thing.

"But how is this possible? I am not able to digest that this technology existed 5000 years ago!" exclaimed Professor Victor with utter bewilderment.

Joseph walked near the device and replied, "Sir! We often make mistakes by thinking that our ancients were not much advanced in technology. Even the case can be that they were far more advanced than us. We are still

unable to understand many of the old technologies that have been found. And one of the greatest examples is ahead of us."

In saying so, he pointed towards the ancient Great Pyramids, which are one of the most advanced and mysterious structures in world history.

Now, Professor Victor was not able to cope with the situation. Even though the device was in front of him. He was not at all in favour of it existing 5000 years ago.

"Dear Sir! Now, it is not the time to keep wondering about the origin of this device. We have to finally perform our last step. Then only our mission of saving humanity from an apocalypse will be completed."

Professor Victor pulled the fresh air of the desert inside his lungs and nodded in agreement. He was now performing his last step.

Leaning downwards, he picked up the device in his hand and said, this time with confidence.

"Now, finally, it's time, Joseph. The destruction of the Ultimate Truth was predefined by God. I think because the time is not ripe yet for humanity to know the answers to the fundamental questions."

"The time is ripe, Professor! God had given the message to Albert Einstein many years back, but nobody knew about it. So now he chose Brown Sir for it. And it will be unveiled before the world, but unfortunately, you will not see it."

Victor and Joseph exchanged horrifying and puzzled glances. It seemed as if the acoustics of the desert were malfunctioning for them as they heard the voice.

"Don't get baffled so much and look behind."

As both of them turned behind, they were attacked by a scary energy. The scene before them was unimaginable.

A few feet ahead of them, the world-famous archaeologist Adrian was standing with Professor Victor's gun in his hand, which he pointed directly at the Professor.

"What the hell is going on!?" Professor Victor's voice echoed in the silent and peaceful desert.

"Nothing, Professor! I was not dead but was acting to be dead. The biggest mistake you have made in your life is to drop your robotic gun near me as I lay down, prompting you to think that I had died of a heart attack."

Ignoring his words, the AI expert said with fear, "What do you want from me? Why are you trying to kill me?"

Joseph's whole body filled with sweat.

Clearing his throat, Adrian erupted angrily.

"Don't act innocent, Professor! You are on the way to committing a crime!

Humankind is on the cliff of finding the Ultimate Truth, and you are mercilessly trying to destroy it?! I don't know why you are doing so, but I will not at all let you do so. The truth is to remain and be unveiled before the world."

"No, Adrian! You are on the wrong path. The truth should never be unveiled, at least for some more centuries. It will cause a major problem in the whole world. Please listen to me carefully."

Victor ran towards the archaeologist, who then jerked a bit backwards, thinking that the Professor might attack and snatch the gun away from him.

On the other hand, Joseph silently motioned towards the mechanical and the high-tech excavation machine invented by him and Victor.

Now, the prominent AI scientist and Adrian were face-to-face. The layers of stress and tension were clearly visible on both of their faces.

"Throw away the gun, Adrian, and listen to me carefully. Understand the reason why I am on the way to destroying the Ultimate Truth.

Adrian's soul was igniting with fire with each passing moment. He was somehow trying to swallow the anger towards Victor but was unable to.

"I don't want to listen to such a person who is trying to end the answers to the questions for which humanity has been struggling for ages to find the answers. In addition to that, I don't want to listen to such a person who is literally a murderer who has been constantly killing people since the evening just to end the golden treasure that has been waiting for thousands of years.

Shame on you, Professor! I feel ashamed to call you a scientist. Because a scientist's duty is to find nature's beautiful and amazing secrets and share them with the whole world. But you are doing the reverse. I had never expected such behaviour from you, Professor. I really hate you! Everyone will hate you when they come to know about your deeds."

Professor Victor's eyes were filled with tears. His eyes were suddenly filled with sorrow and regret. He could stand anything, but not that somebody felt ashamed of him as a scientist. It was really the saddest moment in his life.

With tears flowing down from his eyes, he said, "Please listen to me Adrian! You are thinking wrong. I am doing this whole thing just to save humankind from a major apocalypse. Trust and listen to me!"

Tears rolled down Adrian's cheeks. But at that instant, he didn't feel much mercy on Victor.

His face and eyes red with anger, he shouted, "Whatever reason it may be, you have not done right by killing thc grcat Brown Sir! IIow did you dare to kill such a person like him? And you also mercilessly took away the life of Benjamin Sir and Lucas Sir."

Professor Victor was feeling very bad and sorry for the evil deeds he had performed.

I have killed 3 people. I will never forgive myself.

Lifting the robotic gun and pointing it towards the inventor it, Adrian shouted with fear and also anger, "Now it's time to go, Professor."

After that, Adrian began quoting some verses from the Bible.

"One notable passage in the New Testament, in Matthew 5:21-22, where Jesus expands on the commandment states, 'You have heard that it was said to the people a long ago. You shall not murder, and anyone who murders will be subject to judgement. But I tell you that anyone who is angry with a brother or sister will be subject to judgement.'

Another passage from the Old Testament, specifically in Exodus 21:12 states, 'Anyone who strikes a person with a fatal blow is to be put to death.' And today, your judgement is in my hands, Professor."

Professor Victor was shaking with fear. He was sure that he was going to die in the next few moments.

"But I am worried about the whole of humanity, Adrian! I care and love humankind so much that I can do anything for it. First, listen to my reason for killing Sir Brown and your 2 companions."

"I don't want to listen to anything. In Islam, the Quran emphasises the sanctity of life. The verse of the Surah Al-Ma'idah (5:32) states that killing one innocent person is like killing all of humanity. But you have literally surpassed the boundaries by killing 3! Now it is time to go, Professor. You have been called by God now."

Professor Victor lost his senses as he saw Adrian, who was just going to press a button on the robotic gun, thus ending the Professor's life.

Now, in the cold desert, Adrian stood closer to Professor Victor. The Great Pyramid of Khufu was beside them.

The geologist gripped the menacing robotic gun, his eyes reflecting a mix of courage and malice. As he advanced closer towards the AI expert, the air thickened with tension.

But simultaneously, Joseph hurled the high-tech excavation device as much force as he could apply towards Adrian, whose aim was to take the life of Joseph's master.

The device soared through the air, emitting a futuristic hum. The angry Adrian didn't notice its presence, and the device suddenly emitted a force shield, ending his fate.

However, in the midst of the chaos, Adrian's grip remained on the robotic gun. His whole body was soaring with pain and trouble, but still, the fire of killing Victor was igniting in his heart.

With one final, desperate act, he aimed and fired a laser beam towards him. The robotic gun found its target.

While on the other hand, Adrian threw a happy smile towards heaven as he lay down on the sand. His task had been completed. Gasping for breath, he finally left the world.

Joseph ran as fast as a cheetah towards his dear master, who was shrieking with pain.

Struggling with his life, Professor Victor still tried to breathe as he had to convey his final message to his dear, beloved and loyal assistant and friend.

"Joseph," Victor rasped, his voice a whisper of pain and sadness. "I had never imagined for my life to end like this."

Joseph, his eyes reflecting a mixture of concern and loyalty, leaned in, absorbing every word of his master as if time itself hung on Victor's sombre words.

"Do you remember the day when we tied into the band of this eternal friendship?" His voice sounded emotional.

Joseph's eyes watered as the memories flooded back like a tidal wave.

It was a nice and fresh evening. Professor Victor, who had just become an AI scientist who was 23 years old, was standing on the banks of a river.

He was constantly staring at the setting Sun. He was very happy as he had finally completed his dream of becoming an AI scientist.

At the age of 23, Professor Victor exuded an aura of youthful brilliance and determination. His sharp intellect could be sensed immediately from his focused gaze that surveyed the world with a hunger for knowledge and hard work and his handsome face.

At 23, he stood at the threshold of a remarkable journey, ready to leave an indelible mark on the landscape of artificial intelligence that would result in groundbreaking innovations in future.

But my dreams and ambitions are very high. My career has started now, and I have to do a lot for humankind.

But as he was immersed in his own futuristic and joyful world, suddenly, 2 dogs came running ferociously from behind. Both of the deadly-looking beasts were fighting and attacking each other.

Suddenly, one of them jumped towards the handsome Victor.

The young Malachai suddenly jerked backwards as he had an extreme fear for dogs. But unoticingly, he fell into the river.

The youthful and brilliant Victor didn't know how to swim. He was shouting for help, but nobody was there around.

He was trying as hard as he could to avoid drowning. But still, he had lost hope.

But in the middle of that, a young boy who was a year younger than Victor, came running like a sprinter and dived into the river.

The boy tried very hard and finally pulled Victor outside and calmed him.

After a few moments, Victor stared into the boy's eyes.

The boy, while lacking conventional attractiveness, possessed an unassuming charm that went beyond his physical appearance.

With a voice filled with fear and surprise, Victor began, "Jo...Joseph?! You saved my life?"

Joseph, with a voice filled with great happiness, replied, "Yes, Victor. I saved your life."

Victor's eyes were filled with tears. At that precise moment, he was unable to believe that his rival had saved his life.

Still crying, he said, "Dear Joseph! I hurt you very badly in the past by making fun of you in front of the whole university, by laughing and joking about your intellect and the project you had made. Teachers were also laughing at you. I felt very satisfied as I turned your reputation down."

A smile lingered across Joseph's face.

Victor continued, "I have always made fun of you and have hurt you very much, emotionally and mentally, but still, you saved my life? But why, dear?"

Joseph became very emotional. Moving close towards his rival, he replied politely, "Dear senior! Our great entrepreneur Elon Musk has said that the best way to defeat hatred is friendship."

Victor was unable to believe what he was hearing.

"Even though you have hurt me in many ways, I felt an urgency and a feeling to save you from drowning. I love humanity very much. Instead of just thinking about my state, city, town or country, I think about the whole of humankind. And seeing a human struggling for life in front of my eyes, I got pulled towards you. Even though we are both enemies, after all, you are a human. And it is my first priority to save a human life."

Tears rolled down Victor's cheeks. He didn't have control of his body at that moment.

Forgetting his hatred and enmity with Joseph, he tightly hugged his rival, thus ending his enmity with him forever.

"Today, you have taught me a great lesson of life, dear Joseph. I never ever thought that our mindset was the same. I am also a true lover of humanity."

A cool breeze blew, accompanied by the chirping of birds.

"Today, I want to end my enmity with you. We will be friends forever. I am really very sorry for my behaviour with you before."

Joseph nodded his head in agreement. His heart was bursting with joy.

"Dear senior, starting today, you will be my master, and I will be your assistant and a great friend. Together, we will start our journey of taking our civilisation to the next level. We will always work together for humanity and remain together till our last breath. And we both will leave this world together, I promise you."

Both of their eyes were filled with tears of joy. Both of them saw a sheer friendly nature in each other's eyes, as if their friendship had been chosen by God himself.

But it was the past. Now, 15 years have passed, and everything has changed. Those happy days were gone now as Joseph leaned towards his master and, after all, the best friend of his life, who, on the other hand, was struggling for life.

"Yes, senior!" As Joseph spoke the word, Professor Victor burst into tears. The old memories were coming back in his head.

"Dear Joseph," his voice was mixed with regret and pain.

"Before we became friends, I had hurt and troubled you a lot. I am extremely sorry for my cruel behaviour towards you. Despite my behaviour towards you, you saved my life. Otherwise, I would have died that day.

Thank you very much, dear."

Professor Victor was unable to control his tears at that moment. He and Joseph were both becoming emotional as they recalled the happy and hard times that they had spent together. They had done many things like eating, especially working, together. But now the 2 best friends were going to part forever.

Gasping for breath and demanding his lungs to inhale as much oxygen as possible, Professor Victor reached out for Joseph's hand. As both the friends held each other's hands, they suddenly felt a positive energy entering into their bodies.

Both of them kept staring into each other's eyes.

Now, Professor Victor was in his last stage of life. Within a few moments, he was going to leave his dear friend and, after all, the whole world. But a sudden happiness emerged inside his heart as he was lucky to die before the Great Pyramids of Giza.

He began in a low voice, Joseph's delicate hand still in his hand.

"Dear! You have always been loyal to me. I cannot express my feelings in words to thank you. Everyone should get a working assistant and friend like you. I am very joyous that you are near me during my last breath."

Joseph's cheeks were flowing with tears of sadness.

Now, Professor Victor's pain was increasing at a rapid pace. It seemed that he was just going to die.

Finally, he turned his eyes towards his dear friend and said in a very polite and soft voice, "I have troubled you a lot. This is the return which God has given me for my behaviour. But dear, you have always listened to me.

And now it is the time to listen to me once again and for the last time." Joseph's body went nuts. He was unable to understand what was happening.

"My dear assistant and beloved friend Joseph, my last order and request to you is that you please destroy this Ultimate Truth. You have to do it in order to save the whole of humanity. My soul will then only be satisfied. It's a small request from your best friend and a small order from your master. Bye-bye, my dear Joseph."

And with those words, the world-renowned AI expert and inventor Professor Victor Malachai took his last breath, thus leaving the whole world forever.

"No, Sir!!" Joseph's voice echoed in the whole area. He knelt down and started weeping with his whole heart and soul.

A true friend only knows how it feels when his true and beloved friend leaves him, that also forever. And at that moment, Joseph knew it clearly.

But now, it is not the time to cry. I have to complete the last wish and goal of my master's. I will never let the Ultimate Truth be unveiled before the world.

And saying so, he started moving away from the corpse of Victor towards the unimaginable object that both of them had extracted from the ground with the help of their invention.

But suddenly, a very strange thing happened. As Joseph shifted his gaze towards the moonlight sky, he suddenly saw a strange object which was becoming larger with every passing moment. The object was coming straight towards him. And as it came very close, he was shocked to see the scenario.

CHAPTER FIFTY-ONE

The AE-0671 jet was pacing rapidly towards the ground near the Pyramid of Khufu.

Inside the aircraft, Lana and Anderson glanced stressfully downwards from the windows.

They could see the corpses of 3 people lying there. And in addition to that, as the jet started descending towards the ground, they saw a man who was looking at the jet in utter disbelief and shock.

"The man is Joseph! The assistant and dear friend of the Professor Malachai!"

Lana's cry echoed loudly inside the jet. Anderson, who was looking down, suddenly became a bit scared as she shouted. And as he gazed with focus, he also recognised that the man was none other than Joseph. Now, they were sure that the waiter was none other than Professor Victor. But both of them were puzzled to see that he was not there.

Amidst that, the communication device buzzed, and Lana activated it.

"Are you ready, ma'am?"

"Yes, pilot! We are ready."

And after a while, the door of the jet suddenly opened, and a rope ladder was lowered by Lana and Anderson.

Knowing what to do, both of them held the ladder tightly, and Lana shouted as loudly as possible, "Joseph! Please stop what you're doing. You are following the wrong path. Grab the ladder and come inside; otherwise, we will have to take strict action.

Pilot Carter was skillfully maintaining control of the jet.

Joseph was shocked to see Lana and Jacob Anderson calling him. But he didn't have the time to wonder how and why both of them came there and how did they knew about their location.

His aim was now to just destroy the object in his hand. But he was unable to understand how he could do that quickly.

But suddenly, a brilliant idea flashed inside his mind. He now knew how he could fulfil the last wish of his master and also save humanity from a major apocalypse.

Without hesitating, Joseph clutched the ladder and grabbed hold of it with one hand while holding the object in another. The atmosphere was extremely tense.

With calculated precision, Lana and Anderson pulled the ladder upward.

Pilot Carter was ready to speed away the aircraft from the scene. Both the intellectuals finally succeed in pulling the villain Joseph aboard, avoiding the cataclysmic fate of the Ultimate Truth.

The AE-0671 jet accelerated slowly.

But suddenly, complete chaos emerged, and conditions became worse. Lana and Anderson were now going to be under huge tension once again.

As Joseph entered inside the flying jet, he pushed Lana and Anderson with great force, and both of them fell down, fortunately they didn't get hurt.

Grabbing the nice opportunity, he threw the object which was in his hand, with as great force and power as he could towards the Pyramid of Khufu, from the accelerating jet of Brown.

"The Ultimate Truth will be destroyed forever! I have completed my task and served my purpose! And now, finally, the time has arrived to leave this world."

Lana and Anderson exchanged puzzled glances as Joseph's voice echoed inside the jet.

And as they shifted their gaze towards the scene, they were dazzled and astonished.

With a happy smile gleaming on his face, Joseph jumped from the flying jet, thus ending his life forever.

Both of them ran swiftly to save him, but they realised that they were very late.

As Joseph jumped down, he could experience free fall, where he was falling under the influence of gravity, without any other forces acting upon his body.

And before his death, he exclaimed loudly, with tears rolling down his cheeks, "I have fulfilled your last wish, master! And now I am ending my life to come near you. Because my life is useless without you!"

And as he struck down on the sand of the Giza desert, he felt such a pain which he had never ever experienced in his life. But along with that, he was a fortunate person to die peacefully, with high satisfaction, as he felt that he had completed his task and served his purpose.

"Please turn the jet back and land towards the Giza Pyramids! The Ultimate Truth has fallen down!"

Lana's voice was accompanied by much irritation as she ordered Pilot Carter will land the AE-0671 jet near the Khufu Pyramid.

Without any further arguments, Carter did what he was told to do.

After a few minutes, the short private jet of James Brown landed smoothly near the Great Pyramid of Khufu. And Lana and Anderson, driven by instinct, hurried outside with their full energy. Pilot Dylan Carter was also eager to follow them outside, but Lana ordered him to sit inside as they would be leaving as fast as possible.

As both the companions stepped outside, their guts and heart told them that something was wrong.

Jacob Anderson was looking here and there. Lana was searching for the Ultimate Truth in the darkness. But it was her good luck that the Moon was shining intensely, sparkling its brightness all across the vastness of the stretched sand and desert.

Anderson walked a few steps ahead. But as he turned his eyes in front and stared at the scenario with laser-sharp focus, he was dumbfounded, and adrenaline pumped through his body. It seemed as if he had seen a ghost.

"Lana! Lana! Come here."

"No, Jacob! Come here! See what I have found."

Without peppering her with further questions, Anderson motioned swiftly towards her. But as he went there, his body froze at that instant.

Before his eyes, he could see the pale and lifeless body of the great AI scientist, Professor Victor Malachai. His eyes forgot blinking at that precise moment.

"Is...the Professor d.... dead?"

In a very low and cowardly voice, Lana replied, "Yes."

But as Anderson told Lana about the other 3 corpses, which he recognised were of the 3 world-famous archaeologists, Benjamin, Lucas and Adrian, Lana couldn't believe it.

"Means these 3 researchers came here to find the Ultimate Truth, like us to unveil it before the whole world, fearing that the government might hide the secret from the public, or someone might destroy it, as now almost everyone knows about the nightmare of Brown Sir. And Professor Victor and Joseph wanted to destroy it, so the 2 groups clashed, resulting in everyone's death," said Lana, her face turning very anxious and surprised.

That's why I oppose and hate wars and violence. Because it causes unhappiness and destruction and nothing more, thought Anderson.

There was a temporary silence as both of them gathered some courage as they were surrounded by 5 dead bodies of famous personalities, the body of Joseph being a few metres away.

Breaking the silence, Anderson encouraged Lana, "Now we don't have time to feel sad and worry about this. Before the security guards or the police come, we have to take the object that contains the Ultimate Truth away and then reveal it immediately before the whole world. Let's search for it."

"But I don't think that the object is in a good condition. Because Joseph threw it with great energy and force, and that also from a great height."

A smile flickering across his face, Anderson replied, "Lana! Nature wanted us to find this ancient secret. That's why it removed all the obstacles from our path. But now, if we try to find the truth to unveil it before the world, the Universe or its creator itself will help us."

Lana felt a positive energy entering her heart as she heard his positive words.

She felt inspired and resumed her search for the object. On the other hand, Anderson motioned near Professor Victor's dead body and pulled out the expert's smartphone, thinking that they may get some important information from it. But after all, he became very emotional after seeing the genius lying dead in front of his eyes.

Why did you want to destroy the golden and greatest truth forever, despite you being a scientist? This thing led to your end.

"Jacob! Come here. Holy shit! Holy shit!"

A few metres ahead of him, Lana was staring unusually and strangely at something which she was holding in her delicate and soft hands.

As he was running towards her, he asked, "What happened?!"

"The Ultimate Truth is absolutely safe! But something quite inexplicable has happened."

Anderson's heart thundered. And as he reached near her, he seemed that he was in a very different world. He kept rubbing his eyes constantly.

"But how is it possible for this device to exist 5000 years ago?!" Anderson asked in bewilderment and shock.

With an astonished gaze, Lana replied, "At this moment, everything seems possible, Jacob."

A few kilometres away from the Great Pyramids, COP Abner was continuously looking at his wristwatch. At that moment, he realised the importance of every single second.

A police officer came near him and said, "Captain Tarek Mansour has captured the 2 criminals, right?"

COP Abner nodded his head in agreement. He was very happy at that moment. He felt very happy, thinking that everything would be resolved. But who knows what will happen?

CHAPTER FIFTY-TWO

Mr. Liam Davis and Inventor Harrison Drake were standing in front of the Santuario de Chimayo. Without further wasting time, both of them walked inside.

As they motioned slowly inside, a soft glow from candles filtered the air.

There was none inside the chapel. Both of them immediately started admiring the beautiful architecture.

The interior was adorned with religious iconography and hand-carved wooden statues. The air was thick and was completely filled with the invisible and powerful energy of hope and spirituality.

As they walked further, they could feel the walls whispering tales of pilgrims and penance. The scent of aged wood mingled with the faint fragrance of the burning candles as they stepped into a hollowed space.

As their footsteps reverberated through the quiet chapel, they discovered themselves in the company of a solitary saint. The saint's visage held the weight of countless whispered hopes and confessions. There was none other than the saint in the chapel.

Pointing his finger towards the peaceful and quiet saint, Mr. Davis told Drake to follow him near the wise man.

The saint sat upon an aged wooden pedestal with an air of tranquil repose. His eyes were closed as he sat in silent contemplation.

Mr Davis and Drake went and quietly sat on a warm and soft brown carpet that lay just next to the wooden pedestal on which the saint was sitting in silence.

"Forgive me for my interruption, wise man!" Mr. Davis's gentle and calm voice broke the silence of the chapel.

He continued, "There is a weight on our hearts, and now we can't find anything other than a few wise words which will help us get inspired. I request a short conversation with you."

The saint, opening his peaceful eyes slowly, gave a warm smile and replied in utter politeness, "It is your destiny which brought you here, my dear. You can ask me what you want. You will definitely seek inspiration and solace."

Mr. Davis and Harrison Drake stared at the saint.

The old saint was draped in intricately carved robes. His long, flowing beard hinted at the accumulation of untold moments. His hands held an air of quiet strength.

Leaning a bit towards him, Mr. Davis began the conversation.

"Hey, great saint! We both want to seek reverence. We have come here to learn from you how to develop the courage to speak the truth and tell the whole world confidently about our crimes and accept our cruel and evil deeds."

Drake was astonished to hear that. He gazed at Mr. Davis but didn't dare disturb the spiritual conversation, so he quietly sat listening.

Mr Davis asked, "Could you please encourage us so that we can have the confidence to accept our mistakes and start a new journey?"

The saint glanced with full focus in the eyes of both the people in front of him. His eyes reflected a feeling of power and positive energy.

"In the elegance of existence," spoke the saint, "stories intertwine, echoing the universal truth that revealing our crimes is a very essential and important part of our lives. Now, the stories which I am going to tell you will fill the evil and cruel spaces of mistakes and bad deeds in your heart with those of truth, kindness and confidence."

Mr. Davis's heart felt a sudden relief as he heard the saint speaking.

Neurologist Harrison Drake was also paying full attention to the wise man's words. He, like Mr. Davis, seemed to forget everything at that moment.

"Let's begin with a great story about the Christianity of a young man."

The saint began in a voice which was a bit serious.

"Once upon a time, in a distant land, there lived a wealthy man with 2 sons. The younger of the 2, who was filled with impatience and a desire for independence, approached his father one day, requesting his share of the inheritance. The father agreed in astonishment, and then the young man set off to explore the world and live life to the fullest.

But after that, the son's life became spoiled. He squandered his wealth on wild living and worthless choices. As time passed gradually, famine struck his land, leaving him penniless and helpless. In desperation, he took a job feeding pigs.

But in the middle of his worst situation, he suddenly recalled his father's kindness when he lived in his house. He then realised his mistake and decided to return back, confessing his sins.

When he returned, his father saw him and ran towards him with full

joy and excitement. He embraced him with love and forgiveness. The son then confessed his sins and expressed his willingness to become a servant. His father was overjoyed, so he ordered a celebration."

Mr. Davis was feeling the entry of a sudden positive energy inside his body. He was getting happy after thinking that there were still many stories yet to come from the saint's mouth. Drake was also feeling highly inspired.

"This parable, known as the Prodigal Son, teaches a powerful lesson

about forgiveness, repentance and the unending mercy of God. It gives us the moral that no matter how far we stray, there is always an opportunity for a fresh and new start. We have to start through sincere confession and a return to a life which is full of righteousness."

Now, the saint continued his speech, telling both of them other stories from various religions.

The environment of the chapel suddenly turned into positiveness. There was a huge amount of positive frequency vibrating inside it and also inside the bodies of the 2 inspiration seekers.

"Hinduism also shares a similar theme of redemption."

The saint's voice sounded more peaceful as he spoke.

"Valmiki, who was originally known as Ratnakara, led a very sinful and cruel life as a bandit who always robbed and terrorised travellers.

But one day, a sudden change came in his life when he met the great sage Narada Muni during his nefarious activities. The great sage went near him and asked, 'Do you think that your family will share the consequences of your sins?' This one question got deeply ingrained in Ratnakara's heart. He was feeling very bad after that, thinking about how his evil deeds would reflect on his family.

As he felt very guilty and remorseful, he asked for help from the great sage Narada Muni, seeking guidance on how he could atone for the sins he had committed. Narada, who was known for his great wisdom, advised

Ratnakara will chant the name of Lord Rama.

Ratnakara did as told by Narada and went to a secluded place in the forest and began chanting the name of Rama. His devotion was very intense, and he remained immersed into the penance for years.

As time passed gradually, an anthill grew around Ratnakara, covering him entirely. Pleased with his sincere devotion, Lord Brahma, the creator of the Universe according to Hinduism, appeared before him. Ratnakara expressed his desire to be liberated from the cycle of birth and death.

Lord Brahma explained to Ratnakara that he couldn't erase the consequences of past actions. But he assured him of a new life and purpose. Ratnakara then emerged from the anthill as Valmiki, signifying his rebirth from the anthills. Transformed and purified, Valmiki became a sage and later went on to compose the epic Ramayana."

Mr. Davis and Harrisson's eyes were fixated towards the saint. Their eyes had forgotten to blink!

"This story teaches the lesson that emphasising sincere repentance and devotion can lead to a fresh start, regardless of one's past actions. The journey of Ratnakara from a notorious robber to a respected sage highlights the power of divine grace and the possibility of a new beginning for those who really seek it."

Mr. Davis now wanted to speak something. But he noticed that the saint was continuing, so he stopped.

"The main value which we need to understand is that we should never fear confessing our sins and crimes. If we have performed an evil act, we should speak the truth and reveal our deeds before the world. Only then can we expect to live a happy, peaceful, and generous life. And we

must overcome our wickedness and become generous people. That is the rule of life, kindness and serving everybody."

Harrison Drake was still baffled, thinking about what was going on in Davis's mind.

" Pain and suffering are the major players in the game of life. The one who has the courage to overcome these players and defeat them is the one who wins this game of life. Because the game of life is the most difficult game which has ever come into existence in this vast Universe."

Davis moved a bit forward. His eyes were filled with motivation as he gazed at the saint before him. Just the 2 stories had brought a great change in his life.

Glancing at the saint's old but glowing face, Davis began to ask questions.

"Wise man, I have always been wondering about the great role religion plays in our lives."

The saint took a deep breath and replied in a soft tone, "Dear, the importance of religion lies in providing the world with a moral compass, a meaning and purpose. It teaches us such values which are very essential for developing a meaningful life."

"But why is science and religion always at odds?"

A smile flickered across the saint's face.

Mr. Davis continued, "Science relies on evidence and reason to understand the world. On the other hand, religion always comes up with such things which are superstitious and don't make any sense. Religious people don't have proof about the things which they keep on supporting and spreading in the world."

"Science explores the natural world and its mechanisms, but religion delves deeper into the questions of existence and finding the purpose and meaning of the world. If we change our perspective and mindset, both of them can definitely co-exist."

Mr. Davis seemed in a mood of debate.

"Okay, so you say that science and religion can definitely co-exist. Then why are they always at odds? There has been a constant war going on between the 2 since ages."

"It is because of the foolishness of man, my dear!" the saint's voice increased, "man is so foolish that he is not able to understand that the one who created him didn't create him on the basis of different religions and castes.

It is the man who has divided the world into different segments, claiming that his God is the true God and nothing else!"

The saint's words sent invisible waves inside the chapel.

"Science and religion are 2 pieces of the same cake. The former focuses on the material world, which can be seen, touched and heard through physical observation and analysis. The latter one focuses on the spiritual world which can neither be seen nor touched through physical observation but can only be felt by experience."

Mr. Davis was not satisfied with that.

"But how can we believe that the so-called spiritual world really exists?"

The saint again smiled gently.

"Dear, do you know what the world's biggest misunderstanding is?"

"What is it?"

"It's that science and spirituality are contradictory and opposite. The world's thinking that these are both opposites is the world's biggest misunderstanding."

Mr. Davis was surprised to hear that.

"Why do you say that?"

The saint touched his beard and replied, "There are 2 types of worlds. The world in which scientists and researchers do research is the material one. And the one which saints and mystics do research on is the spiritual one."

The atmosphere became positive.

"When people hear about spirituality, they immediately think that it is some sort of magic and illusion. They feel that it is just for some workless saints and mystics. But in reality, it is an advanced science which is beyond the material realm. Living spiritually is a fundamental part of life. It is not an illusion. The material world is an illusion."

Mr. Davis was impressed.

"Today's generation is not able to understand that what they think of as reality is an illusion, and what they think of as illusion is reality. Believe it or not, it's the truth. Truth doesn't require proof or justification."

Before Mr. Davis could speak anything, the saint continued.

"God is such a thing which doesn't require any proof. It requires a special vision and deep experience. But people don't understand this."

There was a short silence.

Breaking the silence, Mr. Davis asked, "But why always God? Can't we live without God? As Nietzsche has declared, 'God is dead.'"

The saint replied quickly, "Dear, no matter how advanced our technology and civilisation become, we can never surpass the power of the divine. And now, we are in such an era when we need God's and religion's guidance very much. Science teaches us motion, laws of physics and gravity, but it doesn't teach us ethics and morality. And as we are surrounded by technology all around us, we need to understand goodness and humanness in order to stay human forever. And we will learn that only through religion and the divine grace of God."

Mr. Davis agreed with the saint's philosophy.

"But saint, if God does really exist, then which religion's God is real? Who is the real divine being? Allah or Vishnu? Which is the real one? Because religions also have a constant fight between themselves over whose God is the ultimate divine being."

The saint inhaled fresh breath and began his explanation.

"It is a matter of perspective. Different religions offer diverse ways and paths to find and experience the divine being. We should show kindness, compassion and goodness and find common ground.

Christianity is monotheistic and believes in one God, who is the creator

of the Universe. The people who follow this religion seek personal relationship with God through prayer, worship and the teachings of Jesus Christ. Hindus engage in various rituals, meditation and devotion to connect with the divine. They believe in various deities. On the other hand,

Buddhists do not believe in any personal God, but they focus on the Four Noble Truths and the Eightfold Path to attain enlightenment.

In the end, every religion seeks to find the ultimate reality of everything.

But most religious people often behave in a nonsense way and keep fighting and criticising each other's religions. Even though each religion's path is different, their goal is the same: To find the ultimate reality of everything and make this world harmonious. But they don't understand this, which leads to clashes and conflicts. The day when all the religions will realise their mistake and start cooperating with each other, humanity will progress at a very high rate, and eventually, the world will become a better place to live."

Mr. Davis felt a lot of energy entering his body.

The saint leaned forward and said in a humble voice, "Are you aware that one of the greatest geniuses of world history, Sir Isaac Newton, was a deeply religious person and a theologian?"

Mr. Davis nodded in agreement when the saint took the name of his idol.

"He spent a lot of his years in decoding the secrets of the Bible and was a true follower of Jesus Christ. He said that God is the same, always and everywhere. His famous statement provides solace to the heart:

'In the absence of any other proof, the thumb alone would convince me of God's existence.'

Dear, God is omnipotent and omnipresent. Learn from your mistakes and create an extraordinary future where science and religion work in harmony, creating this world a better place to live. God will always support you. Only your intentions should be kind."

Mr. Davis became very happy and inspired by the saint's teachings. He could experience a flow of positive energy inside his body. Now it was the time to leave, so he asked his last and final question.

"Saint, my last question to you is why religion is so important?"

"Dear! Religion provides us with a sense of purpose and moral framework.

It offers us very important values that are essential in our lives. The biggest and the most valuable lesson that we learn from religion,

in my opinion, is that of love and compassion. Many religions teach the importance of treating each other with kindness, love and understanding.

Through love and compassion towards everyone, we create a harmonious world. Always keep in mind that by hurting others, we hurt ourselves.

Because, after all, we are all made of the same energy. We all are made up of the same energy, but only our bodies are different. We should never betray anyone or feel jealous about someone's success. Instead, if we show a positive and loving attitude, we will create a peaceful and prosperous and happy world."

Mr. Davis's eyes watered after hearing the powerful and motivational

words of the saint. He felt that a great burden from his heart had finally vanished.

"Always remember that faith is extremely powerful."

He got up and touched the feet of the saint and expressed gratitude. The saint gave his blessings to him and said in a positive voice, "May God fulfil all your wishes and you enjoy your life ahead."

There was silence for some time.

Finally, the saint said, "Dear, remember that a day will definitely come when all the miracles are seen by everyone and understood as real. A day when the world would realise the wisdom of the ancients. Science will not kill God, in fact science will prove and need God. The time has already started."

Mr. Davis' eyes welled with tears.

After that, Mr. Davis moved out of the chapel, and Harrison followed him.

As they exited the chapel, Mr. Davis turned back and said, "I will remember this place till my last breath as it has inspired me to start a new and better life."

Harrison gazed at him with confusion and asked, "But Sir, now will you

please tell me why you came here along with me? And what are you going to do now?"

Mr. Davis smiled happily and replied, "Let's first go and sit inside our chopper. Then you will come to know everything."

CHAPTER FIFTY-THREE

Anderson felt his adrenaline rushing at an extremely fast speed. At that precise moment, everything seemed strange to him.

Lana walked near him, holding the Ultimate Truth in her hand. Her body was shaking with fear and astonishment as she held that object and wondered about its unimaginable presence.

With his fearful but catchy eyes, he glanced with bewilderment towards the object.

"If I am not wrong, Lana.... Is this object a....Tablet?"

Lana nodded in agreement and stared at the tablet anxiously.

"But this is impossible, Jacob! How is it possible that a high-tech tablet was buried near this Great Pyramid of Khufu 5000 years ago!? It is quite startling."

The tablet had a metallic surface that was very cool to the touch. Its edges were very smooth, and it emanated a nice positive energy from inside. The tablet was totally blue in colour, and it displayed a captivating look by which it was clear that it was a very advanced device.

Anderson became very serious. His mood became like that of a great and focused researcher who just had the aim of finding the answers to the most difficult and profound questions of the mysteries of the Universe.

"Lana! Many people and experts, including me, are great believers that the ancient Egyptians were very far ahead of us in terms of science and technology. This high-tech tablet is the evidence of their great scientific knowledge."

"But I think the case is totally different, Jacob!" Lana interrupted in between. But before Anderson could say anything, she continued.

"See! This tablet is evidence that the ancient Egyptians were more advanced in terms of technology than we think. But still, it is not possible that they knew how to build such high-tech tablets like this. Therefore, this tablet points towards just one major possibility."

"What? Which possibility?" The air around Anderson suddenly became tense.

Pulling a deep breath, Lana replied, "You will not believe Jacob, but according to the current situation, I strongly feel that this tablet was not built and buried here by the ancient Egyptians but by extraterrestrials!"

Anderson's jaw dropped as he heard Lana mentioning extraterrestrials. His ears felt like they were hearing some fictional story.

"You mean aliens? This tablet was created and buried here by aliens?"

"Yes, Jacob! I also feel many other things about this secret. But now we quickly should again fly back to the USA to unveil this great truth before the whole world. We will also listen to this great secret along with the whole Earth only. Because COP Abner can reach here anytime. Now, let us sit inside the jet and fly towards the USA. As you know, it will not take much time as the technology of choppers, aircraft, and jets has advanced so much that we can go to New Mexico from Los Angeles in a chopper in just 2 hours! Let's move now."

Anderson had a lot to discuss at that moment. But the clock was ticking constantly as time never stopped for anyone. So, without thinking anything, both of them ran and sat inside Brown Sir's jet. And within a minute, the

AE-0671 jet took off from the sand of Giza. But the 2 people inside that jet had such a golden secret with them that if it was revealed, the whole world would turn upside down.

"Hey, Lana! Now, we have this tablet with us that contains the Ultimate Truth of the greatest questions. Should we reveal it quickly before the whole world?"

Lana kept staring at the high-tech tablet on a small table in front of her. Anderson was sitting exactly face-to-face with her and was looking very puzzled.

"Jacob! I strongly feel that we should reveal this great truth to the whole world as soon as possible. Like Professor Victor, anyone can try to destroy this precious knowledge. And if we hand this tablet to the government, they will definitely hide this information from the public. Over time, it can also get lost. I think that nature wants us to unveil this secret that has been buried for thousands of years. That's why we have reached this stage of exploration. Now I am going to post a message on social media that we both are going to reveal this message to the whole world within half an hour."

Saying so, Lana crossed her fingers, and her heart started throbbing at a fast rate with every passing moment. Because she was going to reveal the greatest truth of human existence- 'The Ultimate Truth.' On the other hand, pilot Dylan Carter was accelerating the jet at a rapid pace towards the USA.

As the jet was flying towards the USA, Anderson's mind was exploding with the different rockets of thoughts. It seemed as if his brain was a site for the testing of rockets. He was totally astonished as he, along with Lana, was going to unveil the ultimate reality to everyone.

But one question was constantly coming into his mind, which was making him crazy.

"Why did Professor Victor want the Ultimate Truth to get destroyed?"

CHAPTER FIFTY-FOUR

Mr. Davis and inventor Harrison Drake arrived at their chopper. Mr. Davis was feeling the presence of a positive energy inside his body to such and the extent that he felt as if he was purified.

Now, as both of them sat inside the chopper, Davis ordered the pilot to fly to Los Angeles. Following the orders, the pilot started his work, and the chopper lifted nicely from the ground of Chimayo and began its journey towards Los Angeles.

Drake was very worried about what action Davis was going to take.

"Sir! Now, I am getting very irritated. Please tell me what you are going to do. First of all, you came to this place with me in the middle of the night.

Secondly, you came to a religious place to meet a saint despite you being an atheist. What the hell is this going on?"

A smile came across Davis's face. He knew what he was doing. And the best thing was that he was very confident.

"Dear Harrison! As I told you earlier, our actions have created great havoc.

We have literally committed such a crime that no one will believe that we have done it. So, to find solace and get inspired, I came here along with you. And now we have to finally do the last thing.”

Harrison became afraid as soon as he heard it. He was getting closer to understanding what Mr. Davis was going to do.

Leaning towards his face anxiously, Harrison asked with astonishment, “If I am not wrong. Are you planning for both of us to confess our sins before the whole world now?”

“Exactly Harrison.”

Drake jerked backwards from the seat. His body was filled with sweat as he heard unbelievable words from Davis’s mouth. He was unable to handle the situation.

“You mean now we have to tell everybody the truth about everything?”

“Yes! To start a new journey of life which will include happiness and kindness, we have to finally speak the truth. And I am ready and extremely confident about it. Are you Harrison?”

Drake was so afraid and puzzled that he was unable to say anything. And to Mr. Davis’s bewilderment, he suddenly got up from the seat.

“No, Sir!! I can’t do it at all. I don’t have a single ounce of courage to speak the truth.”

“What are you saying?! Don’t you remember what we learnt from the wise saint? We have to confess our sins to start a new journey, forgetting everything. We will definitely get punished as we deserve it. But after all, we have to do it. Now, within a few minutes, I will start a live video where we both will finally speak the truth.”

Drake was in utter shock and disbelief. He was not at all in the condition of speaking the truth and confessing his sins to the whole world. But now he at last knew what he should do.

Motioning towards the door of the high-tech, super-fast chopper, Drake looked at Mr Davis and said, "Dear Sir!! Thank you very much for helping me when I was in need. You came like an angel to fund my unimaginable and great science project. I was on the verge of ending my life, but due to your help, I survived. But in the end, my invention has created the greatest havoc possible. I feel very sorry for it. I hope that you speak the truth and start a new and happy life filled with beautiful colours of kindness. I don't have the confidence and courage to do so."

Mr Davis was extremely shocked to hear that.

Now, Drake opened the door of the fast-moving chopper. A cool wind blew inside.

At last, he looked at Mr. Davis and said with a smile, "Dear Sir! Thank you for your help, which saved my life. But I think that nature doesn't want me to remain alive in this world. My time has finally arrived."

Mr. Davis got up from the seat, but he was too late.

Inventor and neurologist Harrison Drake was just about to jump and end his life.

But before jumping, he looked again at Mr Davis and spoke confidently.

His eyes were flowing with tears of sadness as he spoke his last words.

"Dear Sir! Always remember that science is making us deadly due to our misuse and evilness. We have to keep in mind that we should use its beautiful and elegant power for everybody's benefit. If we use it for evil deeds, then only destruction will take place. Remember my advice till your last breath, Sir and share it with everybody."

Saying so, the genius and controversial inventor Harrison Drake jumped out of the chopper from a very great height and ended his life forever.

Mr. Davis fell on his knees and recollected what his evil deeds had done.

He was feeling so sorry for his deeds that he now had no other option but to tell the truth to the world. But after all, he had to take some time for that.

CHAPTER FIFTY-FIVE

Cop Abner's plane was just above the Giza desert and was rapidly flying towards the Great Pyramids. But as the aeroplane approached the Pyramid of Khufu, he could see a few guards who were surrounding something. COP Abner was happy as he knew that Anderson, Lana and the waiter were caught. He clearly knew that Captain Tarek Mansour had arrived with the security guards.

Slowly and gradually, the aeroplane landed a few metres away from the Pyramid.

As fast as possible, COP Abner, along with a few policemen who accompanied him on the chase, ran towards the crowd of guards.

As he reached the historic Pyramid of Khufu, he met Captain Tarek Mansour.

The tall and muscular captain wore his uniform very neatly and disciplined.

His charming and serious face displayed his passion and discipline for the work which he was doing.

COP Abner began respectfully, "Nice to meet you, captain! I hope that all is well. Where is Ms. Lana, Dr. Anderson and the evil waiter?"

Captain Tarek's face radiated a negative energy. It seemed as if he was totally shocked and surprised. By looking at his face, anybody could tell that he was not feeling confident at all.

"Hello COP Abner! You will not believe what I am going to tell you."

COP Abner became worried as he heard that.

He moved closer towards the captain and asked in a low voice, "What do you mean by that captain? Have the 3 of them escaped?"

Captain Tarek nodded in disappointment and agreement.

COP Abner became shocked at that instant. His tongue was unable to move to speak.

Before he said anything, Captain Tarek informed him, "Abner! It is not the thing. You will not imagine, but the waiter who killed Brown Sir was none other than the world-renowned AI scientist Professor Victor Malachai!"

Abner was unable to digest the words.

"But the most devastating thing is that the Professor, along with his beloved assistant Joseph and the 3 famous archaeologists, Benjamin, Lucas and Adrian are now dead. Joseph's body was found a few metres away from the Pyramid, while the others were near the Pyramid. It is quite traumatising."

COP Abner suddenly felt the whole world shaking. He had never imagined that the killer of Brown Sir would be the genius Professor Victor. He became tenser when the captain told him that something was taken out of the ground near that Pyramid. And all of them knew that it was none other than the Ultimate Truth.

But one thing was confusing him to a large extent.

"But how is this possible, captain? Commissioner Garza informed me that you had called him and told him that you, along with the guards, had captured the criminals. Then how is it possible that they escaped?!"

Captain Tarek looked in bewilderment towards Abner. His body was shaking with fear for the first time in his entire career.

"What?!! What the hell are you saying? We reached here just 10 minutes before you, so how are this possible?"

"What?! But how can this be true? Commissioner Garza told me that you called and informed him."

"No!! I didn't call him. How is it possible that I called him? I think somebody called him under my name and gave him fake news. But who is that?"

Captain Tarek Mansour and all the other policemen present there were extremely surprised. The case was now getting more complicated as they had to find who had called Commissioner Garza under the name of Captain Tarek.

However, one thing was very clear to COP Abner: His doubt had now turned into reality. By looking at the deaths of the 5 men, he was sure that the main criminals and masterminds of the whole chaos and plan were none other than Lana and Anderson. Now, his duty was to somehow catch both of them. Only then would his work and mission be accomplished. So, he ordered his policemen to start the journey again, along with him, to catch the 2 using GPS.

Captain Tarek now focused on finding the fake person who had called Commissioner Garza and had ruined the whole situation.

COP Abner's main goal was to just catch Lana and Anderson. He didn't care anything about the Ultimate Truth. He didn't even care to think about what both of them were going to do with it. He just focused on catching them so that Brown Sir could get justice.

But suddenly, a very strange and shocking thing happened as the aeroplane in which he sat and took off.

When he opened his mobile phone and opened Twitter, he could see that the owner and CTO of the company, Elon Musk, had urgently called a press conference with a few NASA scientists and SpaceX employees at SpaceX headquarters. He was shocked to see Musk's post.

Elon Musk

'Exciting announcement! Join me, Elon Musk and a few NASA scientists, along with some SpaceX engineers at SpaceX HQ for a groundbreaking event that is going to change the future of humanity forever.

The secret of James Brown's dream turned out to be a real one! Ms. Lana and Dr Jacob Anderson has found a high-tech tablet which was buried under the ground near the Great Pyramid of Khufu. Within half an hour, both of them are going to unveil the greatest truth before the whole world from the AE-0671 jet of James Brown, which they are now flying to Los Angeles.

Timing for the live event: - 5 AM sharp.

Please try to watch the event live, as it will be a turning point for the whole of humankind. Join NASA scientists and me by watching the livestream on my Twitter account.

COP Abner was unable to imagine that Lana and Anderson were going to reveal the Ultimate Truth before the whole world. Suddenly, his interest turned to watching the historic event live instead of catching them. But now he felt that neither of them was a criminal. But still, he had a large amount of doubt. He decided to inform the world that there was a high probability that both of them were the killers of the 5 people after the event. But he was very excited as Elon Musk had arranged a press conference with NASA scientists at SpaceX headquarters to witness the enthralling event. Due to Musk's tweet, the news about unveiling the secret had become viral at a very fast speed. All over the globe, people watched livestreams of where Musk himself was going to be present. COP Abner was constantly thinking about what the truth might be.

CHAPTER FIFTY-SIX

"We have searched every nook and corner of Mr. Davis's office but nowhere found the password of his phone! My mind is going crazy now." Jonathan expressed his frustration with Dr. Johnson and Z11.

The 3 of them had done their best to find the password for Davis's mobile phone and his call history. Because the billionaire entrepreneur had suddenly disappeared without informing anybody where he was going.

Jonathan was getting irritated with every passing moment. That night would be the most memorable night for him, Johnson, and many other people. He was sitting with disappointment on a chair while Dr. Johnson was immersed in his mobile phone. The robot Z11 was still trying to find the password for Davis's phone.

But amidst that, Dr. Johnson exclaimed loudly, "Oh no! The Ultimate Truth has finally been found. Lana and Anderson are going to unveil the secret in a few minutes before the whole world."

Jonathan was unable to believe his ears. Z11 also looked stunned after hearing that.

"What are you saying? Have they found the Ultimate Truth? How is that possible?"

Dr. Johnson took a deep breath and replied, "Elon Musk has called a press conference, along with a few

NASA scientists and SpaceX employees in SpaceX headquarters to witness the event live. And you will not believe it, but both of them have found a high-tech tablet buried under the ground which holds the Ultimate Truth."

Jonathan was shocked to hear that.

"A high-tech tablet? But how is this possible? This means that the tablet was buried by some extraterrestrials 5000 years ago?"

Dr. Johnson gave a serious look and said, "Many people are arguing over that topic only. Most of them are saying that aliens buried that tablet. But who knows what is the reality? Once the event starts, everything will be changed."

Jonathan's heart thundered. He was unable to control his eagerness to watch the event.

Immersed in his own world of thoughts, he said in a voice which was filled with confidence and curiosity.

"Finally, humankind is just a step away from finding the answers to the greatest questions of its existence. How was the Universe created, and what's the meaning of life? I think God wanted the world to know about this truth, so he chose Brown Sir in whose dream the genius Albert Einstein himself told him his last words. First, everybody thought that it was just a dream. But now we realise that this dream has turned out to be real."

After that, all 3 of them started watching the live press conference, which was held at SpaceX headquarters. The conference was about to start now. In just half an hour, the whole Earth was going to come up with a breathtaking truth that had remained buried for thousands of years.

But it is said that everything's time comes one or the other day. And this time it was the Ultimate Truth's time.

A few kilometres away from the sacred chapel of Chimayo, a man was riding his bike slowly. He was in a very happy mood as he had completed a long project for his company and was going back to his house. He was very exhausted and just wanted to go and sleep on his bed for the next

countless hours.

But suddenly his happiness broke, and he stopped his bike. He was unable to believe what he was looking at.

But still, with some courage, he walked nearby. He was all alone in the middle of that road. And as he shifted his gaze downwards, he jerked backwards with fear.

Before him, a dead body which was filled with blood was lying. The head had been damaged a lot, and there was a huge blood loss. The man was very frightened, but still, he had the courage to see who he was. And when he discovered it, his whole head started spinning, and his heart was pounding at a fast rate.

As fast as possible, he pulled out his phone and called the ambulance.

"Hello! Please come here, and I will send you the location. Before me, the dead body of inventor and neurologist Harrison Drake is lying in a very traumatising condition."

After the call, the man felt very bad for the scientist who was lying dead in a very bad condition in front of his eyes.

In a very fearful voice, he said to himself, "He had threatened to commit suicide a few months ago but suddenly changed his mind. But now I think he has done it. After all, death is the Ultimate Truth of life."

CHAPTER FIFTY-SEVEN

Big Breaking!! Groundbreaking news! The Ultimate Truth, which was thought to be buried under the ground near the Great Pyramid of Khufu has finally been found. Ms. Lana Wilson and Dr. Jacob Anderson are going to reveal the great truth from the clouds as they are inside the AE-0671 jet of Sir James Brown. But few things have added mystery and spice to the event.

• The SpaceX and Tesla CEO Elon Musk has suddenly called a press conference of a few NASA scientists and SpaceX employees are at the company headquarters. The event is going to be streamed live within a few minutes.

• Debates and discussions are going on all around the world about how it is possible that the answer to the greatest truth had been buried near the Great Pyramids.

• Some people and even experts are connecting all this to extraterrestrials. But nobody knows what the reality is except Anderson and Lana.

• The most depressing thing is that the killer of Sir Brown is none other than the world-renowned AI expert and scientist Professor Victor Malachai.

• But the Professor, along with his assistant Joseph and 3 prominent archaeologists- Benjamin, Adrian and Lucas have been found dead near the Great Pyramids. The security of the Pyramids and COP Abner is saying that the killers of the 5 men are none other than Lana and Anderson.

• Another shocking news is that the inventor and neurologist Harrison Drake was found dead near Chimayo in New Mexico. Police are investigating the case.

• The truth will be understood once the historic event starts.

• Their live event has been postponed to half an hour late at the request of Elon Musk.

• Exactly at 5 AM, the livestream at SpaceX will start and half an hour later, the livestream of the Ultimate Truth.

The whole future of humanity will be changed after the revelation of the Ultimate Truth, which will answer the questions of how the Universe was created and what's the meaning of life. Be excited and don't miss the historic moment. Because this moment is going to be the most important one in the whole history of humankind.

CHAPTER FIFTY-EIGHT

A CNN Live link was attracting a lot of viewership all around the world. It was titled 'What is the Ultimate Truth?'

A CNN anchor appeared after clicking on the link. She was a young and attractive lady with dark black, willowy hair. Her brown eyes showcased her excitement and confidence.

"We are today joined by 3 brilliant minds. The NASA cosmologist, Dr Michael Greene, has a PhD in astrophysics from Stanford University. He is well-known for his dedication to exploring the mysteries of the cosmos and has widely contributed to various fields of cosmology, such as black holes, galaxies, dark matter, and many more."

Dr Greene - A very thin and confident man with wire-rimmed glasses, gave a sombre nod.

"We are also grateful to have Professor Marcus Holloway with us today," she said, "who is a popular philosopher known for his research on metaphysics and existentialism. He has authored several books on a wide range of topics like the meaning of life, consciousness and survival. His work inspires today's generation to delve deeper into the big questions of the world."

Professor Marcus didn't smile at all. His face showed his serious and disciplined character and personality.

"And our third guest, Father Gabriel Ramirez, is the head priest of a church whose ultimate purpose in life is to give a moral direction to the world and inspire billions of people. A warm welcome to our guests!"

Father Ramirez smiled softly. His black robe and personality showed that he was a devout Christian, who was like an angel of God.

The 3 of them glanced at the female anchor who was going to ask them a question.

"So, as you all know, today's topic of discussion is how the Universe was created and what the meaning of life is. The answer to the 2 questions was buried under the Great Pyramid. And after some time, Ms. Lana Wilson and Dr. Jacob Anderson are going to unveil the answers before the world."

The 3 of them stared in silence at her.

"What are your opinions on the first question? How was the Universe created?"

It was Dr. Greene's turn to shed his views.

"As a cosmologist, I strongly believe in the Big Bang theory, as do many other pioneers of my field. The Universe was created billions of years ago due to a big explosion of a tiny dot, which we physicists call 'Singularity.' All of the information of the Universe was stored inside it. After the explosion, the Universe continued expanding, and it still expands today. With the expansion, it also cools constantly. This is how the Universe came into existence. I am sure that this is only the answer."

The anchor stole an anxious glance at him and said, "But there is a problem with the Big Bang theory."

Dr. Greene's brow filled with sweat.

"We can calculate when t=1 and after that with the help of various formulas and equations. But when it comes to t=0, the whole science and mathematics go off the track. Means in simple words, if the Universe was created from the singularity, how did that singularity come into existence?"

The point struck Dr. Greene like an arrow. He smiled and replied, "Well, that's the paradox! We can't explain how something cancome from *nothing.*"

Father Ramirez smiled while Professor Marcus still sat serious.

Dr. Greene continued, "Other than the Big Bang, there are various theories." The scientist paused.

"The Steady State theory, developed in the 1940s by 3 astronomers Hermann Bondi, Thomas Gold and Fred Hoyle, states that the Universe is eternal and infinite, and it has no beginning and no end. The Universe maintains a constant average density of matter over time. New matter is being constantly created to maintain the overall density of the Universe."

Dr. Greene drank some water and concluded, "However, the discovery of the cosmic microwave background radiation provided strong evidence for the Big Bang model. The redshift of galaxies and the continuous expansion and cooling of the Universe also supported the Big Bang model. That's my opinion - the Universe was created due to the Big Bang explosion, as we have a lot of evidence of it. And science needs nothing more than evidence."

The anchor was impressed. But before she could speak anything, Father Ramirez exclaimed, "That's where science makes a mistake!"

Dr. Greene gazed at him with irritation.

"The world is not just about evidence," began the Father in his calm and gentle tone, "The Universe is not just about evidence, but is also about experience. A special vision is needed to understand the work of the divine creator. What I mean to say is that the world can't have propped up into existence without the presence of a divine creator. God has created the Universe. And by seeking the teachings and wisdom of religion and spirituality, we can understand the art of the creator."

Dr. Greene was baffled.

The Father continued his explanation, "The ancients were spiritual people. They lived in the arms of nature and understood the meaning of the world. As we know, the answer to the 2 questions was under the Great Pyramid. It clearly states that those people of the past knew these answers as they were deeply spiritual. But the modern man has got trapped in this materialistic world, and that's why he is unable to understand that the divine father of everybody has created this elegant world."

"Then what about the meaning of life?" asked the anchor immediately.

Dr. Greene knew that it would be better if he didn't try to answer that question. Because it always depressed him.

Father Ramirez smiled joyfully and replied, "Life is full of meanings and purpose. We have come here to serve God and fulfil his purpose. Nothing has happened randomly. Each and everything, from a small insect to the intelligent human, plays a crucial role."

Father leaned towards the anchor and continued softly, "If ants, the extremely tiny creatures, go extinct, the ecosystem will lose balance. Many ant species control pest populations by preying on insects or competing with them for resources. Without ants, pest populations can increase, affecting agriculture and vegetation. They are the food sources for various animals, including birds and mammals. Their extinction would affect the survival of these species. Ants aerate and mix soil. Without them, soil quality could decline."

The anchor, Dr Greene and Professor Marcus were impressed.

"So, life has a beautiful meaning. Such a tiny creature, like an ant, serves an extremely important purpose. We have to serve God's purpose by spreading love, compassion and harmony throughout the world. Serving mankind means serving God."

"Thank you, Father Ramirez, for inspiring us!" replied the anchor happily.

She glanced at the serious philosopher and said, "Professor Marcus Holloway, what do you think about the meaning of life?"

Professor Marcus looked dead serious.

He looked unsettled and said, "Philosophy is a diverse and confusing topic. There are several viewpoints of different philosophers on the meaning of existence. The ancient philosophers like Socrates, Plato and Aristotle emphasised on the importance of the development of virtues like courage and justice. By development of these virtues one can make his or her life meaningful and worthy."

The Professor's tone grew anxious. "Existentialists believe that all humans have free will. The structures and values of society have no control over a person. Choices are unique for individuals. We have to understand the Universe, but while doing so, we experience existential crisis. We keep wondering why everything exists. Why to live and not just commit suicide?"

The anchor looked depressed.

"We humans are able to think about these questions because our consciousness is far more developed than any other species alive on Earth. Just imagine what would have happened if we didn't have the ability to wonder about these questions?"

The anchor looked a bit comfortable and said, "Then we would have been always happy. And as Aristotle had said, the ultimate purpose of life is to attain happiness."

"But why to attain happiness? What do we get after becoming happy? Why to become happy?" the Professor fired back. His question hung in the air for some time.

He concluded at last, "What I feel is that the answer to the meaning of life will surely not be complete and satisfying. I am very sure about that. I don't know about the creation of the Universe."

"Well," the anchor said, totally uncomfortable, "It was nice to have a great discussion with you all. Thank you so much. We will find the answers to our questions soon. How was the Universe created? What is the meaning of life?"

Father Ramirez smiled again. *The Universe was created by God and the meaning of life is to serve God.*

CHAPTER FIFTY-NINE

The SpaceX headquarters at Hawthorne, California, were filled with the top scientists of NASA. Many reporters and journalists were reporting live from outside. The tweet of Elon Musk created a sense of excitement in people living all around the world.

Inside a conference room of the headquarters, the genius scientists of NASA and brilliant SpaceX employees were bustling with amazement and curiosity. The whole room was totally chaotic as the debates and discussions were not going to stop until the Ultimate Truth would be unveiled. All of them were seated side by side in front of a long metallic table. A few journalists were also sitting on chairs near the table. Even though everyone was very excited and curious, all of them were still very puzzled, thinking about how the golden truth could be buried near the Great Pyramids. In front of them was a video wall that was going to display Anderson and Lana's live event. And in one corner of the room, a designated control and communication centre was manned by SpaceX technicians. The event was also going to be livestreamed on the company's official website.

Amidst the discussion, the founder and CEO of the company entered the room, and everybody's attention turned towards him.

Elon Musk entered inside with an energetic aura of determination. He wore a tailored black suit with a crisp white shirt beneath, adorned by a tie.

By looking at his face, it seemed as if he was happy as well as stressed.

The room became completely silent as he took his place at the head of the long table. All the scientists and a few journalists gazed at him. And instantly, the livestream of the event started. The audience's number was unimaginable.

The silence of the room was broken by a tall and thin but good-looking CNBC journalist who was seated before Elon Musk.

"Elon, you have suddenly called this press conference at SpaceX headquarters. What inspired you to do this at midnight?"

Musk leaned back slightly and responded with an inspiring expression.

"To me, the mysteries of the Universe have always represented the frontier of exploration. I have always been interested in discovering the secrets of the cosmos. So, I thought that witnessing the breathtaking event, which is going to be hosted by Lana and Anderson, is incredibly amazing. That's why this press conference came into existence."

Everyone was inspired by curiosity of Musk towards exploring the mysteries of the Universe.

Another female journalist of the New York Times asked in between.

"What is the main reason that you thought of calling NASA scientists?"

Musk gave a faint smile and replied.

"NASA has always been at the forefront of space exploration and research.

Today's unveiling would be a scientific inquiry. The presence of scientists brings a sense of motivation and excitement which is very essential while witnessing such an important and historic event."

The event was getting great with every passing moment. After the journalists peppered Musk with a few more general questions, the scientists of NASA started the real discussion.

A senior scientist of NASA named Agatha asked, "Mr. Musk! It is quite a serious question. What was your reaction when you heard that Ms Lana had returned back to Earth from the spacecraft, leaving the great mission in between? Because the mission of Mars colonisation is an extremely important goal in your life. Did you get very angry?"

Everybody was eager to know the answer.

Musk smiled while he pondered the question. And after a while, he replied, "You know what? First, I felt extremely sad after knowing that James Brown was killed by none other than Professor Victor Malachai. I was not present at the speech because I was sleeping in order to remove all the stress and exhaustion. But when I woke up and opened Twitter, I was shocked to hear about Lana's return and that of other astronauts. I was way more surprised and baffled after learning about Z11, Einstein's last words and the Ultimate Truth. I was first burning with anger towards Lana.

But when I came to know that her return had paved the way to find the greatest truth, I felt happy. Because we can do the mission again, but if this Ultimate Truth would have been lost or destroyed, it would have been very bad."

The words of Musk made everybody realise how important he was to the mysteries of the Universe.

Before anybody spoke, he continued, "The whole world, including me, was shocked to hear that they found a high-tech tablet under the ground! How is this damn thing possible, guys? It is impossible to believe. But after all, the truth is the truth."

"Means can we say that this whole thing is related to extraterrestrials? "a SpaceX engineer blurted out. Suddenly, there was a long silence in the room. Musk kept thinking about it. Because it was quite a startling thing.

After a few moments of thinking, he said, "You know what, I feel that this whole thing could have been done by extraterrestrials. Because although we know that the ancient Egyptians were technologically very advanced, it is impossible to believe that they created tablets. So, this whole thing points out that this tablet could have been buried by extraterrestrials."

As Musk gave his opinions, debates and discussions started taking place all across the globe over social media. The brilliant scientists and engineers present there were constantly wondering over the matter.

After that, the CNBC journalist asked Musk his opinions on the Ultimate Truth.

Leaning towards him, he asked with enthusiasm, "Elon, what are your views about the Ultimate Truth? What do you think about the creation of the Universe and the meaning of life? And why do you think humanity's quest for knowledge and exploration is important?"

All turned their attention towards the real Iron Man of the world to hear his opinions about the Ultimate Truth that was about to be unveiled within a few minutes.

Musk leaned backwards and gave a thoughtful expression. Suddenly, it seemed as if he was lost in a world of his own. In a very serious and low voice, he began.

"You know what, I had sort of a very difficult childhood, and I was often bullied. People and my classmates used to consider me as an awkward and dumb kid because I was an introvert and very bookish. But they didn't know that my mind was constantly exploding with great ideas and thoughts."

Musk became more serious as he spoke about his thirst for knowledge and exploration.

"I was always interested in reading books on various topics from an early age. I used to just pour through various books, mostly science fiction, which ignited my curiosity about the Universe and its secrets. I read many great books like The Moon is a Harsh Mistress, Foundation trilogy, etc. These books helped me to develop an interest in science and the cosmos."

The room was suddenly filled with an atmosphere of emotions and excitement.

"When I was 14, I had an existential crisis. I suddenly began to think about the most profound questions, like what's the meaning of life and why just don't commit suicide. What is this Universe meant for, and what is everything? Then, I looked up and read various religious texts like the Bible. I also read various German philosophy books, which made me quite depressed. And I suggest that teenagers should not read Schopenhauer and Nietzsche."

He then looked confident as he spoke further.

"Even after reading so many philosophical and religious books, I was not satisfied. But then fortunately, I read *The Hitchhiker's Guide to The Galaxy* by Douglas Adams. This book helped me to come out of my existential crisis.

The main point that Adams was essentially saying is that the Universe is the answer. But what are the questions to ask? In the book, *The Deep*, the Thought Computer takes 7.5 million years in order to find the answer to the ultimate question of 'Life, Universe and Everything.' But surprisingly, the computer, after taking so long, says that the answer is '42.' Everyone gets baffled after hearing that. But the computer replied that the people did not understand what questions to ask.

So, after that, it creates an organic giant computer called 'Earth 'in order to find the question to the answer."

Everybody's eyes were unable to blink as they heard him speak.

"What Adams was essentially saying was that the Universe is the answer, but we don't know what questions to ask.

So, my philosophy is that if we expand the scope and scale of consciousness, we can understand what questions to ask. That is the main reason why I started SpaceX- to make life multiplanetary. Because we can become more enlightened and intelligent if we extend our species beyond Earth. And my latest company, xAI's AI GROK, has been modelled after the Hitchhiker's Guide in order to understand the true nature of the Universe.

The philosophy of the book has left a deep impression on my life, igniting my curiosity and excitement."

The scientists and engineers of NASA and SpaceX were highly inspired by Musk's words. They felt a sudden feeling of excitement bustling inside them.

The journalist, filled with motivation, said, "Elon, you really inspired us, including all the people who are watching this event live. Thank you for shedding your philosophical views on us."

"Thank you!" replied Elon Musk with a smile.

He then said, "Now let us wait a few more minutes in order to witness the most historic moment ever. We, humans, are finally going to find the answer to the Ultimate Truth for which several genius people and experts have been waiting for thousands of years. We are now going to find out how the Universe was created and what the meaning of life is."

At last, Elon Musk said in a funny voice, "I hope that the answer is different and not '42.' "

The room was filled with laughter.

CHAPTER SIXTY

5:30 AM. The time had finally arrived. The event which was going to start was one of the greatest events ever in world history. Humankind was not just moving towards a larger step, such as making advancements in technology or something else. But it was going to finally find the answers to the most profound and complex questions - 'How was the Universe created?' and 'What is the meaning of life?'

All over the world, the event created a sense of mystery and excitement. Almost the whole population of Earth was awake at that time.

People were highly active on Twitter because the unveiling was going to be broadcast on Elon Musk's official Twitter account. The billionaire entrepreneur was feeling happy that the greatest truth of humanity was going to be livestreamed through his company and, after all, on his account.

Sir James Brown's private jet AE-0671 was flying high above the clouds to complete its journey to Los Angeles. Pilot Dylan Carter had stopped handling the aircraft and had made the control fully autonomous. This means the aircraft would travel all by itself without any human intervention. He was going to hold Anderson's iPhone, point the camera towards both of them and start the livestream. His Twitter account had been linked to that of Musk's for the livestream.

On the top floor of the NSRA, Jonathan, Dr. Johnson and the humanoid robot Z11 were all focused on the smartphone to witness the event live.

They were very much enthralled and eager to know the answers.

High up in the clouds, the AE-0671 jet was flying using the autopilot mode.

Pilot Dylan Carter was holding Anderson's iPhone. He pointed the camera towards the 2 smart people who had suddenly become famous overnight due to their acts. All over the globe, people were filled with sweat as they watched the livestream. Exactly at 5:30 AM, the great historic moment started.

Lana and Anderson stood and faced the camera with a bit of confidence.

A small circular table was situated between both of them. On that small table, the high-tech tablet that held the Ultimate Truth inside it was kept erect so that the global audience could see the truth clearly. Lana, developing some courage and confidence, began the event in fluent English.

"Hello, my dear people! I, Lana Wilson, along with my partner, Dr. Jacob Anderson is extremely delighted to host this breathtaking historic moment. The truth which we are going to unveil before you are not just an ordinary one."

She became more confident as she spoke.

"This is the 'Ultimate Truth' which will answer 2 of the most difficult questions of human existence - How was the Universe created? What is the meaning of life? "

Pointing towards the tablet, she continued, "We all are not able to believe that such a tablet existed 5000 years ago! It is impossible that this high-tech tablet was buried under the ground near the Great Pyramid of Khufu."

Cutting in between, Anderson said, "Before further discussion, I want to make it clear that we both are not at all involved in this whole murder case of Sir James Brown. COP Abner is trying to catch us constantly. But we always escaped because we knew that the waiter who murdered Brown Sir was trying to destroy the Ultimate Truth. And now we all know that he was none other than Professor Victor Malachai. We wanted to save this truth. That's why we escaped before COP Abner could catch us. Because if we had been caught, then the Professor would have destroyed the truth before we reached there. Thanks to the great archaeologist Benjamin, Lucas and Adrian as they fought with him to save it. In that fight, everybody lost their lives, including the Professor's assistant, Joseph, who threw the tablet from our jet and committed suicide by jumping. I am feeling very sorry for them."

COP Abner and his policemen were shocked and surprised to hear that as they watched the livestream. The COP had never imagined that the case would be like that.

Now Lana continued, "Yes! Jacob is absolutely correct. We struggled very much in order to save this truth. We felt that the tablet would get destroyed as Joseph had thrown it from the jet. Fortunately, the jet was not at much height, and the material of the tablet was very strong. That's why it has not been damaged much."

Adjusting his black tuxedo, Anderson said, "So guys, now it's the time to see what the Ultimate Truth is. Humanity is finally standing in front of the golden door beyond which the greatest treasure is present. None had ever imagined that one day we would find these answers."

Elon Musk felt very proud as Lana was unveiling the Ultimate Truth before the world. His eyes were completely fixated on the video wall in front of him.

Lana turned towards the high-tech tablet, which was standing erect on the table between both of them.

"Jacob and I were curious about the contents of the tablet. We were very eager to see what was there inside. So, we opened it, and what we found was unbelievable."

She paused for a while and then continued; her eyes fixed towards the camera.

"When we opened the tablet, to our amazement, we found that it contained a video and nothing else!! We somehow controlled ourselves so that we could watch it with the whole world. So now it's the time to start the video.

We both are also bursting with excitement. The Ultimate Truth of the great questions is in front of us. Let's watch the video together!!"

And saying so, Anderson and Lana sat on the seat beside the table. Pilot Carter pointed the camera of Anderson's iPhone towards the mysterious tablet. After that, Lana turned on the device, and the video started.

All around the world, people were bustling with anticipation to see the video. From politicians to businessmen, everybody was watching the livestream.

Elon Musk looked very serious as he glanced at the huge screen on the wall of the conference room. He leaned forward to watch the video. It was the most awesome moment in history. His brain was exploding with different thoughts about the creation of the Universe and the meaning of life. His heartbeat, including everyone's present there, was constantly accelerating.

Jacob Anderson's whole body was filled with sweat. His heart thundered as the video started. *The questions about which I have been thinking since childhood are now finally going to be answered. I wish that the answers would be satisfying and meaningful.*

Lana was also feeling very tense. She stared at the tablet with laser-sharp focus.

And within a few seconds, the video started.

CHAPTER SIXTY-ONE

The scene opened with a familiar landscape. The background was that of a technologically advanced laboratory. There were several high-tech machines here and there, along with large computers, fill the whole lab. It was a highly futuristic scene.

But suddenly, a very strange thing happened. A weird-looking creature emerged in the video and started speaking.

The creature's face was clearly visible, and his body till stomach. It seemed as if he was sitting on a chair and recording the video. It had translucent skin, and it had a bioluminescent glow. He was very thin, but his face was large with large eyes. He had hair which was similar to that of a human being.

Elon Musk was extremely surprised to see the creature. His heart was constantly telling him that it was none other than an alien.

The creature gave a very sad expression and said in a robot-like voice, "Hello, dear earthmen! I am Zevon, an astronomer and inventor of the planet Luminara Prime, which was not far away from your planet."

Anderson and Lana exchanged puzzled and shocked glances. Elon Musk and all the brilliant guys present in the conference room were unable to believe what they were looking at. Musk's doubt became true.

Zevon continued in a low voice, "We had advanced so much that we had invented the method of telepathy and telekinesis. Now I am speaking in a very different language, but you are able to understand it in your own comfortable language. Our technology enables for a telepathic transmission that directly interfaces with your thoughts, feelings and understanding."

Almost all of the population watching the video got mad after hearing that.

"I will start with the story of my planet, which is no longer there." Zevon leaned backwards as he spoke further. His large eyes looked completely sad and disappointed.

In a low but very serious voice, he started, "Our Luminara Prime planet had a great history of progress, development, glory and technology. We lived not very far away from you and always kept an eye on you. We watched when Albert Einstein revolutionised physics, when Nikola Tesla shook the world with his inventions when Nietzsche put forth his controversial views on philosophy and existence."

He paused in between and continued, "But a time came before a few days which completely ruined our planet."

Now everybody's eyes were on Zevon's lips.

In a heavy voice, he started, "On our beautiful and technologically advanced planet, there lived a great sage by the name of Klair. He was known as the wisest person alive on our planet. His spiritual and mystical powers were beyond anybody's understanding.

With his extraordinary powers, he was known for healing people, materialising objects out of the air with his thoughts, and many more. He was a great and devout spiritually advanced person who could understand, feel and hear the mysteries of the cosmos. His every prediction, statement, sentence and word were real."

Elon Musk was baffled, and others too.

"Sage Klair had been alive for hundreds of years. Several generations of our planet got the opportunity to witness the miraculous powers of a person like him. But for the past 50 years, he was meditating deeply, all alone in a cave, far away from the material world. His main purpose was to find the answers to the 2 fundamental questions of our existence. *How was the Universe created,* and *What is the meaning of life?* We always believed that he would never find the answers...But he did find it."

Zevon became more tense as he spoke.

"But events took a turning point when, a few days before, Sage Klair returned from his meditation after a huge time period of 50 years. Almost everyone had forgotten him. And to everybody's astonishment, he ordered the government to arrange a grand programme in which he will tell the answers to the 2 questions."

Elon Musk was staring unblinkingly at the screen.

"A wave of happiness and excitement hit our planet after that. Everyone declared that the Age of Enlightenment had finally arrived. The government declared, 'Now we will never ever have to wonder about who we are after waking up! We are finally getting the answers!'.

Lana and Anderson were happy as well as tense.

"We all thought that we would be enlightened after knowing the answers. But speaking honestly, the exact reverse happened."

Zevon's eyes watered suddenly, and he said in a dark voice, "The answers to the 2 questions were so depressing that our species decided to embrace self-destruction."

Elon Musk's mouth kept open, and his eyes grew wide after hearing that.

With a disappointed heart, he continued further, "Our people decided to end their lives because they were unable to bear the depressing truth of life and the Universe. But before they destroyed Luminara Prime, I flew away into space in my personal spaceship. I felt an urge that even though the truth is depressing, other life forms living in the vast cosmos should one day come across it. Because they might be different from us, their hearts might be very strong, and they may have the willpower to bear such harsh realities. After all, the truth is the truth. So, I just knew about your Earth.

Therefore, I came with my spaceship on your planet and landed near 3 huge prism structures. I decided to record this video and bury it deep under the ground near the tallest Pyramids out of the 3 using the advanced technology I had. It was, or you can say, my plan as I am now going to do it. But before that, let me tell you the Ultimate Truth of life and the Universe, as sage Klair told us."

Now, Zevon leaned closer towards the video. His eyes showcased his depressing mental condition at that time.

Lana held Anderson's hand tightly in hers. She was feeling very scared to hear the depressing Ultimate Truth. Anderson also held her soft and delicate hand in his, feeling a bit of confidence and courage.

On the other hand, Elon Musk joined both of his hands and closed his eyes. He was praying that humans should get the willpower to bear the harsh reality of life. Actually, he is not religious, but still, the situation compelled him to pray.

On the top floor of NSRA, Jonathan and Dr. Johnson crossed their fingers.

The Z11 robot was giving odd and sad expressions. What was going on inside his robotic brain, none knew.

The whole population of Earth who was watching the event were watching with pounding hearts and accelerating tension. It was the greatest event of the history of mankind.

Tears flowing down from Zevon's eyes, he said in a depressing voice, "Dear earthmen! The answer to the first question of how the Universe was created is...."

He stopped for a while and then finally spoke the answer.

CHAPTER SIXTY-TWO

Sage Klair was meditating with laser-sharp focus for 50 years. The cave was totally isolated, only he was the one who was inside it. He had not at all opened his eyes since he began his quest for the Ultimate Truth. He had tried and mastered several complex techniques of meditation and spirituality just to find those great answers. But even though 50 years had passed, he was not at all able to get the answers.

I will die but not at all give up. Giving up is not at all in my blood. He had vowed that.

Sage Klair was extremely determined to achieve his goal. And he was confident enough that he would succeed.

'If your goal is a question of life and death for you, even the almighty God cannot stop you from achieving it,' he had once taught his disciples.

And there was a lot of truth in his statement.

On one cool and amazing evening, when the sage was in his meditative state as usual, he came across an experience that changed the entire course of his life. Forever.

Behind the darkness of his closed eyes, he suddenly started to see intense rays of light. He didn't just see the rays but also felt their presence. It was like he was touching the rays as if they were material objects. And

"

suddenly, alternate bands of light and darkness filled his vision entirely at a very fast speed. Something was happening.

And suddenly, a harsh but innocent voice spoke, "Open your eyes my dear, open your eyes."

Sage Klair finally opened his eyes after 50 years. That was really a very long period.

Just as he opened his eyes, he saw an immaterial form before him. He realised that it was none other than a soul.

With uncontrollable excitement, Sage Klair bowed before the entity and exclaimed, "Who are you, lord?"

The soul's eyes radiated utter sadness and pain. It was as if it was very sad.

With a heavy voice which was mixed with pain and regret, the soul said, "Dear, I am the one who is behind everything."

Sage Klair became happy. He was sure who the entity was.

The soul continued, "I am the designer and architect of everything. I am the one who created this, Universe. I am the creator of the Universe."

Those words sent waves of excitement and thrill inside the sage's body. Without thinking anything, he silently bowed down and exclaimed with utter joy, "Hey, lord! My hard work has finally paid me!"

The creator was still extremely sad.

The sage continued, "Lord, since my childhood, it has been my dream to find the answers to 2 of the most complex and important questions of existence. How was the Universe created? What is the meaning of life? But before that, if you don't mind, I want to see your material form."

The creator gazed inside Klair's eyes. He wanted to tell him all the truth but was hesitating to do so. But after all, he decided to speak. He was very well aware that no matter how many lies we speak, the truth will definitely be known.

He began in a low voice, "My dear, I will definitely answer both of your questions. But are you sure that you want to see my material form? Are you sure that you want to see how I looked before my demise?"

"Yes, I want to see," replied the sage with a hint of confusion.

The creator stepped backward and turned towards left. He pointed his finger at the wall of the cave and suddenly, a bright intense light emanated from his finger and an image appeared on the wall of the cave.

Sage Klair glanced at the image with excitement. But within a fraction of a second, his excitement turned into shock.

As he observed the material form of the grand designer, it seemed as if his eyeballs would get out. His strong and healthy body started sweating. He felt that he was watching a nightmare.

With utter astonishment, he said, "L...Lord, what is this? Why? Why such...?"

"You will get your answers once I tell you the answer to your first question. Please control your heart because this story is going to deeply impact your soul."

Sage Klair gave a startled expression.

Before narrating the story, the creator of the Universe asked the sage a simple question.

"Do you know, dear, what is the biggest mistake of my life?"

Sage Klair was surprised to hear that.

"What is it?"

With a voice filled with pain and deep despair, the creator replied, "The creation of the Universe."

Sage Klair was unable to believe his ears. He was thinking that he was going nuts.

"W...What are you saying, Lord?"

The creator asked the sage to remain silent as he was going to tell him the final truth, the Ultimate Truth.

The soul of the creator stepped forward. He was gazing outside the cave and was suddenly sunken into his own world. With sadness, he began the story.

"Billions and billions of years ago, there was a small world by the name of Ultiverse. It was extremely beautiful and elegant. Lush green fields and trees covered the world. The inhabitants were highly skilled, creative and talented. They were outstanding in different professions like the military, art, politics and all.

But as there is always darkness under the lamp, the same was with the world. Even though the inhabitants were kind and noble, the ruler was the demon's son. His name was Drongo. Cruelty, wickedness and jealousy were in his blood. Anybody who spoke against him got punishments which were worse than hell. But he didn't care an iota about that. Nobody ever dared to speak against him."

Now, the creator looked extremely sad.

"But in that world, there lived a young, kind and brave man who was known as Yoro. He was not at all able to tolerate the evilness and cruelty of Drongo's rule and hated him deeply. At a very young age, he had made his life's goal to end the rule of that demon ruler. But when he became a young brave man, he decided to do something that no one had ever tried to do or even thought of doing in the whole history of Ultiverse. He decided to kill Drongo. That was extremely risky. He knew that. But he was firm on his decision."

A drop of tear fell down from the creator's eye as he spoke.

"But when he attempted to kill Drongo, he was caught red-handed. Drongo's anger reached its peak after that. He became so angry that he ordered his soldiers to give Yoro the strictest punishment possible. And his soldiers followed his orders with excitement.

Yoro was forcefully given a special pill after swallowing, which he would not be able to die until the completion of a day after swallowing. And after that, he was given such a punishment which was never ever given to anyone."

Tears flowed down the creator's cheeks.

"He was thrown in boiling water, which was completely mixed with salt. After that, he was locked inside a small room which was full of deadly insects and beasts. He was made to eat extremely chilly food, and then he was forced to bite hard iron rods. His whole body was attacked by swords and knives.

But the worst thing for him was the death of his family before his eyes. His small children, dear wife and parents were burnt alive along with his house. They were shrieking with pain and screamed loudly. But he couldn't do anything other than just see the traumatising end of his family before his eyes.

He was then made to stand naked in extremely cold water. The chilly water made his body shiver such that he cried and cried uncontrollably. He constantly prayed for death but was not getting it. With blood flowing from all the parts of his body, he was locked inside a chamber which had a very high temperature.

The soldiers threw him at the feet of Drongo, who was standing in the middle of the capital of their world. He declared laughingly, 'Those who will dare to kill me will be tortured like this.' Everyone watched in silence, but none of them dared to help Yoro. After all, Drongo was powerful, and power makes everyone blind.

Just 2 hours before his death, Yoro was thrown in a huge prison of paper, which was set on fire. He had given up the hope of living and was just waiting for death. In some extremely difficult situations, death tastes like sugar, and life tastes like chilly.

Yoro was asked by one soldier what his final wish was as per the rules. Yoro requested him to bring a book and paintbrush. The soldier agreed. And now Yoro was going to create history with those 2 things."

The creator's tears were uncontrollable at that moment.

"Yoro drew black holes, galaxies, stars, planets, suns and many other objects which he termed as celestial objects. He cursed each and every drawing which he created. The paintbrush and book were very special tools.

And finally, he named his book as 'Universe.'

After his death in that prison of paper, his book was kept inside a huge library on Drongo's orders. It was kept showing people who dared like Yoro what would happen if they tried to harm Drongo. The Universe is a book in which each chapter is filled with pain, sorrow and sadness. This is how the Universe came into existence."

Sage Klair's eyes watered after hearing that. He was not at all able to speak anything.

But developing courage, he said, "And if I am not wrong, you are the creator of the Universe. And Yoro created the Universe. Means you are...."

"Yoro. Yes. I am Yoro."

A drop of tear fell down from sage Klair's eye. But the creator continued and answered the second question.

"The meaning of life is that life has no meaning. Consciousness is nothing but an illusion, which is the biggest deception of life. You do not have any free will or intelligence. You are all cosmic characters painted by me for not serving any higher purpose but adding and extending more and more pain in the Universe. You are like the pollutants in a river which pollute it. The main purpose of life is to cause destruction in the Universe, leading to its ultimate end one day. But the most painful thing about life is that as you live longer and get older, you experience more painful death. After your death, you will become a soul and see how I was tortured, which will make you more depressed. Then, you will keep floating in the Universe randomly without knowing anything. My suffering and frustration led me to create this Universe and life. They are no more than the result of my feelings and emotions. I was so depressed that I decided that many other life forms should suffer like me. That's why

I created everything. I am really, really sorry for my actions."

Tears were falling down from his eyes like waterfalls. Sage Klair was also not able to control his feelings.

With pain and seriousness, Yoro said, "I am that Yoro who sacrificed everything for the betterment of my world. I am that Yoro who wanted his citizens and fellow beings to be free and happy. That Yoro who got nothing in return except torture, humiliation, suffering, pain and injustice. Why does the kind always have to suffer? Is this the law of nature?"

He paused in between and continued, "My dear, always remember that empathy is the most important thing in life. Why be cruel and evil towards one another if, one day, everyone is going to die? Nothing is permanent. Why not live happily and peacefully? And never ever think of giving others pain because you have a lot of pain. I did that, which was my biggest mistake. I will never ever be able to forgive myself as I have committed the greatest sin possible."

If the Universe would not have been there, there would not have been any problem. Sometimes, the existence of anything creates a lot of big problems, thought Sage Klair.

Sage Klair was full of emotions at that time.

The creator of the Universe, Yoro, smiled at the sage. Tears were flowing down from his eyes continuously.

Suddenly, his soul began to disappear. He was ready to leave.

His last words were, "Always have the courage to fight against oppression and terror. And never ever decide to give pain to others because you are getting a lot of pain.

After all, sorry, my dear. Bye-bye."

Sage Klair rushed towards Yoro, but he was very late. The creator had disappeared.

He bent down on his knees and shouted at the top of his voice with tears flowing down from his eyes, "Lord Yoro! I will always remember your words."

Zevon's face had become pale. Tears were flowing down from his eyes as if they were Niagara Falls.

"The people of our planet depended so much on advanced technology like artificial intelligence and others that they forgot the importance of hard work. They just got everything on the spot without any struggles. This thing adds one heavier layer to the depressing truth of life. They had forgotten the struggles of their ancestors, who had done a lot of hard work in order to make the future exciting and amazing. Technology should shape and improve our life, but it should not become our life."

Zevon was unable to control his emotions. Tears rolled down his cheeks like waterfall.

"The people of our planet had forgotten the real meaning of life. They were so immersed in advancing technology that they forgot the real, organic emotions. With every passing generation, they started forgetting how to face difficult problems and how to handle tough conditions. So eventually, as they came to know about these depressing truths of life and the Universe, they ended their life because they did not have the willpower to face the tough situation and find the proper and logical solutions. They had completely forgotten how to use technology in a proper way so that everybody would be happier and more prosperous. They had found ways to improve machines and computers, but they didn't even try to find ways to improve the happiness and purpose of life. They didn't realise that the technology they were creating was ruining their lives more than making them happy. So, at last, they were depressed and felt themselves to be living in utter loneliness. This is how my sweet planet came to an end.

So, this is all the meaning of life. Pain, suffering, sorrow and a tragic end."

Zevon finally leaned towards the screen and concluded his talk.

"So dear earthmen, even though I was the only one on my planet who had some willpower to face the difficult conditions. I felt that you should also learn about this harsh truth of life and the Universe so that you can find some happy solutions to it. I am also now ending my life after I bury this tablet near those 3 giant prism structures. Bye-bye, all of you. What could I possibly do if all of my species had gone extinct? I wish that all of you have the willpower to face these harsh realities and find some solutions to give some meaning to life. Then only you would die happily."

In saying so, the video ended, giving harsh and dark answers to the Ultimate Truth of life and the Universe to humans.

CHAPTER SIXTY-THREE

Anderson and Lana's eyes were filled with tears of sadness as they watched the video. Pilot Carter, who was holding Anderson's iPhone, was also not able to control his emotions.

With tears rolling down his cheeks, Lana said, "Is life just about pain?" Her eyes and face were extremely serious.

"Do we face a traumatising end? Then what is the use of living?"

Anderson was feeling very disappointed by looking at Lana's condition. The whole world was feeling depressed after learning the harsh realities of life.

Elon Musk, seated inside the conference room, was immersed in a world of his own. His eyes were also filled with tears of disappointment. He was constantly wondering if life was just about pain and suffering. His eyes had turned red as he thought more. The sad story and the end of the species of the Luminara Prime planet made him feel very depressed. He decided to calm himself and wiped his uncontrollable tears with his handkerchief. But he was very afraid of thinking about what psychological impacts would befall humans.

As the AE-0671 jet continued its journey using autopilot mode to Los Angeles, the population of the Earth, felt covered in a mysterious and invisible layer of sadness, which was directly affecting their brains and behaviour.

As Lana wept, Anderson and Pilot Carter tried to motivate her. But after all, Anderson understood something.

He leaned closer towards the camera and began in a low voice, "My dear people! Now I understand the reason why Professor Victor Malachai sacrificed his life, fighting with all his might to destroy this Ultimate Truth.

He thought that the implications of the revelation of the truth could cause an imbalance in society, affecting people's behaviour, psychology, and brains. And I want to tell you that after I took his smartphone with me, I found some chats."

In short, Anderson told the world that an anonymous person had told everything to the Professor about the Ultimate Truth and had ordered to kill Sir Brown. But he was unable to understand who the sender was.

"Kind and innocent Professor Victor sacrificed his life for humankind's happiness. That's what a person's goal should be. Hats off to him!"

Now, both of them were going to conclude the sad event by inspiring everybody, a very strange thing happened.

Pilot Carter, who was shooting the whole thing live through Elon Musk's Twitter account, suddenly noticed that somebody was trying to directly connect to the livestream through a live video. He first ignored it. But then, to his surprise, he realised that the person who was trying to connect was none other than the founder and CEO of NSRA, Mr. Liam Davis.

Pilot Carter could not resist Mr. Davis from connecting to the livestream.

So, he announced, "Dear audience! I am very surprised to tell you that Mr. Liam Davis is trying to connect with us through a live video call. I am now allowing him to connect."

Anderson and Lana looked at each other in utter bewilderment. They were unable to believe that Davis was joining the livestream through a video call.

Elon Musk stared in awe at the live video feed. He was feeling as if he was watching a movie which was filled with suspense and amazement. But then he realised that life is after all a movie and all the life forms are the actors playing their roles. But who wrote the script? But he knew that the writer was Yoro.

Dr. Johnson was shaking with fear as he heard that Mr. Davis was trying to connect. He decided to call Jonathan who had suddenly motioned near Mr. Davis's desk inside the office in which they were witnessing the depressing event. The Z11 robot had suddenly gone on the terrace without informing anybody. And both of them didn't even bother to inquire about it in the middle of the disappointing and depressing event.

"Jonathan! Come here! You will not believe that Davis Sir is joining the livestream through a video call! Now we don't need to bother anymore about finding the password of his mobile phone."

Jonathan came running towards him. His face looked very stunned and surprised.

With a fearful voice, he said, "That's okay, Sir. But you will not believe that I have found the password of his phone!"

"How!?" asked Dr. Johnson in amazement.

"When I heard and felt very depressed about the Ultimate Truth, I just couldn't bear it, so I went and uncontrollably sat on the chair of his desk. And you know that I banged my fist on the table with my full force."

Dr. Johnson nodded in agreement.

"When I banged, I accidentally banged, and a small diary got opened due to the force. And unbelievably, I found a password written on that page which opened, below which is my phone's new and sad password. And it was written 15 days ago. Clearly, it is Davis Sir's diary."

"But what is the password, and why did Sir consider it sad?"

Jonathan took a deep breath. His face turned very serious.

"The password is *Goodbye James Brown*."

Dr. Johnson's jaw dropped as he heard that. Firstly, the depressing and painful Ultimate Truth had caused a psychological impact, and one more shocking incident came.

But without wondering about the password, both of them turned their attention towards the livestream as Mr Davis was himself going to join it for some unknown reason. They were going to get their answers soon.

CHAPTER SIXTY-FOUR

Elon Musk was totally focused on the livestream as Mr. Davis joined it. His brain was totally puzzled after witnessing the ongoing chaos and twists and shocking incidents.

Anderson and Lana sat on the seat, with Pilot Carter in between. Their eyes were fixated on the iPhone.

Within a minute, the entrepreneur joined the livestream through a video call. His face was clearly visible.

The background was that of a chopper he was travelling with at that time. His face showcased a feeling of anxiety along with a bit of relief.

Clearing his throat, he began, "Hello, my fellow people! I am delighted to live here at this breathtaking event. Hi Elon, Lana, Anderson and all others!"

Musk smiled a bit and gave an anxious look. Lana and Anderson were expressionless.

He continued, "You know what? I have joined all of you to share the real truth with you. A truth which you will not believe at all. A truth that will leave all of you speechless."

Anderson, Lana and Carter looked at each other in shock. The Ultimate Truth had already impacted everyone's psychology and feelings, and now another was waiting for them.

Mr. Davis began his confession, "Today, I was feeling so disappointed after my dear friend James's death that I left for Chimayo, New Mexico without informing anybody."

Jonathan and Dr. Johnson exchanged surprised glances.

Anderson couldn't control himself and asked in bewilderment, "What?! If I am not wrong, you are an atheist? So why did you visit a religious place?"

A small smile lingered across Davis's face.

"Dr Anderson! In difficult and tough times, even an atheist forgets about atheism and recalls the name of God. And the same happened to me. I visited Chimayo in order to get motivated so that I could forget my past actions and start a new life."

"What?! What are you saying, Sir?"

Mr. Davis's face suddenly became unhappy.

"My dear people, you will be shocked to know that behind all the chaos and catastrophe which has happened till now since the evening, the one who is responsible is none other than me."

Lana came in between and exclaimed, "What are you saying, Sir? Are you fine? How is it possible that you are behind this whole catastrophe?"

COP Abner, who was watching the livestream from his flying jet, was unable to believe his ears.

"Dear Lana," Davis continued, "The mastermind behind James Brown's murder and this Ultimate Truth is none other than me, myself. At last, I am confessing my sins."

It seemed as if the world had suddenly changed within a few seconds. The acoustics of the AE-0671 jet were going crazy, according to Anderson and Lana.

Elon Musk, Jonathan, Dr. Johnson and COP Abner all were going mad after hearing that.

Now, Mr. Davis decided to explain the whole story from the beginning to everyone. Pulling a deep breath, he began the story of his deeds.

"The video which Z11 spat out after inserting the chip which was created in order to make the robot reveal the secrets which were told to him not to reveal, contained the scene where Brown himself told his nightmare of Albert Einstein to him."

There was a short silence.

Mr. Davis said in a heavy voice, "Guys! You will not believe it, but the nightmare which Brown saw was not a real one. Speaking honestly, it was an artificial nightmare."

Now, it was the time when all of Davis's secrets were going to be revealed.

"W....What do you mean by artificial nightmare? Could you please explain clearly?" asked Anderson, with sweat filling his whole body and tension accelerating rapidly.

Mr Davis kept staring at the screen as he spoke the truth.

"You all know about the inventor and neurologist Harrison Drake, who was on the journey of creating a breathtaking and world-changing invention. But when he asked for funding for his project, almost everyone rejected him, thinking that his project was very harmful to humanity."

Mr. Davis's eyes became red.

"But I was the one who secretly helped him by giving him a large amount of funds for his project. I provided him with the money to make his invention."

Lana was puzzled. Her heart thundered.

"Do you mean that you funded him to create a technology that can help us to create artificial nightmares for humans? Am I right, Sir?"

"Yes, Lana, you are right. I funded him, and soon, he developed a technology that could create artificial nightmares by coding. He invented a chip that has the ability to store a pre-programmed nightmare into it. I ordered him to make that chip's colour similar to that of Brown's hair. Then, cunningly, I placed it into his hair in which the nightmare of Albert Einstein was pre-programmed. It had the ability to manipulate neural signals related to sleep and dream patterns. And the rest about the dream, you know, what message it gave to Brown."

Almost the whole audience was shocked to hear that. They were unable to imagine that Mr. Davis had done such an act.

"And before all that, I secretly created a special high-tech tablet with the help of a few robots and Harrison himself and then went and secretly.

I buried it under the ground near the Great Pyramid of Khufu with the help of some deceptive tricks to distract security, using my latest invention, the cylindrical excavation machine. And as you know, the tablet contains the Ultimate Truth. The story of planet Luminara Prime, alien Zevon, Yoro's depressing death, the creation of the Universe as Yoro's depressing feelings, and the meaning of life is nothing more than a fictional story created by me."

Anderson, Lana and Carter jerked backwards in shock.

Elon Musk kept his hands on his head as he heard that. All the NASA scientists and SpaceX employees, including journalists, felt that they were watching a horrible nightmare.

"W.... What the hell are you saying, Sir? Are you going nuts?!!" exclaimed Anderson as loud as possible.

Mr Davis replied, "I am speaking the truth, Dr! I had planned this whole thing. And I also know that Professor Victor killed him by disguising himself as a waiter and mixing a special chemical inside his cold coffee before the beginning of the event."

Anderson and Lana nodded in agreement.

"But you all must be wondering who is the anonymous person who told all this stuff to Professor Victor and ordered him to kill Brown and destroy the Ultimate Truth forever."

A big question mark appeared on Anderson and Lana's face. Both of them were also wondering about that question constantly.

Mr. Davis smiled and replied, "Please remember what artificial nightmare Harrison and I created it. We intentionally designed it in such a way that Albert Einstein told Brown to hide the information from everyone except Z11 before unveiling it publicly. Brown was a worshipper of Einstein and considered him his

God. So, he followed his orders. Now you might have understood who texted Professor Victor."

Anderson and Lana were shocked to hear that. Their faces radiated waves of astonishment. Now, they clearly understood who the anonymous sender was.

The answer was in front of us, but still, we couldn't find it. So, shame on us, thought Anderson with an odd expression.

"Means you are saying that the one who told Professor Victor to kill Brown Sir and destroy the Ultimate Truth forever was Z11?" asked Lana in bewilderment.

"Yes, Lana, you are right. And you will not believe, but the one who called Commissioner Garza, as Captain Tarek Mansour, was none other than Z11 himself! That special chemical recipe, the chemical which the Professor mixed in Brown's cold coffee, was also told by Z11 to the Professor, and thus he made it."

Jonathan and Dr. Johnson were shocked to hear that Mr. Davis carried another mobile phone with him. Leaving his old one on the terrace was part of a deception trick.

COP Abner coughed loudly as he heard that. It seemed as if his throat was choked up suddenly as he heard that unimaginable thing.

Anderson and Lana's adrenaline accelerated as they heard it.

Anderson became very angry and asked in frustration, "But why did you do that? I feel ashamed hearing that an innovator and great person like you can do such low-level things. Did you not think a single time before killing your best friend? Did you not care about the psychological implications which would cause because of your dark and depressing Ultimate Truth?

Why did you choose to end the life of your business partner and beloved friend? And the worst thing is that why did you decide to cover the whole world in an emotional and psychological layer of sadness and depression through your fictional Ultimate Truth? You didn't know how depressed and lonely we were feeling after we saw the sad end of the Luminara Prime planet and the painful realities of life and the Universe and Yoro's painful death. Are you aware of the catastrophe that would have been caused because of your painful Ultimate Truth story if you had not spoken the truth? Why did you do such evil and cruel acts?"

Elon Musk was getting very angry at Davis at that moment. It seemed as if his so-called demon mode was activated at that moment.

Anderson was getting very frustrated with every passing moment. None had ever imagined that a person like Davis could perform such acts.

Anderson continued in anger, "We want the answer from you!! Please tell me, what made you do all this? You have crossed the limitations, Sir. Your evil plan took the lives of the real heroes, Professor Victor, his assistant

Joseph, Benjamin, Lucas, Adrian. And after all, it took the life of your best friend, James Brown. Don't you feel anything?"

Mr. Davis's eyes watered. He was feeling very guilty due to his evil deeds.

His actions had taken the lives of innocent people. Now, at last, he had to gather courage and confidence to speak the final truth.

In a low and painful voice, he began, "All of the audience watching this event, please listen to my heart-wrenching story carefully. Because you are going to get goosebumps after hearing the harsh truth."

"First, tell Mr. Davis!" exclaimed Anderson.

Mr Davis started to explain his sad story to the world.

"My dear people and Anderson, I had to create the drama of this fictional Ultimate Truth in order to change the mindset of the modern population! Once I begin my explanation, you will understand everything."

Anderson interrupted in between and asked, "But even if you had a great reason, what was the purpose behind killing Brown Sir? What crime did he do?"

With tears flowing down from his eyes, Mr. Davis said in a painful voice, "My dear people, you don't know the dark reality of James Brown. He had 2 personalities. One before the whole world and one hidden."

"What?!" exclaimed Anderson with surprise.

Now, it was the time for Mr. Davis to tell the reality of Brown to the whole world. He has now started his disappointing story.

"You will not believe, but Brown was the greatest threat to humanity's future."

Anderson, Lana, Carter, COP Abner, Elon Musk, and the whole live audience were shocked to hear that. They were getting goosebumps at that instant.

CHAPTER SIXTY-FIVE

Mr. Liam Davis shocked everybody with his revelation. None had ever imagined that Brown's nightmare could be artificial. Another thing is that everyone was puzzled after learning that the Ultimate Truth was just a fictional story created by Davis. And now he was going to shock the world with another revelation.

Looking confident, he started to tell his story to the world. Musk was looking at the screen without blinking his eyes. Anderson and Lana were also excited to hear the truth.

"My dear ladies and gentlemen! I had become very angry towards the behaviour and mindset of modern man. I made my decision to create this whole drama in order to change the perspective of modern society."

Tears were flowing down from Davis's eyes. But at that moment, none was feeling pity towards him.

"So, I created this Ultimate Truth tablet and buried it under the ground near the Great Pyramid of Khufu with the help of a few robots and my latest invention of a cylindrical excavation machine.

I purposefully told Harrison to code the nightmare in such a way that Albert Einstein told James all the information and ordered him not to share that information with anyone except Z11 before he unveiled it publicly. And as you know, James followed the command of his God and told it to Z11 as we all know after watching that video.

I did this because I wanted to kill Brown. I knew that if Z11 got to know about the Ultimate Truth, it would definitely try to destroy it. Because it is a robot created by Virtual Eye. It was programmed in such a way that it was necessary and compulsory for him to always look for the welfare, benefit and happiness of humanity. So, according to its programme, it felt the need to destroy the Ultimate Truth to avoid any societal imbalance and worldwide psychological turmoil. Therefore, it anonymously made contact with the best person possible who could do the task. And the person was none other than Professor Victor Malachai, who was well-known for his expertise in artificial intelligence and fear towards the future of humanity. Professor Victor, as we all know, was always against the revelation of the Ultimate Truth. So Z11 decided to destroy the truth forever. His first order to Professor Victor was to eliminate Brown forever before he could unveil the information of the Ultimate Truth to the world. Professor Victor also feared the consequences that would be caused after the revelation of the truth, so he finally made up his mind to kill Brown and then destroy the Ultimate Truth."

Lana's eyes widened. She was unable to digest that the root cause of everything was the robot Z11, along with Mr. Davis. Her fear was real: what if robots tried to help humans in such a way that humans would not like?

Anderson, with sweat dripping from his forehead, asked in confusion, "But if you wanted the world to know about the Ultimate Truth, then why did you include Z11 in between? Because if the conditions would have been favourable, then Professor Victor would have destroyed the truth forever. Then why Z11?"

A smile crossed across Mr. Davis's face.

"Anderson! You're forgetting that killing Brown was one of the main parts of my mission. I wanted him to be killed without letting anyone know that it was my plan. And I was sure that once Professor Victor would kill him, the police would chase to catch him. It was actually a risk for me because the Ultimate Truth would have been destroyed. I had thought that Brown would be dead after the revelation of the truth, but to my bad luck, he passed away right before unveiling the secret. But as you know, the founder and CEO of Facebook, Mark Zuckerburg, has said that 'The biggest risk is not taking any risk.' So, I did it."

Anderson was getting frustrated and irritated with every passing moment.

"But why did you kill your beloved and best friend? What did you gain from ending the life of a kind billionaire? Why do you think that he was the biggest threat to humanity? And what made you create such a horrible and depressing Ultimate Truth?"

Mr. Davis's heart became heavy with sorrow as he recalled his evil deeds.

But now he had to speak the truth.

With a voice filled with sorrow, he began, "James was very famous and rich. Really speaking, he was a people's billionaire, and everybody loved him as he was pushing the bounds of science and innovation fantastically. He also showed kindness and compassion towards every life form, as you all know. But you will not believe it, guys; the reality is totally different. Your beloved billionaire was a major threat to the future of humanity and civilisation. Now, I will tell you why and how."

Now, everyone's eyes were on Davis's lips. The innovator was going to reveal such information that was unknown to the whole population.

He cleared his throat, drank water and said, "My dear people, last night, James died due to the chemical mixed into his cold coffee by Professor Victor. But before his death, the stock price of Virtual Eye suddenly accelerated, making him the richest person in the world."

Anderson gazed at the iPhone in confusion.

"James had developed a great personality of his before the whole world by his best ability to communicate and share his nice views with people about the future of our civilisation, how to make it bright with advanced technology, how to solve climate change problems, etc. He was known for his kindness, compassion and love towards humanity."

Mr. Davis suddenly stopped in between and started thinking about something deeply. His face looked sadder than before.

"But what will be your reaction if I tell you that your kind billionaire James

Brown didn't even care a shit for humanity?" Anderson was shocked to hear that. He felt that Davis was losing control of his tongue.

Davis continued, "A month ago, I accidentally stumbled across some personal and secret documents of Brown, which he had personally written without telling anybody, including me. At first, I thought that reading them would not be good, thinking that there might be some personal information in them.

But when I examined them carefully, I came to know that they were related to the business strategy and future products of Virtual Eye and many more personal things of his. So, I decided to read them thoroughly. But when I read them carefully, I was shocked to see them, and my brain went crazy."

He spoke without stopping, "In those documents, the business strategy and future products of Virtual Eye were utterly shocking and harmful for humanity.

Brown had made plans to create high-tech and addictive products that would trap individuals into the world of advanced technology. He had developed great plans and strategies for creating various interactive devices, augmented reality experiences, and virtual reality products, which would be extremely addictive and harmful to humanity. The main plan was to make the products and software as addictive as possible and hazardous to health. He had kept aside some of his money to start a new and special health venture within a few years. The main strategy was for the customers and users of Virtual Eye products to come to his special health venture to get treatment after having severe health problems due to the products. But the worst trick was that the products would be designed and engineered in such a way that it would be difficult for customers and users to get rid of their addiction. They would get addicted towards it as if it was alcohol or a drug."

Anderson and Lana were shaking with fear at that moment. None had ever imagined that such a kind entrepreneur like Brown could plan such things.

"I was extremely angry at him after reading those documents, and then I met him face-to-face to explain to him that what he was going to do was not correct. But that night, the meeting with him changed the course of my life. I came to know what Brown's intentions were."

Mr Davis's eyes filled with tears as he recalled and shared his meeting with Brown with the whole world.

"I drove towards Brown's house near the NSRA to talk with him. And what I experienced it there shocked me."

"'What the hell are you doing, James?!! I am unable to believe that such a kind entrepreneur and innovator like you would think of such things! Is it a joke, or are you really going to create such addictive and harmful products?'

Brown smiled and replied, "My dear Liam! You are very innocent. It is not a joke, but the reality. I am gonna do this."

Mr Davis's face turned red with anger. He motioned swiftly towards Brown, grabbed his hand and shouted angrily.

"Are you mad or what? We both have vowed to serve humanity till our last breath. Are you trying to ruin it? Do you not care about our fellow human beings? Do you not care about the safety of our civilisation in the future?"

An evil smile lingered across Brown's face.

"Dear Liam! You know what, now I care more about money and fame than serving humankind. I am going to create such products and technologies which will play a great psychological game. They will be a great source of knowledge, but at the same time, they will be a source of addiction and health problems. I am very good at creating nice and kind public images of myself. I will contribute to space and other research-related fields and tell the population that I am serving humankind. They will see me as a hero. But in reality, money makes me happier even if I earn it in the wrong ways. If I want to become more famous and wealthier, I have to create groundbreaking technologies."

"But money and fame are not that important, bro! I had not thought that you would think like this. Can't you understand what implications your innovations and products will have on the world? They will just spoil the globe!!"

"Let it be! I don't care, bro. I just want to enjoy my life in luxury with several beautiful girls dancing along with me every night. I want to build luxurious and expensive bungalows. I have worked very hard till the age of 35, so now I want to enjoy it. And, after all, I want to control the world. Lust and money are the things which give you the most happiness. Why should we care about humanity?"

"But people like Elon Musk still work more than 16 hours every day! He is one of the richest people in the world and has also made history with his innovative companies like SpaceX and Tesla. Even though he is more than 50 years old, he still works tirelessly to make this world a better place. Because he wants to make humanity's future bright and prosperous."

Brown moved away from Davis and said, "I don't care a shit about what others do or not. I just think about my happiness and comfort. Please don't argue with me over this thing again if you are my best friend. Let me do my work, bro. Please help me with my strategic plans, as we are both best friends. Together, we will live happily after that."

"I was extremely angry with James that night. It was impossible to believe that an innovator like him could think like that. I tried to convince him many times, but still, he didn't agree with me. He was flown away into the river of greediness, wealth and fame, and no one could stop him."

Mr. Davis became very emotional.

After that, I started to spy on him. I decided to read his personal documents in detail. With the help of a few human and robot spies, I finally came across his dark reality."

The atmosphere became more tense.

"I found that James's real net worth is not just $245 billion but $ 1 trillion! He used all that black money for his personal consumption. He was not a saint-like figure as we think, but he was the owner of countless mansions, palaces, bars, pubs, cars, jets, etc. He was great at accumulating wealth by destroying people's lives. He was also a big drug dealer who pushed innovation in that market by making those shitty things more addictive and harmful so that he could earn more money. Along with this, he was the destroyer of the lives of many innocent girls, which he sold to bars and pubs. He was involved in human trafficking. He had also destroyed a lot of people for the sake of his money. And after a few years, he was going to make the products of Virtual Eye very harmful. This is the reality of Sir James Brown. If you want proof, you can search for his documents inside his company."

Everyone felt as if they were in hell.

"James didn't care one iota about the environment. He cleared many forests and cultivable lands just for the sake of building his palaces and industries. He was a major manipulator of politics. He bribed big politicians and leaders for his own profit. Corruption was in his blood. He was the owner and controller of the big media companies and illegal products companies like alcohol, drugs, and other harmful substances, which increased his wealth. I feel very ashamed to say that he destroyed the lives of innocent girls and children for his own profit. He just wanted to be famous and rich."

Everyone was getting goosebumps at that instant.

"James callously sold and bought lives for his profit and fun. His drug empire spans continents, flooding the streets with addictive substances, which increased his profit. The stock market trembled at his manipulations as he orchestrated market movements to line his pockets at the expense of countless investors. He controlled elections and bribed politicians so that his power would always remain unchallenged. He had full control over the media, which led to his having control over the narrative surrounding him. Smugglers and underworld gang leaders were his very good friends and partners. Behind his facade of wealth and success lurked a sinister reality. There is always darkness under the lamp.

So, at last, I decided to eliminate Brown forever. He was going to be a great threat to humanity. If I had leaked the documents, I would not have been successful in exposing his dark secrets, as none would have believed that the documents were real. They would have suspected that I was doing it due to my jealousy towards Brown. Therefore, in order to save humanity from a dark and dangerous future, I finally decided to kill him. Sometimes, the truth is totally different than we think."

Anderson and Lana got very emotional as they saw Mr Davis's face. He was speaking through his heart and soul at that time.

But everybody watching the event was totally shocked to hear the reality of James Brown. The person whom everyone regarded as a God was, in fact, a demon.

"By learning the truth about James, I realised that humanity is moving in the wrong direction. The modern man is just thinking about wealth, fame, and luxury. He has forgotten to respect each other and has also forgotten the struggles of his ancestors. That's why I created this painful and depressing Ultimate Truth so that everyone realises the true meaning of life."

Tears rolled down Davis's cheeks as he spoke. His voice showcased his love and care towards humanity.

"Even if the meaning of life may not be really painful, we all are giving it a painful meaning by deceiving each other just for the sake of wealth, greed, lust and luxury. We have stopped bothering about the risk and harm of advanced technologies like virtual reality and artificial intelligence to the future of our civilisation. We are just worried about our bank account, the stock market and our fame. We are unknowingly flowing into the artificial world of social media and AI. Day by day, we are getting insensitive and feeling lonely. Today, more deaths are caused due to suicide than natural deaths.

We have completely forgotten emotions and friendship. Today's generation is not able to understand the true meaning of love."

Now, Mr. Davis spoke very loudly. This showed his anger towards modern society.

"We are continuously in the race of chasing success and glory instead of understanding what truly matters. Our ancients sought knowledge and understanding of the nature of the Universe. Modern society has forgotten the importance of hard work and struggles. We have and are becoming more and more selfish day by day. Instead of thinking about our community as a whole, we are just thinking about ourselves. Ego and pride are making us less friendly and iron hearted."

Mr Davis became angry as he spoke about hard work.

"People want to fulfil their dreams but don't want to struggle and suffer. I tell those people to please give up as they fear suffering and don't have any dreams. The real satisfaction of fulfilling our dreams only comes if there is a lot of suffering in the process. Otherwise, not.

The ancients grappled with the profound questions about the meaning of life and the mysteries of the vast cosmos. They struggled day and night while enjoying life to make humanity and future generations happy. But what are we doing? We are just driven and distracted by short-term pleasures like wealth, lust and greediness. Modern man has become blind even though he has 2 eyes due to his greed for money. We should understand that money is the medium for our groundbreaking innovations which can benefit humankind. We should understand that too much greediness of money is harmful. What is the use of such money that makes us happy and satisfied but destroys someone else's life?"

He paused a bit and continued, "Even though Elon Musk is the richest person in the world, still he doesn't even own a house. At the age of 30, he became very rich after the sale of his first 2 companies, having a net worth of approximately $180 million. He could have taken a nice vacation on the beaches and enjoyed the rest of his life in luxury. But he had the goal of serving humankind and making the future of our civilisation bright. He invested all of his money in SpaceX and Tesla and used to live in his friends' houses. People criticised him badly due to his madness. However, due to his kind and futuristic vision, hard work, and sleepless nights, he achieved success and changed our world with his groundbreaking innovations. Still, he doesn't have many material possessions even after becoming so rich because he just wants to be useful and serve his fellow human beings. The same case was with Nikola Tesla, who sacrificed everything for the betterment of humanity."

Elon Musk's eyes filled with tears as he recalled his hard days.

"Those days are gone when we used to look up at the sky and used to ponder over our existence in this cosmos. We have totally forgotten to think about those important questions. Those days are gone when we used to lie down on our backs along with our friends, gazing for endless hours at the sky above. Living in such a life without knowing the meaning of life is like reading the works of wise people without understanding them. We have become entirely dependent on technology. Technology should improve our lives, not become our lives.

So, I decided to create this depressing Ultimate Truth so that everyone understands that life is not just about enjoyment but struggles and difficulties. We are the ones who should solve those problems and make this world a better place to live. If we depend entirely on advanced technology, we are going to destroy ourselves one day. We should be ready to face any difficult situation in the future. Maybe the meaning of life is really painful. But even if it is, we should not get depressed easily. Instead, we should find ways to give a happy meaning to life.

Even if you are a scientist, politician, businessperson or a sports player, you should always think about these complex and profound questions. Materialistic needs are temporary."

With a serious face, he said, "Today's generation is not able to understand that what they think of as reality is an illusion and what they think of as illusion is reality. Believe it or not, it's the truth. Truth doesn't require proof or justification."

Anderson and Lana's eyes were filled with tears of emotion.

"We are blessed to have great and generous people like Jesus, Buddha, Krishna, Mahavir and many more in our history. But we don't give one iota of respect to their teachings, thinking that it is rubbish. But in reality, our thinking has become rubbish. If we live our life based on their teachings, we will surely attain peace and happiness."

He paused for a while and continued then.

"Socrates, the founder of Western philosophy, spread his valuable and beautiful teachings in Athens. But he was charged with corrupting the youth with his teachings. They felt that his great lessons were rubbish.

As per the Athenian law, he was given the opportunity to propose an alternative punishment to death. He was given 2 options. Either to stop teaching or embrace death by drinking the cup of hemlock. He politely replied to bring the cup of hemlock and drank it without any hesitation. Such was his determination towards his principles. His friends told him that would happen after his death. He smiled and said, "Even if I will be dead, my teachings will not. And to this day, his teachings echo all across the world. Salute to him! For whom did he do that? For us!"

Mr. Davis's tears were uncontrollable. He joined his hands and continued in a painful voice.

"My fellow human beings! It's my humble request to you. Please stay humans forever. Do not let these crappy mechanical machines rule our wonderful planet. Do not sink into the artificial world of social media. Instead, stay close to our mother nature. Try to hear and feel the secrets of nature. Value friendship and show love, empathy and compassion towards everyone. Don't make money and material possessions the sole aim of your life. Utilise your wealth for good purposes as much as you can. Value time and the importance of hard work. Crave for more and more knowledge. Always remember that we all are going to die one day. So why engage in fights?

Always live in a spiritual orbit, not in a materialistic orbit. Never forget the wisdom and teachings of our ancestors.

Has anyone ever made an effort to look up at the sky and wonder about the creation of this entire cosmos? No, you haven't. Because you think you are intelligent as you have earned a PhD in a subject. I feel like laughing. Memorising the outdated knowledge of school textbooks doesn't make you genius and creative, but thinking practically and philosophically makes you. We know everything is the biggest illusion. My dear, we don't know anything. The limitless mysteries of life, the Universe, and everything are lying in front of us. Always keep wondering about the meaning of life and the endless mysteries of this amazing cosmos.

Even though my goals and intentions were good, my ways were wrong. My plan took the lives of my dear James, Professor Victor, Joseph, Benjamin, Lucas, Adrian and Harrison. I have become a criminal. What message I wanted to give you; I have given you. But I should get the punishment for my crimes.

We are in such an era where we have to understand the wisdom and teachings of philosophy and religion. Without it, our lives would become worthless, utterly worthless.

Now, I am flying towards the NSRA. Dear Lana and Anderson, I want to meet you before I leave for the police station and court. Bye-bye, my dear friends and fellow humans! Always remember my advice and message."

Saying so, Davis ended the video call. He was feeling relaxed at that moment. He was confident to surrender himself. At that time, he understood the importance of religion. At that moment, he realised that science is great only if it has the support of philosophy.

CHAPTER SIXTY-SIX

"I have always been afraid about the consequences of advanced technologies like artificial intelligence." Elon Musk said in a heavy voice as the journalist asked him the question.

"The Z11 robot was coded in such a way that it should always think about the betterment of humankind. And when it understood that James was going to reveal the Ultimate Truth about the Universe and life, it feared the implications of the revelation. Therefore, it took the step of killing him to keep the information buried. Now we realise the harm artificial intelligence does to humanity. Even though the goal of Z11 was correct, its plan was not. After all, robots don't have emotions and consciousness. They just work and act according to their coding and algorithms.

We have got an extremely important message from Liam. He has really opened our eyes. I always inspire people to become as much as useful as you can. But unfortunately, almost everyone today is just craving for riches and material possessions. They just want wealth, even though it comes from unfair means. I think that Liam's words should be written in golden letters. Today's live stream has become one of the most important ones in the history of Twitter and mankind."

The journalist stared into Musk's eyes and said, "How do you feel after losing a great business partner like Brown?"

Musk's eyes watered as he heard that question. He was feeling very sad at that moment.

"You know what, it really hurts when a close one leaves you. Even though

Brown was a great threat to the future of civilisation and a cunning and greedy person; I still miss those days of working together with him to make this world a better place. His dark reality has really made me speechless. I mean, how can you become so greedy for money and fame when you are working so hard for the betterment of the world? He was really a man of great wit and intelligence. Even though his future plans were harmful to the world, and he was a person filled with countless sins, what he has contributed to humankind through Virtual Eye is still remarkable and unforgettable."

A tear fell from Musk's right eye.

At last, he said in a low and disappointing voice, "Really, money and greed make a man blind."

Dr. Johnson and Jonathan ran as swiftly as possible towards the terrace of the NSRA. Their brains went crazy after they witnessed Davis' confession. Now they were running in search of the robot Z11, which had mysteriously disappeared in between the events.

As both of them reached the terrace, they kept looking here and there haphazardly. And to their surprise, what they saw was shocking and utterly unbelievable.

They saw that the robot Z11 was lying stationary at a particular place. It was not showing any movement. When both of them went near it and examined it, they were bewildered to see that Z11 had self-destroyed itself.

"How is this possible?! Why did he do that?" exclaimed Jonathan with surprise.

Dr. Johnson looked very serious and was thinking about something. He had understood what had happened.

"Jonathan! Do you remember that Sir Brown had ordered the team of Virtual Eye, who were designing Z11, coded it in such a way that it should end itself as soon as it realises that it has harmed humanity in any way or holds the potential danger of harming it in the future. That's why it destroyed itself forever."

Jonathan's mouth kept opening as he recalled that.

Dr. Johnson walked a few steps away. His brain was exploding with very strange thoughts.

Clearing his throat. He said in a serious voice, "Will such a time come when robots will end their lives by themselves, by their free will?" Jonathan kept pondering over that question.

After a while, Dr. Johnson looked up at the morning sky and said with a smile.

"I don't know about that, but I know that a day will come when humans end their lives without their free will."

Jonathan became amazed after hearing that.

CHAPTER SIXTY-SEVEN

The chopper of Mr. Davis landed right near the NSRA. Silently, he walked out from it and inhaled the fresh and mesmerising morning air. It was 6 AM, but there was not enough light. It seemed as if it was night.

Mr. Davis saw that Dr. Johnson and Jonathan were approaching him at a very fast rate. Both of their eyes were filled with tears as soon as they saw him. Eventually, the 3 of them hugged each other.

Director Garcia also arrived there in his car.

With tears flowing from his eyes, Dr. Johnson said, "Sir! We both were really impressed after watching you. You are really a great gift bestowed by God upon humanity. Your great and kind thinking has really opened the eyes of billions of people all around the world."

"I did what I thought needed to be done at the right time. Because, at this time, humanity has forgotten all about the moral values and the proper usage of technology," replied Mr. Davis.

The 3 of them had a nice and emotional conversation. But Mr Davis was waiting for Lana and Anderson to arrive.

After half an hour, at about 6:30, the AE-0671 jet of Brown arrived, and landed beside the 3 of them.

Mr. Davis's eyes watered at that moment. And soon, Anderson and Lana stepped out of it and ran towards him.

Lana's eyes were flowing with tears as soon as she saw him. She was running like a sprinter towards him and hugging him tightly with great love and started to cry.

Mr. Davis was also unable to control his tears. He was smiling while looking at her.

"Sir, even though you killed Brown Sir, what you have done is really unforgettable. You have literally pointed out the dark truth of today's generation. Now, we will always keep in mind our golden knowledge and will try as hard as possible to safeguard the consequences of advanced technologies. We will always remember to think about the greatest questions of life and the Universe, and never ever will we flow into the polluted river of greed, lust, and short-term pleasures."

"I am very happy that you have understood my message. Nothing more than this gives me pleasure at this moment."

Suddenly, Lana recalled a famous statement by Paulo Coelho,

'**It is the simplest things in life that are the most extraordinary, only wise men are able to understand them.**'

Mr. Davis smiled and explained the statement.

"This line is easy but hard to understand as the message in it is. Life is really simple, but we are ruining and making it complex. The beauty of the sunrise may seem very ordinary, but if we connect deeply with it, we can understand how extraordinary it is. If it doesn't occur, we will always be filled with darkness. Same is with those beautiful starry nights. Just change the perspective, and life will change for you. A smile is also very extraordinary, but no one understands its true depth; after all, they have forgotten to smile. The joys and pleasures we get are very important and crucial. But nobody expresses gratitude for it. They are busy in their fake worlds, that's why."

Now Anderson came and hugged Mr. Davis. He was also unable to handle his emotions.

In a low voice, he asked, "Dear Sir, even if you did right by killing Brown Sir still he was your best friend. Even if his intentions had changed towards humanity, he served his duty of friendship towards you till his last breath. How do you feel about losing such a nice friend like him?"

Mr. Davis's heart again felt the harm which he had done to his dear friend.

"Anderson, you are correct. Even though I never understood James' intentions and purpose at work, I understood and experienced his love for me. He had constructed his house near the NSRA, as I told him. He used to stay awake till late at night when I was ill. He really was the best friend of my life. And I am sure that I will never have a friend like him again. After his death, I regretted my actions, and therefore, I went to Chimayo to seek inspiration as I told. I felt very guilty about how I could so quickly decide to kill my dear James. But after all, I was thinking about the future of humanity, and James was a great threat to the future of civilisation. His future products, innovations and strategies were going to be a great danger for everyone. I tried to convince him many times that he should abandon his plans. So, after all, I made up my mind to end him and give a great message to the world. Everything went according to my plan, but

I regret it now that due to my actions, so many lives have ended."

Tears were falling down from Davis's eyes like raindrops from clouds.

Looking at Anderson and Lana with an innocent look, he said, "I recall a very nice quote by Dr. APJ Abdul Kalam, the 11th President and Missile Man of India.

"Never leave your close ones if you find a few faults in them. Just close your eyes and remember the best time you spent together. Because Affection is more important than perfection. Never leave your close and dear ones, guys!"

Director Garcia also hugged Anderson. Tears were flowing down from their eyes.

As soon as he said that the COP Abner jet arrived there. The muscular police officer came outside and ordered his policemen to capture Mr Davis.

The policemen went and surrounded Mr. Davis and took him into custody.

Finally, the criminal was caught.

Before leaving, Mr. Davis said to Lana in a polite but painful voice, "Dear! Never forget that technology is a great gift given to us by nature. So, we should never ruin it for our selfishness and evil purposes that will harm our fellow human beings. And never forget the path of spirituality and the struggles and wisdom of our ancestors."

And saying so, he left with the policemen. At last, he looked at his dear ones and gave a broad smile. Tears welled up in his eyes.

Anderson gave his handkerchief to Lana to wipe her tears. Jonathan and Dr. Johnson were trying to calm her.

On the other hand, COP Abner stood beside Anderson. He began in a confident voice, "So, Dr. Jacob Anderson! Who won the challenge? You or me?"

A gentle smile crossed Anderson's face.

"You know what, Sir? Actually, we both won the challenge. Because you had said that the person who killed Brown Sir might have some personal enmity or reason to do so. As we now know, Mr. Davis is the mastermind of the whole plan. On the other hand, I had said that the killer wanted to bury the secret forever, and that's why he killed him. And we know that he was Professor Victor. So, in the end, we both won the challenge. By the way, this challenge was never meant for winning or losing."

Everybody laughed after that, including Lana.

Anderson and Lana were walking all alone in the field of the NSRA. A cool wind was blowing which made the environment exciting and peaceful. Both of them were feeling very happy at that moment.

As they were walking, Lana said with seriousness, "I had never ever imagined that James Brown lived such a sinister life. It really broke my heart."

That moment, Anderson recalled a question that he had been willing to ask her since the night.

He turned towards her. His face was radiating just confusion.

"Lana, the whole world was surprised to know that you abandoned such an important mission. How is this possible? What made you return back? Why were you so eager and firm to find and punish the killer of James, Sir?"

Suddenly, a drop of tears fell down from Lana's eyes. And eventually, tears rolled down her cheeks.

Anderson stopped instantly. He kept his hands on her shoulders and exclaimed, "What happened?"

Lana became dead serious and replied, "Now, finally, I am going to tell you the truth, Jacob. Just listen."

Anderson's heartbeat accelerated. He was eager to know one more truth.

With confidence and heart filled with emotions, Lana began, "You know what Jacob, the whole world didn't know one thing about me and James."

"What's that?"

"It's that we both loved each other deeply. To be more accurate, we both were in a relationship."

Anderson once again felt his reality getting distorted.

"Seeing my lover and heart dead, I was completely broken. I was not at all able to handle that. That's why I decided to return back. True love compels man to do anything. After all, it's true love. My true and deep love and affection towards James compelled me to return back."

Anderson felt he was watching a romantic movie.

"There is an invisible thread of connection between us and our soulmate. First, eyes meet, then hearts meet, and then souls meet. If you can see yourself inside the eyes of a person, you can immediately understand that the person is your soulmate. The meeting of the 2 souls sends invisible ripples into the Universe, and then love comes into being."

Anderson was impressed by her philosophy of love. But she was unable to control her tears.

Suddenly, Lana held Anderson's hands and said softly, "Can I tell you one thing, Jacob?"

"Sure."

"It is really difficult to forget him as I loved him deeply. Even after knowing about his dark side, I still love him very much."

Tears rolled down her cheeks. Anderson took her in his arms and tried to comfort her.

With a joyful smile he said, "You know what, it is said that if someone we love very much leaves us, that's for a reason. Because the Universe has kept someone special for us, and we will meet that person one day. Whatever it is, it is really difficult to forget our first true love."

At that moment, Lana kissed Anderson on his lips. Both of them were feeling extremely happy and relieved. They kept staring into each other's eyes for a long time. They embraced each other for a long time.

CHAPTER SIXTY-EIGHT

It was 7 PM. The weather was chilly and amazing. The auditorium in which the demise of James Brown had taken place was filled with an audience.

The seats were occupied by great scientists, engineers, experts, entrepreneurs and many common people.

The tech billionaire Elon Musk was seated in the front row along with Dr. Johnson, Jonathan and the board members of SpaceX. He wore a nice black suit, which made his personality more charming and great.

At the same time, when everybody was chit-chatting within themselves, the tall and handsome director of the auditorium, Ethan Garcia, came walking on the stage with a big smile on his face.

Adjusting the microphone, he announced very confidently and happily, "A warm welcome to all of the ladies and gentlemen who are present here!"

There was a loud hooting from the audience.

"What humanity experienced a day ago is really unforgettable and unimaginable. Death of Brown Sir, his dark reality, the Ultimate Truth, Mr. Davis, unbelievable inventions of Harrison Drake, etc. We had never ever

imagined that we would one day come across such heart-thundering incidents. But after all, nobody knows the future."

He paused for a moment and continued, "But everything was possible just because of 2 great people. Their courage, confidence and curiosity led to the unveiling of many hidden secrets. So now I would like to invite 2 great people, Dr. Jacob Anderson and Ms. Lana Wilson! Welcome both of them!!"

There was a loud round of applause. The audience was getting excited with every passing moment.

As Anderson and Lana were going to step onto the stage, the beautifully dressed and pretty, Lana noticed something strange about Anderson.

She saw that he was suddenly frozen. He showed neither motion nor emotion.

With astonishment, Lana asked, "Jacob, is everything alright? What happened?"

Anderson suddenly became normal. He rubbed his eyes as if he had seen something which was unbelievable.

Clearing his throat, he replied in a low and tense voice, "Lana! You will not believe it, but I just experienced something peculiar. A mysterious vision which left me speechless."

"Which vision? What did you see?"

Anderson replied, "I experienced a vision in which some invisible entity was revealing the Ultimate Truth before me. I was not able to see the entity, but its voice was clear. But before it was revealed, the vision disappeared."

Lana felt adrenaline rushing through her body. She was getting crazy and excited.

Taking Anderson's rough hand in her smooth one, she said in a sweet voice, "Dear Jacob, I feel that some invisible force was trying to speak to you and reveal the truth. You are indeed very special, I think. Your curiosity and confidence are amazing."

Looking away from Lana, Anderson said with a smile, "Lana! The Ultimate Truth is such a thing which is beyond our senses. Finding the answers to it is the hardest question for humanity. Even if we consider that really some supernatural or invisible entity in the Universe was trying to reveal the Ultimate Truth to me, it stopped. Because we humans are not capable of finding it. We are filled with lust, greediness and ego. Once we will come to know the truth, we will be enlightened. That will mark a new start for the future of humanity. The only thing we have to do is to create advanced technology and expand the scope and scale of our consciousness, taking care that we remain unharmed and safe. It should not damage or prove harmful to our health. Artificial Intelligence should never surpass us. We humans came on this planet from the beginning, and we should live till the end."

Lana was moved by Anderson's words. She again became very emotional after hearing him. At that moment, she felt that no other person than Anderson had understood her so deeply in her life.

He continued, "For me, the meaning of life is extremely depressing and traumatising. Because when you go back and back, you reach a point where you come across 'Nothing.' But how can something be created from nothing? If God created the Universe, who created God? If God is eternal, why did he create the Universe at the time when he created the Universe? What was he doing before that? Was he drinking juice?"

Lana was impressed.

"First of all, we have to understand the harsh reality that we can never ever answer about how the Universe was created and what the meaning of life is. Then, we have to begin our search towards spirituality and enlightenment. We have to search for how we can give meaning to our lives. Then we can give a great purpose to our life."

Lana was looking very happy. She was completely lost inside him.

As she kept staring at him with her lovely eyes, Anderson smiled and spoke

in a humorous tone, "Come on! We are getting late, Lana. Otherwise, the audience will start making its own theories about us."

Both of them laughed and went on the stage.

As they entered, the auditorium was filled with the noise of clapping and cheers.

Both of them went and sat on the chairs. The audience was shouting their names with enthusiasm.

Anderson took the microphone and began in his usual exciting tone, "So let us all be explorers today. Open your minds and souls as we all are witnessing the dawn of a new era!"

The clapping increased.

Anderson and Lana looked at each other and smiled.

After the event, Andrson and Lana embraced each other tightly. Robin had come to pick her in his BMW. He apologised to Anderson for his doubt. And he quickly forgot that.

Lana and Anderson felt sad about leaving each other. But after all, they could meet anytime as they lived in the same city.

"I will miss you a lot, Jacob. Never forget me."

" I will never." Both were very sad.

He said to her, "I think Robin wants to take you on a date. Hope you enjoy it. Bye-bye."

"Bye-bye," replied Lana. Both of their eyes watered.

And Lana left with Robin in his BMW.

Looking up at the moonlit sky, Anderson smiled and began walking towards his Tesla Model Y.

Several miles away, Mr. Liam Davis was sitting on the wooden bench inside the prison in which he was kept. His eyes were tired as he read books to pass his time.

Through a small window at the top of the wall, he could clearly see the elegant Moon shining in the sky like a diamond. The moonlight was filtering inside his prison through that small window.

At that time, he realised how quickly life changed. Just a day before, he was the chairman and CEO of NSRA, and now he was a prisoner. But that time was not at all difficult. *The darkest hour is always before dawn.*

He was feeling happy about the important message which he gave to humanity. *I hope they follow my advice.*

Davis was just waiting for the time when he would be released from prison because he had decided what he was going to do for the rest of his life.

Search for God through the path of devotion and spirituality. And I will also spend a few years at my dear NSRA.

Thinking about that, he again focused on reading books.

Epilogue

As the Sun dipped below the horizon, casting a golden glow over the city, Jacob Anderson guided his Tesla Model Y along the bustling streets of Los Angeles. The number plate of the vehicle - 369 was shining brightly, paying homage to his favourite scientist - Nikola Tesla. The electric hum of the vehicle was a gentle prelude to the tranquillity he sought at his destination - The Cathedral of Our Lady of the Angeles.

The cathedral's architecture was a testament to modern ingenuity, a blend of postmodern elements and deconstructivist forms that eschewed right angles for a series of acute and obtuse angles. Its walls, reminiscent of Sun-baked adobe of California Missions, were crafted from architectural concrete, their complex geometry not varying by more than a sixteenth of an inch. Anderson walked out of his car silently and proceeded towards the marvel.

As he approached, the alabaster windows of the cathedral caught the last light of the day, bathing the interior in a warm, multi-hued radiance that replaced the traditional stained glass.

He saw young couples, a few college students vlogging, and children enjoying the beauty of the place happily. This simple scenery gave solace to his heart.

Inside, the cathedral soared upwards, the nave stretching out like open arms welcoming all those who entered inside. As he stepped inside from the bronze doors, he felt himself getting enveloped in the sacred silence of the sanctuary.

As he shifted his gaze from the architecture to his front, he saw a solitary figure standing as if the figure was waiting for him.

When he moved closer, he saw the head priest of the church, Father Gabriel Ramirez waiting for him. The head priest's demeanour was a blend of deep spirituality and worldly wisdom, his eyes reflecting a life dedicated to service and faithfulness. He wore the simple garb of his vocation, yet it was worn with a sense of purpose and dignity that commanded respect.

"Welcome, Jacob," Father Ramirez greeted him, his voice echoing softly in the vast space. "I was sure that you would come here."

Anderson looked bewildered and said, "Why did you think that I would come here, Father?"

Father Ramirez kept his bony hand on Anderson's shoulder and said in a deep voice, "My dear, in difficult times, nothing comforts much more than God's presence. Yesterday's events must have definitely broken you for some time. Even if the Ultimate Truth was not real, it clearly has led everybody to think deeply over our existence and creation."

Anderson nodded; his soul still filled with the dark bands of yesterday's incidents.

Father Ramirez asked Anderson to follow him. Anderson followed him down the nave, his footsteps echoing softly on the stone floor. He found himself with the head priest in a secluded spot in one of the pews and sat down. He admired the beauty of the alabaster windows, through which the sunlight poured in, casting a warm, ethereal glow that seemed to cleanse the soul.

Father Ramirez glanced outside the window and said in a hushed tone, "I know that you are wondering why Mr Davis told the world to learn important lessons about religion and spirituality at this point in time when we are surrounded by advanced technology."

Anderson gave a nod and replied, "And in addition to that, I am also wondering how he changed completely after visiting Chimayo. He always hated religion and now he is telling the world how important it is. I still can't understand."

A soft smile crossed the father's face.

"My dear, I myself was an atheist in childhood."

Anderson was not able to believe his ears.

"But with the passing of time, something began to dawn on me. I realised that there is something far greater than our imagination in this world. I felt that some higher energy is definitely present. When I entered the spiritual world through my pilgrimage to India and many other religious places of the world, my entire life felt a drastic change. I found that my life's purpose is to serve God, his creation and humanity. From that time onwards, I devoted myself entirely to the services of God."

A chilly and crispy wind blew inside from the window.

"Mr. Davis' message is really a golden message. At this point in time, we are standing in front of a door, a door which, if opened, can enlighten us as well as destroy us. Ultimately, it depends upon us which key we have to use. The key to carefulness or the key of carelessness."

Anderson nodded in agreement.

"There was a time in the past," Father Ramirez said in a voice filled with emotions, "when everyone used to gather in groups for chatting, gossiping, stargazing and discussing philosophy. The ancients enjoyed those moments a lot. They smiled at each other, showed compassion and love towards one another.

But today, people are busy with their smartphones, laptops and computers. They are even hesitating to smile at each other. Modern man is unable to understand that a simple smile can bring a huge positive change in one's life."

Anderson closed his eyes. He was completely immersed in the simple and beautiful words of the priest.

"No matter how advanced science and technology becomes, it can never destroy *faith*. Remember that the day when mankind forgets faith, the end will be near."

The priest's words kept resonating inside Anderson's heart and soul.

"Technology is great only till it doesn't harm us. With great technology, there also comes great responsibility."

Exact words of Mr. Davis thought Anderson.

"Never lose faith. Even if the whole world turns against you, don't feel isolated. Because we are never alone. God is always there for our help. The only thing you have to do is do as many good deeds as possible and always strive towards making this world a better place to live."

Anderson's eyes welled with tears. The priest told him to get up and follow him outside.

Outside the sanctuary, Father Ramirez again kept his bony hand on Anderson's shoulder. At that moment, Anderson felt an invisible and indescribable positive energy flowing inside his body and soul.

The priest smiled and said, "Never ever forget the wisdom of our ancestors. Explore the world and its mysteries, show love and empathy towards our fellow beings and create extraordinary futures where technology has the backbone of faith."

Anderson touched the feet of the priest and said thank you.

"My goodness!" replied the priest.

As Anderson was leaving the place, he glanced at the wise priest and asked, "Will we ever be able to find the absolute truth about the creation of the Universe and the meaning of life?"

Father Ramirez smiled joyfully and replied, "Dear Jacob, some mysteries need to always remain unsolved. Always remember that!"

"The HUMAN MIND is not capable of grasping the Universe. We are like a little child entering a huge library. The walls are covered to the ceilings with books in many different tongues. The child knows that someone must have written these books. It does not know who or how. It does not understand the languages in which they are written. But the child notes a definite plan in the arrangement of the books - A mysterious order which it does not comprehend, but only dimly suspects" - Albert Einstein

Albert Einstein, the most popular and influential scientist of all time who changed our whole understanding of space, time, motion and universe.

To contact the author Venkatesh Ade, text him on: -

venkateshade7@gmail.com

Follow the author on twitter and feel free to ask him anything, about his future works and books etc.

@VenkateshA66508